RETHINKING FEMINISM IN IRELAND

BLOOMSBURY OPEN ACCESS

An ebook edition of this book is available open access on bloomsburycollections.com. Open access was funded by the Bloomsbury Open Collections Library Collective.

Bloomsbury Open Collections is a collective-action approach to funding open access books that allows select authors to publish their books open access at no cost to them. Through this model, we make open access publication available to a wider range of authors by spreading the cost across multiple organisations, while providing additional benefits to participating libraries. The aim is to engage a more diverse set of authors and bring their work to a wider global audience.

More details, including how to participate and a list of contributing libraries, are available from bloomsbury.com/bloomsbury-open-collections.

RETHINKING FEMINISM IN IRELAND

Camilla Fitzsimons

BLOOMSBURY ACADEMIC
LONDON • NEW YORK • OXFORD • NEW DELHI • SYDNEY

BLOOMSBURY ACADEMIC
Bloomsbury Publishing Plc, 50 Bedford Square, London, WC1B 3DP, UK
Bloomsbury Publishing Inc, 1385 Broadway, New York, NY 10018, USA
Bloomsbury Publishing Ireland, 29 Earlsfort Terrace, Dublin 2, D02 AY28, Ireland

BLOOMSBURY, BLOOMSBURY ACADEMIC and the Diana logo
are trademarks of Bloomsbury Publishing Plc

First published in Great Britain 2025

Copyright © Camilla Fitzsimons, 2025

Camilla Fitzsimons has asserted her right under the Copyright,
Designs and Patents Act, 1988, to be identified as Author of this work.

For legal purposes the Acknowledgements on p. 201 constitute
an extension of this copyright page.

Cover design: Eleanor Rose
Cover image © Vince Cavataio/Getty Images

This work is published open access subject to a Creative Commons
Attribution-NonCommercial-NoDerivatives 4.0 International licence
(CC BY-NC-ND 4.0, https://creativecommons.org/licenses/by-nc-nd/4.0/).
You may re-use, distribute, and reproduce this work in any medium for
non-commercial purposes, provided you give attribution to the copyright
holder and the publisher and provide a link to the Creative Commons licence.

Bloomsbury Publishing Plc does not have any control over, or responsibility for, any
third-party websites referred to or in this book. All internet addresses given in this
book were correct at the time of going to press. The author and publisher regret any
inconvenience caused if addresses have changed or sites have ceased to exist, but
can accept no responsibility for any such changes.

A catalogue record for this book is available from the British Library.

Library of Congress Cataloging-in-Publication Data
Names: Fitzsimons, Camilla, author.
Title: Rethinking feminism in Ireland / Camilla Fitzsimons.
Description: London ; New York, NY : Bloomsbury Academic, 2025. | Includes
bibliographical references and index. | Summary: "Rethinking Feminism in Ireland
offers a radical approach that sees feminism as a practical philosophy that seeks
to combat all forms of oppression. Exploring a number of topics including political
activism, the world of work, queer and trans-rights activism, gender-based violence,
and reproductive rights, the author sets out a fresh approach to the future of
feminism using case studies in Ireland to to illustrate global issues. Including
interviews with 30 people involved in feminist activism in Ireland, this book uses
Irish history and political developments to create a collaborative, collective feminist
effort with a global outlook"–Provided by publisher.
Identifiers: LCCN 2024050803 (print) | LCCN 2024050804 (ebook) |
ISBN 9781350501126 (hardback) | ISBN 9781350501119 (paperback) |
ISBN 9781350501133 (epub) | ISBN 9781350501140 (ebook)
Subjects: LCSH: Feminism–Ireland.
Classification: LCC HQ1600.3 .F55 2025 (print) | LCC HQ1600.3 (ebook) |
DDC 305.4209415–dc23/eng/20250304
LC record available at https://lccn.loc.gov/2024050803
LC ebook record available at https://lccn.loc.gov/2024050804

ISBN:	HB:	978-1-3505-0112-6
	PB:	978-1-3505-0111-9
	ePDF:	978-1-3505-0114-0
	eBook:	978-1-3505-0113-3

Typeset by Integra Software Services Pvt. Ltd.
Printed and bound in Great Britain

For product safety related questions contact productsafety@bloomsbury.com.

To find out more about our authors and books visit www.bloomsbury.com
and sign up for our newsletters.

For my mum

CONTENTS

Chapter 1
THE TROUBLE WITH FEMINISM ... 1

Chapter 2
FEMINISM AND ELECTORAL POLITICS ... 25

Chapter 3
FEMINISM, WORK AND TRADE UNIONS ... 53

Chapter 4
FEMINISM AND TRANS LIBERATION ... 77

Chapter 5
CONFRONTING GENDER-BASED VIOLENCE ... 101

Chapter 6
REFRAMING REPRODUCTIVE RIGHTS ... 127

Chapter 7
DOING FEMINISM ... 155

Notes ... 168
Bibliography ... 181
Acknowledgements ... 201
Index ... 202

We are still such a long way from achieving gender justice. The advances we have made seem so fragile. Gender inequality has become so normalized within our society that I sometimes wonder how we can ever achieve the kind of world I would like for future generations.

– Founder of a feminist network in the midlands

Chapter 1

THE TROUBLE WITH FEMINISM

'Say her name – Savita' was the chant from the thousand-strong crowd that trailed through Dublin city centre on a wet October afternoon in 2022. The march had been organized by the socialist feminist group ROSA to mark ten years since the death of Savita Halappanavar, a migrant woman living in Ireland who died of septicaemia in a Galway hospital whilst miscarrying. She had repeatedly asked for an abortion but was denied one because doctors could detect a foetal heartbeat. One senior nurse told her that her request was being denied 'because Ireland is a Catholic country'. Four years after a referendum that did remove that ban, many speakers at the march used their platform to outline how, because of ongoing barriers to abortion care, the same thing could easily happen again.

'One, two, three, four, we won't take it anymore. Five, six, seven, eight, separate church and state' marchers shouted as they demanded an end to religious influence, especially in schools and hospitals. Some protesters carried banners emblazoned with the message 'Make Our Maternity Hospital Ours' referencing the government's transfer of ownership of Ireland's future flagship National Maternity Hospital to a private company with a Catholic ethos. Such was the anger at a rally six months earlier, veteran feminist Ailbhe Smyth had promised to 'lie down in front of the diggers if it came to that' to prevent the project from going ahead.

On O'Connell Street, the ROSA-led march passed a protest made up mostly of Iranian women who were standing in solidarity with their own country's feminist uprising against strict control of their freedoms. The catalyst for Iran's insurrection was the death of Mahsa Amini, a 22-year-old woman who died from injuries inflicted whilst being detained by the country's morality police for infringing strict hijab regulations. Over six weeks later, the unrest in Iran was showing no sign of abating. Women of all ages and backgrounds were symbolically cutting off their hair in an act of open defiance against the theocracy's strict rules and were demanding fundamental reform as people of all genders joined large street protests to oppose the weight of religious fundamentalism on their lives. As the March for Savita and the protest for Mahsa Amini crossed paths, each group applauded the other loudly. Later on, Hasta Yavari, a young Kurdish-Iranian woman living in Ireland addressed the crowd outside City Hall proclaiming, 'I'm here for Savita, for Mahsa Amini, and all the women who've lost their lives because of misogyny'.

At the same time as the Dublin march but 100 miles northwards, hundreds congregated in the rain outside Belfast City Hall as part of the 'Women Demand Better' rally which was organized by Unite the Union. The spark that lit that mobilization was the closure of Regina Coeli, a former Mother and Baby Home but more recently a hostel for homeless women that was owned by the Catholic Legion of Mary. Eleven months earlier, its managers had announced the hostel would shut its doors because the religious order didn't have the half a million pounds needed for essential repairs. The closure was bitterly opposed by staff and residents who occupied the building in an attempt to have the decision reversed. Their action only ended when Northern Ireland's housing executive promised to rehouse those affected in a better facility. Nearly one year on, and with no clear timeline on when this would happen, the 'Women Demand Better' rally wanted this promise to be upheld and sought actions on the reasons why record numbers were ending up homeless in the first place. Protesters also called for something to be done about the cost-of-living crisis and on male violence against women. They demanded proper pay and recognition for the essential and often invisible work carried out by women and appealed for decent healthcare.

The next day, on 30 October 2022, around 250 protesters gathered outside Cork Maternity Hospital to register their objection to government plans to significantly reduce access to home birth services. Under proposed new rules, anyone who lives more than a thirty-minute drive from a maternity unit would no longer be eligible for the scheme despite there being no medical evidence to support this arbitrary decision. The protest was supported by the groups Midwives in the Community and AIMS Ireland (Association for the Improvement in Maternity Services). It came less than six months after a different protest outside the same hospital. That rally had focused on a discovery that donated organs from deceased babies were incinerated without the knowledge and permission of parents. They had been assured that the remains would be returned to them for burial once certain tests were carried out, but this didn't happen.

The same week that protesters rallied in Dublin, Belfast and Cork, Holly Cairns now leader of the Social Democrats (hereafter Soc Dems, a centre-left political party) led a private member's bill in the Dáil (Irish parliament) that sought urgent changes to a controversial redress scheme for the survivors of Ireland's notorious Mother and Baby Homes, the last of which closed in 1996. Tens of thousands of women were detained in these Catholic-run and state-supported institutions where they endured high levels of cruelty. Many of the children who were born into these institutions died prematurely, endured unsanctioned vaccination trials and/or were trafficked through illegal adoptions including to the United States.

In the days before the Soc Dems launched their counterproposal, the then Minister for Children and Green Party TD (elected member of parliament) and now leader of the Green Party, Roderic O'Gorman had defended the legally binding *Mother and Baby Institution Payment Bill* (2022) by stressing low burdens of proof and emphasizing that every woman who was institutionalized could seek compensation. Not so for 60 per cent of those born into these Church-run institutions who wouldn't get a cent. This is because anyone who spent less than six months in a Mother and Baby Home is excluded from the compensation scheme even though the key harm has been recognized as the lifelong impact of the separation of mother and child. The minister also didn't acknowledge how his much-maligned recompense scheme was based on a widely discredited final *Report of the Commission of Investigation into Mother and Baby Homes* (2021), which had excluded hundreds of hours of survivor testimonies that had been volunteered as part of a state enquiry into how people were treated in these cruel institutions. He also kept quiet about the fact that, a few weeks earlier, he had shelved his own plans to review these testimonies; a promise given following spontaneous protests by survivors' organizations when the report was first published. Instead, he and his government colleagues continued to ignore sustained protests both inside and outside the Dáil when, in February 2023, they knowingly voted to deny compensation to around 24,000 living survivors and consciously dismissed high levels of recorded abuse in boarding out placements and adoptive homes.

Had any of these busy activists fancied a night out in between protests they might have enjoyed an event running at the Irish Museum of Modern Art (IMMA) where *!Women Art Revolution* was being screened, a film that chronicles over fifty years of women's arts-based protest across the world. Or they could have tried *A Mary Magdalene Experience* – a short film about the reaction of a working-class community to a fictionalized politician getting 'me-too-ed' on the internet which was written and directed by artist and activist Grace Dyas. Had they waited a couple of weeks, they could have caught an Abbey Theatre double-bill of Tara Flynn's one-woman show that details the impact of online abuse after sharing her abortion story, then the drag queen Panti Bliss sharing tales from their life as an LGBTQIA+ activist.

These examples are just a snapshot of near-continuous protests, talks, demonstrations, campaigns, marches, petitions, boycotts, art projects and lobbying that continue to happen on a range of issues that particularly affect the lives of women. Feminist activism isn't just on the rise in Ireland, but there have also been uprisings in Algeria, Argentina, Chile, Korea, India, Mexico, Nigeria, Poland, Scotland, South Africa and many more countries around the world. Such is the international uptick in activism, where some people are dubbing this a 'fourth feminist wave'. Quite the turnaround from just a few short years ago when it was common for feminists to be dismissed as irrelevant and when it was routine for some people in the public eye to denounce them as little more than disillusioned man-haters.

Why I wrote this book

I've been back and forth about whether to or not to write a book about feminism, the reasons for which will become evident throughout this chapter. It's not because I too think feminists are man-haters, far from it. And it's not because women and girls don't face a particular type of inequality in social, political, intellectual, cultural and economic attainment. The World Economic Forum call this inequality the 'gender gap' and tell us that, at the current rate of change, it will take 134 years for this gap to close which is about five generations beyond the 2030 Sustainable Development Goal (SDG) target.[1]

There are many ways that the gender gap manifests in day-to-day life. Women's freedom is more likely to be curtailed including the right to work, to go to college and to travel independently. Sometimes this is because of laws that prevent them from doing so. Other times it is because of cultural norms, coercion within intimate relationships or care burdens, or because girls are more likely to be the first in a family to be taken out of school to help with domestic and care work. The charity Oxfam has assessed the global value of women's unpaid care work if it was evaluated at minimum wage and cost this at US$10.8 trillion per year.[2] Even the climate crisis disproportionately affects women and girls who are in greater danger when they are forced to migrate.[3]

Women and girls are also much more likely to be impacted by interpersonal gender-based violence, something that cuts across all countries and cultures. This takes many different forms and is best understood on a spectrum. At one end, there is the low-level hum of harassment that many women and girls put up with, often on a daily basis. At the other end are much more serious acts of violence that deny people safety and sometimes even life itself. In today's world, many people have a much better understanding of how gender-based violence can be physical, emotional, financial and psychological. Words like 'gaslighting', 'love bombing' and 'red flags' are now part of everyday vocabulary. Yet, the issue is still not taken seriously enough by governments across the globe. Instead, it is mostly tolerated, or ineffectively addressed through under-funded, stretched services and law-and-order approaches that, as Chapter 5 will discuss, often do more harm than good. Some people only get exercised about male violence against women when it is weaponized against migrant men – a racist trope that is only applied when those who are accused are people of colour and when the imagined victims are white. This feigned concern for the safety of women is mystifying for those of us who have intercepted the literature far-right agitators have distributed, which seeks to curtail the movements of women and girls through curfews. Or when we've been there when they interrupt vigils for victims of gender-based violence. The far right doesn't care about women. And their erroneous narrative about racialized men does a disservice to women of colour who can feel hamstrung, including in feminist spaces, when talking about the sexism they endure in racialized communities. They may hesitate because speaking up could throw oil on the white supremacist fire of suspicion that portrays all men of colour as somehow deviant.

Our feminist struggles also extend to the fact that millions of people live under laws that curb their reproductive rights. In 2023, an independent review of Ireland's abortion laws found serious flaws including unnecessary legal barriers that are non-compliant with the World Health Organization (WHO) guidelines on abortion care it also found significant gaps in the availability of services. To this day, seven people, that we know of leave the island every week to access abortions in England and Wales and people probably travel further afield also some people can't travel because they don't have the right travel documents, they don't have the money for flights and accommodation, they don't have the freedom to leave because of care responsibilities or coercion, or because of a disability that makes travel more challenging. So, they buy pills online and take them without medical supervision. Anyone who helps them risks a prison sentence. In countries where pills are difficult to come by, people resort to unsafe abortions which are known to be responsible for tens of thousands of deaths each year.[4] As Chapter 6 will explore in more detail, reproductive rights also extend to the right to have children and to parent them in safety, something which is repeatedly broken in today's world.

Gender-based discrimination is also evident in the workplace where women are routinely paid less for the work they do even when they hold similar roles and have much the same qualifications. Women are less likely to be in positions of power, are pretty much locked out of certain roles altogether, and are often relegated to service work and tasks that are perceived to be more feminine. They are more likely to volunteer or be asked to volunteer for tasks with low promotability and can be reluctant to avail themselves of flexible working arrangements for fear of being viewed negatively by their employers. They also evaluate their own performance more negatively than their male counterparts.[5] Meanwhile, childbirth and childrearing can impact progression in a job or the risk of losing one's job altogether. On top of all this, the global #MeToo movement, which erupted following the exposure of decades of rape and sexual assault by media mogul Harvey Weinstein, has helped expose just how common workplace sexual assaults against women are. The length of time it took for allegations to surface about sexual harassment in the workplace by comedian turned health guru Russell Brand in 2023 shows the extent to which broadcasting corporations still protect male stars even though there had been several reports about his behaviour to senior management.

The two souls of feminism

Broadly speaking, *feminism* presents itself as a social movement that seeks to address these inequalities. However, there are fundamental differences at the heart of feminism that deserve our attention and that this book seeks to expose. In general terms, there are two different approaches to the fight against women's oppression. First, there are feminists who focus on individualized equality. Their goal is for women to take their rightful place at the tables of power and participate as equals in managing an otherwise largely unchanged system aside from some tweaks here and there. More women in positions of power will, it is argued, eradicate sexism because their presence and influence will create more responsive, civilized and equal environments. This liberal version of feminism is sometimes nicknamed 'lean-in' feminism after the corporate feminist Sheryl Sandberg whose book *Lean In: Women, Work, and the Will to Lead* (2013) helped repopularize feminism when it sold millions of copies worldwide. Sandberg argues that, with the right frame of mind and a good dollop of sisterly support, all women can break through the so-called glass ceiling – an invisible barrier of unwritten rules and unspoken biases that prevent them from progressing in public life despite their best efforts.

This book argues against this version of feminism. Certainly, it might speak the language of equality but, as I will demonstrate, many of the actions taken in the name of feminism actually do more harm than good because they diminish the social status and material conditions for many other women and girls. Take, for example, the way liberal feminists rarely incorporate issues such as food poverty, inadequate housing and environmental destruction in the feminist fight despite mountains of evidence that these growing concerns disproportionately impact women and girls. These problems aren't denied, but they are often compartmentalized separately and as someone else's problem to solve. At the same time, liberal feminists frequently exhibit relational trait characteristics of middle-classness or what Stephanie Lawler more bluntly calls 'expressions of disgust' towards working-class existence.[6] This is how Emma Quinn, an activist with ROSA and member of the Socialist Party puts it:

> I know that all women experience sexism on a daily basis, but there is this attitude, and narrative that is pushed in the media, government and the state that middle-class women are more classy, more chaste, more responsible. That they just have to lean in, that they are respectable. And then there's this constant thing about working class women, especially one-parent families and women of colour. 'They are stupid, they are ignorant, they choose a life of benefits, they are irresponsible reproductively speaking, they can't be trusted,' and that is still really common.

This sentiment can be so strong that Emma has witnessed 'less sympathy for working-class women who are victims of gender-based violence and femicide'. She is right that this perspective on working-class lives is continually re-enforced across a range of sites including the media, popular writing and even in academia where it is not uncommon to find literature, mostly by middle-class people, that oversimplifies and homogenizes working-class experiences.

But differences are more than just representative. People do have very different experiences of life that arise from a materialist base. For this reason, the lens I bring to this project is against individualism because, beyond certain parameters, our ability to control our lives is extremely limited. Our gender identity helps set these parameters, but our life chances are also determined by our social class, perceived ability, sexual orientation, ethnicity, exposure to poverty and proximity to the catastrophic impacts of climate change, none of which are mutually exclusive. Certainly, sexism is bad everywhere, including in the boardrooms of power and some of the advances forged by liberal feminists have benefitted all women and girls. Women are statistically living longer, are more likely to be educated than in the past, are having fewer children, are less financially dependant on men and sometimes benefit from more workplace protections than was once the case. But these improvements are not evenly spread and one of the biggest failures of liberal feminism is pursuing a feminist agenda whilst denying that capitalism is not a model for economic progress for all but an oppressive and exploitative system for many.

For the purposes of this book, and as I have already modelled, I describe the first soul of feminism as *liberal* feminism using this as a catch-all expression that includes 'corporate', 'neoliberal' and 'white feminism' which I will discuss in more detail a bit later. Its second soul, within which I include 'radical', 'socialist', 'critical' and 'Marxist' feminisms, will mostly be referred to as *anti-capitalist* feminism.[7] Sometimes these different approaches come together, as happened in Ireland's abortion referendum of 2018, the culmination of a thirty-five-year-long grassroots movement that was built and sustained by radical feminists but involved a united front in its final phase.[8] But there were diverging goals within the campaign with most liberal feminists stressing abortion legality and most anti-capitalists stressing abortion access (a topic that will be explored in Chapter 6). This book acknowledges these moments of congruence and argues for a united front when this is the best course of action. But to imply there is one singular history of feminism with a shared vision for the future is a misleading distortion. For example, the still popular aforementioned 'waves' metaphor is discriminatory and exclusionary. Feminists' waves – the first being the suffragette movement of the 1920s, the second the equality-based movement of the 1960s and 1970s, and the third being a redefining of gender and femininity that began in the 1990s – is a white-centric, grand narrative that heavily relies on the myth of a shared choreography of actions and the same political ambitions. As Lola Olufemi argues, to historically insist on the analogy of waves helps erase dissenting and alternative voices within feminism, framing these as antagonistic, or just not that important.[9]

I was recently reminded of the issues with feminist waves when I was teaching a class called 'Advanced Gender Studies' at the university where I work. Half the group was mostly white and had lived in Ireland much of their lives. The other half was visiting students from a range of countries including Azerbaijan, Chile, Pakistan, India, Syria, Turkey and Vietnam. When I asked people to share their thoughts on the waves analogy, it was immediately clear that it perfectly matched the story of feminism familiar to those native to Ireland. They had never questioned its logic before. For others, it made no sense at all. This is because of how the waves metaphor centralizes the liberal feminisms of imperialist countries and, as some students pointed out, carries an insulting tone that suggests women the world over must follow in the footsteps of their more enlightened white European and North American 'sisters'. Shared sisterhood isn't real. It is a harmful illusion that benefits privileged women or, as bell hooks writes, it is 'a false and corrupt platform disguising and mystifying the true nature of women's varied and complex social reality'.[10]

Sometimes, the language of sisterhood is used by individualist feminists to help them get where they want to go by co-opting feminist struggles. Take the argument that the sisterly thing to do is to elect female politicians into government who will, in turn, make the world a better place (something I discuss more in Chapter 2). This practice mostly pulls women into politics whose proximity to privilege make them more likely to support policies that are compatible with the capitalist status quo. Nevertheless, these women, we are told, somehow serve as an example to other women of what is possible. This was the perspective adopted by Hillary Clinton when she congratulated Giorgia Meloni, the far-right leader of the political party Brothers of Italy, on her election as the first female president of Italy. Clinton claimed her election would 'open doors' for all women because every time a woman is elected head of state this 'is a step forward'.[11] Meloni made much of her identity as a woman and a mother to get elected, but she is no friend to feminism and the assumption that women in politics will act in solidarity with each other is a dangerous one. The only progress her election represents is to model how women, especially mothers, can be a useful front to soften the politics of racism, xenophobia, anti-immigration, transphobia and homophobia; something the sociologist Sara Farris has dubbed 'femonationalism'.[12]

The myth of shared sisterhood also deepens the male–female binary in a way that doesn't appreciate how gender exists on a culturally situated, intersectional continuum. Judith Butler maintains that gender isn't fixed but is reproduced through our repetitive behaviours, or by 'the repeated stylization of the body' which each of us continuously performs.[13] In other words, we *create* masculinity and femininity by behaving in the ways we are expected to behave. Essentialist presumptions run deep. Generation after generation, we are inculcated how to behave through education, religion, the domestic sphere, literature, media, popular culture and just about every aspect of social life. If we paper over this social constructedness, we ignore how gender expressions have differed throughout history and how representations of 'male' and 'female' hugely vary across the globe.

Understanding capitalism

Conscious of the fact that I have made some broad statements about the exploitative nature of capitalism and its relationship with gender inequality, it is only fair that I spend some time briefly explaining how capitalism works and that I do so in a way that is accessible to those of you who are not familiar with the economic analysis anti-capitalists like me typically present. First, it is worth bearing in mind that, although it can sometimes feel like it has been around forever, capitalism as we know it is actually relatively new. Modern capitalism is mostly traced back to the enormous social and economic upheavals of the nineteenth century especially the Industrial Revolution in Great Britain, which Ireland was part of at that time. But it is illusionary to use this as a starting point without bringing to the fore how from as far back as the fifteenth century, British, and indeed Western colonization more broadly, ensured fertile conditions for industrial growth. European colonizers conquered vast regions in Africa, Asia and Latin America where they ruthlessly killed or enslaved their people, stole their natural resources and uprooted their existing social structures. Ireland was England's first and longest held colony and the occupation of Ireland was brutal. Millions of people were evicted from their land or became tenants of English landowners, one million are thought to have died during the so-called Great Famine of c. 1845–52 and another million emigrated, the scars of which are still felt today. There was food available in Ireland at this time including grains and livestock but much of this was exported mostly to Britain rather than being distributed. The occupation of Ireland robbed it of its language and much of its culture whilst anti-Irish prejudice exerted significant influence over British culture. The Irish ruling class were also active participants in the British slave trade and some families made fortunes both from selling slaves to plantation owners and by handling the products of their labour.[14] Their actions directly contributed to the concentration of wealth in urban areas around major ports in Belfast, Cork, Dublin and Limerick, a pattern of geo-economic distribution that largely remains intact today.

Capitalism also wasn't inevitable. It was strategically implemented through certain political decisions during the nineteenth century, including laws that combined small units of land into larger units which were then distributed amongst the few.[15] Many people who had independently managing their own small plot were no longer self-sufficient so were forced into the wage economy where they worked for these early modern capitalists in factories or as agricultural workers. Their bosses drew wealth from their surplus labour meaning people were – and still are – paid an amount that was less than the value of the goods and services they produced. As Karl Marx and Friedrich Engels wrote in the *Communist Manifesto*, they became

> a class of labourers, who live only so long as they work, and who work only so long as their labour increases capital. These labourers, who must sell themselves piece-meal, are a commodity, like every other article of commerce, and are consequently exposed to all the vicissitudes of competition, to all the fluctuations of the market.[16]

Although this is the version of events that matches the Irish experience, the Indian Marxist feminist Kumkum Sangari expresses concern that Eurocentric histories of modern capitalism do not transpose to other parts of the world where transitions were segmented. It is important to note that, in some countries, including India, different modes of production coexisted as did labour slavery, bonded labour practices and wage labour. Class and caste systems overlapped as did different pre-capitalist matrilineal and patrilineal family forms and systems.[17]

Another neglected aspect of Western capitalist formation was its parallel strengthening of individual household units so that domestic and care labour, or *social reproductive labour* could be privatized. Social reproductive labour includes childbearing and child-rearing, elder care, housework and other forms of care work that reproduce and sustain the workforce. Mostly, it is shouldered by women. Its privatization is the context within which Engels described the housewife as 'the first domestic servant, pushed out of participation in social production'.[18] Even a working woman, Engels maintained, must also fulfil her duties 'in the private service of her family'.[19] Anti-capitalist feminists have done important work in advancing Engels work on social reproductive theory and key thinkers include Cinzia Arruzza, Tithi Bhattacharya, Angela Davis, Susan Ferguson, Marnie Holborow and Lise Vogel all of whom acknowledge foundational work done by Engels, as articulated in *The Origins of the Family, Private Property and the State* which he wrote in 1884. This work's anthropological focus demonstrates how, before industrialization, communitarian kinships within which women were more autonomous were common. Engels outlines how technological advances (i.e. better but often heavier ploughing equipment) meant that profits could be drawn from agricultural work. Men were better able to operate these machines, especially when women were pregnant, meaning farming became a masculine endeavour. This doubled down on the notion that the unpaid labour of managing the home was woman's work and therefore a feminine endeavour.[20] Rather than being natural and universal, Engels thus squarely locates the patriarchal family structure, and the essentialized roles within it as an integral part of the social relations of capitalism.

Engels made mistakes and much of his thesis has been roundly criticized by anti-capitalist feminists including his dire prediction that the separation of labour and the copper-fastening of patriarchal inheritance lineage represented a 'world-historic defeat of the female sex'.[21] Arguably the most challenged aspect of Engels's work is his claim of a dual system that separated the *production* of goods from the *reproduction* of people. Lise Vogel goes so far as to suggest this separate treatment for waged and unwaged work, proceeding in parallel, contributes to an overall theoretical weakness in *The Origins*.[22] The Irish-based Marxist feminist Marnie Holborow (2024) succinctly summarizes other shortfalls including his sexist language, failure to fully explain the segregated, pressurized role of the working-class family and how he missed the fact that many women would, relatively quickly, be withdrawn from the workforce. But Holborow also reclaims much of Engels thinking by retaining the economic necessity of social reproductive labour, not as an aside, but an essential ingredient in the capitalist project. Protections for women and children proved essential, Holborow explains, as they 'effectively set the conditions for the reconstitution of the working-class family which would deliver, on an individualized basis, a steady stream of workers – fed and refreshed daily for today and new workers for tomorrow'.[23]

One thing that is certainly clear is that, as Angela Davis writes, 'the housewife as a finished historical product' is a relatively new phenomenon,[24] and one that prevails to this day. In Ireland, women still spend an average of 7.2 hours a week more on care work with 45 per cent of women providing care for others on a daily basis in an environment where 'traditional gendered allocation of housework persists in many households'.[25] Many men do more and sometimes equal housework, but it is still mostly conceived of as women's work. However, as Angela Davis argues, much social reproductive theory perfectly matches the white, middle-class experience, but is alien to the lives of many working-class and racialized women.[26] These women always worked for a wage, including wages for housework and mostly in the service of white middle-class women. Moreover, as the socialist feminist Susan Ferguson outlines, although widespread slavery had been abolished by the latter half of the 1800s, its legacy persisted through segregation, discriminatory economic policies and social practices that ensured industrial growth for mostly white populations, especially in the United States. These systems helped fuel industrial growth by keeping the cost of commodities low, enabling the expansion of widespread 'housewification'.[27] In other words, white women only got to become housewives in the first place because of the exploitation of black and brown women.

The neoliberalization of capitalism

The asymmetric path from the Industrial Revolution to the capitalism that we have today had many twists and turns. The market economy might have flourished for its capitalist beneficiaries in its early years but it soon began to flounder as the first quarter of the twentieth century was marred by financial instability, global conflict and the potential for socialist revolution. As the perpetual growth some presumed would last forever stagnated, Western nations started meddling in their supposedly free market in an attempt to stabilize economies. This was mostly through what is commonly called 'Keynesian economics' which was a set of policies that were modelled on ideas attributed to the British economist John Maynard Keynes. Keynes's way out of economic depression was for governments to spend more money on jobs, social supports and welfare programmes, believing the money it would put in people's pockets would stimulate growth and turn back the clock on recessionary patterns. Some people cling to the notion, even to this day, that Keynesianism was an expression of class compromise by the ruling class. I hold the view that its state interventionist theory was designed to shore up capitalism at a difficult time despite the fact that it too would inevitably run into problems, as happened in the 1970s with the stubborn stagnation of European economies.[28]

When Margaret Thatcher was elected as Britain's first female Prime Minister in 1979, she abandoned Keynesianism and, in tandem with Reaganomics in the United States, revolutionized the British economy by introducing specific fiscal and social policies.[29] Her neoliberal reforms had very particular features, all of which sought to return capitalism to many elements of pre-1920s classical liberalism's laissez-faire economics. These features included the deregulation of money markets, the privatization of social services and the management of national budget deficits through austerity instead of wealth taxes. The thinking behind these policies was – and still is – that any interference in market freedoms is wrong. Instead, a process of new public managerialism would infuse business-logic i.e. value for money, measurability and competition, in public-sector workplaces across the world. The ambition was to create a leaner, hollowed-out state structure that could outsource as much of its work as is humanly possible, be this the provision of housing, education or welfare. Meanwhile trade unions, the entities which organize workers and collectively bargain for decent working conditions, were deliberately portrayed as old-fashioned and even greedy and, as Chapter 3 explains, new laws curbed their activity so they could no longer taint a competitive world order.

The merits of these neoliberal policies and practices we were (and are) told is that if we allow entrepreneurialism to flourish, the wealth that is generated at the top of society will seep downwards and enrich everyone. There will be better and more jobs, public transport that run frequently and on time, and more efficient healthcare and education services. Together these factors will create the conditions for each of us to reach our fullest potential in a world where we are solely responsible for our own lives, regardless of our circumstances. Margaret Thatcher, most notably articulated this perspective in an interview with the magazine *Women's Own* when she stated:

> I think we have gone through a period when too many children and people have been given to understand 'I have a problem, it is the

Government's job to cope with it!' or 'I have a problem, I will go and get a grant to cope with it!' 'I am homeless, the Government must house me!' and so they are casting their problems on society and who is society? There is no such thing! There are individual men and women and there are families and no government can do anything except through people and people look to themselves first.[30]

Notice how Thatcher made sure to preserve the family – the socio-economic unit of capitalist success but pushes hard on the individualist perspective. If you are poor, it is probably because you don't work hard enough or don't avail of the opportunities available to you. If you don't have a job, it's because you aren't resourceful enough. If you don't have somewhere to live, maybe you didn't save hard enough or manage your money correctly, or you aren't ambitious enough. The solution to your woes lies with you, never mind the exorbitant cost of housing.

Thatcher is also credited with popularizing the now broadly accepted discourse that there is no alternative to capitalism. This mantra runs so deep that there can be virtually no support for alternative policies in the corridors of political power. This is despite the steadfast assertions that wealth would trickle downwards not proving to be correct. Instead, David Harvey notes, 'enough contradictions in the neoliberal position to render evolving neoliberal practices (vis-à-vis issues such as monopoly power and market failures) unrecognisable in relation to the seeming purity of neoliberal doctrine'.[31] The free market isn't free. Repeated policy decisions have centralized money and power in the hands of a small number of people who control the jobs, health and housing market, our access to food and our freedom to move across borders. Mostly, these people haven't acquired this wealth through merit but because of a myriad of advantages bestowed on them including inheritance, better education and lots of social and cultural capital. The depth of inequality and the scale of associated problems are staggering. Globally, the richest 10 per cent take home 52 per cent of all income whilst the poorest half earns just 8.5 per cent.[32] In Ireland, our richest 1 per cent hoard 27 per cent of all wealth, a share that has grown significantly in the last ten years.[33] To better understand what these numbers look like in the day-to-day, think about the rising prices of food our supermarkets sell which has directly contributed to the growth in food banks across Europe, one of the richest parts of the world. Mostly, this rising cost of living is blamed on increased transport costs, hikes in the cost of manufacturing food or sometimes even the modest pay rises frontline staff receive. A much less talked about factor is that retailers like Tesco, one of the biggest supermarket groups in Europe, always prioritize profits above all else. In 2022, their annual operating profit in the UK and Ireland alone was almost €3 billion.[34] It took Unite the Union to highlight how, whilst large segments of society were struggling to put food on the table, Tesco was engaging in excessive profiteering and corporate greed.[35]

Another aspect of neoliberal globalization is the management of country-to-country borders which promote the free flow of goods and capital whilst limiting the movement of people. Think about how some of the goods Tesco sell would have reached its shelves on massive container ships, some almost a quarter of a mile long, that continuously move around the world. This practice is justified by the claim that open trade fosters competition, encourages innovation and delivers greater efficiency. Its flip side, aside from the obvious environmental downsides, is that neoliberalism's model of free trade forces millions of people into abysmal working conditions in countries where they have fewer legal protections, meaning companies can get away with paying them a pittance, often in dangerous jobs as they service the hyper-consumerism of the Global North. One example that is commonly drawn out to demonstrate this is fast-fashion, an industry that upholds unrealistic beauty standards for women across the world and one where Tesco is an active participant. In 2013, the world got a glimpse behind the scenes when the Rana Plaza textile factory in Bangladesh collapsed killing over 1,100 mostly female subcontracted garment workers some of whom were manufacturing clothes for the Irish-owned company Primark. This corporate giant has made much of both short- and long-term compensations for families and surviving workers,[36] but like other multinationals, they continue to use deeply anti-union Corporate Responsibility Model contracts that exploit workers in poorer countries. Meanwhile, the pollutants created by cheap, on-trend clothes that are designed to be snapped up at the height of their popularity then discarded soon afterwards, are returned to the Global South where clothes' mountains are now a permanent feature across West Africa particularly in Ghana as well as in Chile's Atacama Desert. Catherine Rottenberg maintains that liberal feminist's capacity to turn a blind-eye to the low-paid, precarious workforce behind this and many other lifestyle choices people make has been part of the re-invention of female emancipation as one where women are now expected to thrive in both career *and* family, effortlessly manage their own work-life balance and control their fertility long enough to make sure they do their bit to drive consumerism forward.[37]

Understanding patriarchy

All feminists draw from theories of patriarchy, and everyone agrees that the oppression of women and girls is not particular to modern capitalism but pre-dates it. In isolation, patriarchy mostly refers to the economic, social and cultural oppression of women by men, something bell hooks calls 'institutionalized sexism'.[38] The expression, as it is used today, emerged from white-Western consciousness-raising feminisms of the 1960s when women realized that, even within the seemingly egalitarian rights-based movements they were part of, male abuses of power were endemic.[39] Its connectedness to, and interdependence with, other structures has been widely debated within feminism, as has its universalization.

Often, the word 'patriarchy' is used in a way that is theoretically weak. For example, Western liberal feminists' call to 'smash the patriarchy' is not only abstract, but reinforces gender essentialism, something these same feminists argue against in other spaces. Sangari maintains this Euro-American take on patriarchy, omits the unequal distribution of power amongst men and the consent or complicity of women in upholding patriarchal power. Or, to use Sangari's own words, 'women can be on both sides of the divisions between oppressed and oppressors, exploited and exploiters'.[40] Her solution is to pluralize to *patriarchies* thus creating a more workable, non-singular concept that holds differences across nation spaces and recognizes other axes of oppression. There is no doubt that different men benefit from different patriarchies and that many men are disturbed by the oppression of women. But some men, across all walks of life, resist equality with women because of the many benefits bestowed on them. These advantages can include occupational rewards, freedom from much unpaid labour, the right to be in charge and the prestige of simply being male. And although many men do not harass or attack women, many men do use violence to control and disarm women. The sociologist Raewyn Connell argues that the masculine dominance patriarchy upholds means that the men who are violent don't necessarily think of themselves in that way and might even feel that their actions are entirely justified and authorized by the ideology of male supremacy.[41] Conversely, patriarchy's feminine coding valorizes women for being good mothers, attentive partners and employees who don't make a fuss when they meet sexism in the workplace. When women do step out of these parameters, the structures of capitalist-patriarchies can push back in the form of misogyny, something Kate

Manne describes a structural pattern of behaviour that controls and punishes women and girls when they challenge the status quo. Manne calls misogyny 'the "law enforcement" branch of a patriarchal order which has the overall function of *policing* and *governing* its ideology'.[42]

As I write, it is hard not to be struck by a growing acceptance of misogynistic rhetoric and behaviours in the public domain in a way that would have been unthinkable even a decade ago. Take Donald Trump's triumph in the 2024 US presidential election which proceeded despite a Manhattan federal jury in a civil lawsuit finding him liable for sexual abuse and guilty verdicts for 'hush money' payments to hide sexual misconduct. Trump personifies capitalism's relationship with patriarchy embodying hyper-masculinity and misogyny and actively seeking to curb the rights of women and also LGBTQIA+ people, migrants and other minority groups. Outside of politics, far-right activists like Andrew Tate and the supposedly more moderate Canadian psychologist Jordan Peterson remain popular. Tate, whose TikTok videos have amassed 11.6 billion views,[43] claims women are the property of men, that they shouldn't drive and that rape victims are responsible for their own attacks. Peterson's pseudo-scientific claims include that patriarchy is natural and normal and that women actively choose lower-paid jobs instead of learning to be more competitive and better negotiators.[44] When these men use misogynistic rhetoric, it widens what other men think it is acceptable to say and do in public, never mind what they might think is okay behind closed doors.

Performing feminism

When feminists buy into the pretence that patriarchy is singular and universal, that misogyny is an individualized trait and that it's okay to ignore the structural role of social reproductive labour, they generalize the lives of mostly white, middle-class Western women whilst ignoring the negative aspects of the political system they support. At the same time they perform feminism by co-opting concepts at the heart of anti-establishment feminism. One of the most obvious examples of this is the deradicalization of the concept *intersectionality*, a term coined by the US civil rights advocate and legal expert Kimberlé Crenshaw, when she sought to articulate the problems with viewing oppressions on a singular axis of either 'race' or 'gender'. Intersectionality pre-dates Crenshaw through the writings of radical black feminists including Angela Davis, bell hooks and Audre

Lorde. Today, this analytical tool is equally applied to other oppressions and discriminatory features like disability, age or sexual orientation describing how these oppressions don't exist side by side but compound each other. Without an intersectional analysis, it is argued, there can be an over-simplification of complex racial, gendered and other dynamics of power. Marxist feminists including Tithi Bhattacharya, Nancy Fraser and Lisa Vogel have discussed the strengths and limits of an intersectional lens, and identity politics more broadly (a topic I return to in Chapter 7) cautioning us against focusing on identity in a way that overshadows economic inequality and the centrality of class struggle. The anti-capitalist feminism I advocate seeks to synthesize both perspectives. It views capitalism as the central feature that gives rise to patriarchy, racism, colonization and imperialism *and* also as the structure that creates working-class exploitation without viewing this latter oppression as a privileged analysis.[45]

Beyond the theoretical, there is no denying that the essence of intersectionalism has been greatly undermined and co-opted beyond all recognition within neoliberal Western feminism. Mostly it has become a symbolic performance of addressing issues through institutional rebranding that is rarely accompanied by concrete changes that might meaningfully impact the realities of structural inequality. The extent to which its mutation has occurred was crystallized for me when I heard the word trip off the tongue of a sitting centre-right Fianna Fáil TD at a National Women's Council of Ireland event when defending his government's response to domestic violence. I shouldn't have been surprised. 'Intersectionality' is listed as one of the values that underpin Ireland's most recent *National Strategy for Women and Girls 2017–2020* where it sits alongside 'inclusiveness', 'generosity', 'diversity', 'respect for human rights', 'non-discrimination' and 'equality'. Strange words from a neoliberal government whose political choices have repeatedly ignored concrete proposals by charities on ways to address a housing and homelessness crisis that disproportionately impacts women, who have repeatedly failed to honour commitments they made through the Istanbul Convention Action Against Violence Against Women and who have made no serious attempt to gender and equality-proof their fiscal decisions despite knowing that women disproportionately rely on the welfare state and are more likely to work for low pay and under insecure working conditions.[46]

Colonizing the language of intersectionalism also has a negative effect on the people who get caught up in its promotion. I am talking about those who get invited into largely unchanged spaces where they are expected to be the face of reform. I asked my colleague Lilian Nwanze-Akobo to tell me about her experiences. 'I get called into spaces a lot, to be the Black face' she told me, continuing:

> At first, I didn't realize that this was what was happening. I really thought people wanted to hear what I had to say – for a change! So, I was delighted! It very quickly dawned on me at some of those functions and panels, when I saw the glazed eyes and the uninterested looks, that it wasn't really about what I had to say. It was about ticking the right boxes. Because, you see, ticking the boxes meant that an institution or group could be seen as doing the right thing. Is there a black face on your panel? Then you understand and are implementing diversity policies. Tick! So, as I sat in panel after panel and meeting after meeting, on board after board, I realized that I was naïve to think that things were going to change.

Increasingly, liberal feminists, including those who perform intersectionality whilst upholding the capitalist system, are described as 'white feminists'. Ruby Hamad, academic, journalist and author of *White Tears, Brown Scars* (2020) describes whiteness in this context as a shifting political concept that refers to the privileges some people enjoy solely because their identity resembles Western European heritage. White feminism can sometimes be dismissed in Irish contexts because of Ireland's own history of colonization and racialization where the Irish were unfairly linked to agriculture and dirt in contrast to the perceived cleanliness of the white British middle class.[47] Or people can argue that it is perfectly reasonable to only be concerned with the experiences of white women because the migration that normalized ethnic diversity in Ireland only began in the 1990s. But what about the ongoing oppression of Ireland's indigenous Traveller population who have long been denied the right to their own narrative and nomadic lifestyle? Instead, their place in society is determined by people who are mostly concerned with the supposed problems Traveller communities create with no appreciation for how their erasure from the dominant history of Irishness has greatly contributed to their oppression.[48] In 2018, following a sustained campaign, Irish Travellers eventually secured ethnic minority recognition. Nonetheless, they remain the most discriminated against people in Ireland in just about every aspect of their lives including health, housing, employment, education and even the right to socialize. Megan Berry, who is a Traveller and an education outreach worker, highlighted the weight of this discrimination when she told me how 'it happens on a daily basis for ourselves' continuing:

When it comes to Travellers in Ireland, it is accepted that people will openly discriminate. And you see that in politics, and in people of authority when they perpetuate stereotypes or if we look at the media and how it portrays Travellers and the lack of accountability and sanctions. The general population is very easily enabled to jump on that band wagon and to come out and be discriminatory.

As a white woman, I can argue against white feminism by refusing to centre the experiences and perspectives of white middle-class women. Indeed, many theorists who write against white feminism reject the crude binary of 'white' and 'non-white' and ask that people don't retreat into their own racialized categories. For example, the journalist and author of *Against White Feminism* (2021), Rafia Zakaria acknowledges the challenges for anti-capitalist feminists who are white when they are unfairly categorized with the very liberals they have fought against for decades. She also asks feminists of colour not to see every flawed interaction as racially motivated.[49] Similarly, the academic and writer Emma Dabiri, who speaks openly about experiencing racism growing up in Ireland, agrees racial binaries can unhelpfully flatten very different experiences, concerns and agendas. The 'white feminists' that I know do nothing substantial to address the plight of Travellers even though Traveller women have a mortality rate that is five times higher than the national average, a suicide rate that is also five times the national rate and only a 13 per cent chance of finishing school, which compares to a national rate of 95 per cent.[50]

Rethinking feminism: An overview of the book

This chapter introduced the two souls of feminism, arguing liberal feminism is a dead end in eliminating gender-based oppression whilst anti-capitalist feminism provides a superior, alternative route to change. I have offered a very broad sense of how capitalism emerged and have outlined its interdependence with patriarchy. It is followed by five thematically organized chapters: feminism and electoral politics; the world of work and the role of trade unions; feminism and trans liberation; gender-based violence including state violence; and reproductive rights and justice. Each chapter sets out a multi-dimensional historical context that recognizes how, typically, history is told from the perspective of privilege. The book's final chapter draws lessons from across each theme to articulate a vision for the future that encourages solidarity across lines of difference and makes the case for a politically charged, praxis-oriented approach that refuses to strip feminism of its substance and potential to contribute to radical change.

As well as theoretical insights from other scholars and secondary readings from a range of sources, this book features insights from over seventy activists I engaged with during this project, some of who you have met in this chapter. Forty-three people responded to an online open call to 'feminist activists' to tell me about their work. I also interviewed thirty-one activists, some of whom I knew personally, others I had interacted with during specific campaigns and others who were suggested to me or, in one instance, got in touch with me directly seeking to be involved. I don't cite everyone I spoke to verbatim, or name everyone explicitly, but our conversations have been immensely informative, nonetheless. Some readers might argue that the purposeful selection of mostly like-minded people is a weakness because it denies liberal feminists the opportunity to express an alternative point of view. But there are other books that fulfil that function, and my aim is to shine a light on Irish-based anti-capitalist feminism, both historically and to this day and to locate this within a wider global context.

Some political parties claim to be feminist, but they aren't. So many 'feminists' in these parties turn a blind eye to wrong doings by their own organizations.

– Dublin-based trade unionist and feminist activist

Chapter 2

FEMINISM AND ELECTORAL POLITICS

In 1876, at a time when the British Empire was saturated with patriarchal values, the married couple Anna and Thomas Haslam set up what many believe to be Ireland's first suffragette society. They called it the Dublin Women's Suffrage Society. Only men were allowed to vote at that time and only if they met certain property qualifications. The Haslams, who were unionists, wanted this to change. With their supporters, they set out to shift public opinion by petitioning Westminster to accept that women were not inferior to men and therefore deserved an equal right to vote.[1] The couple may have been the first to seek the franchise for women, but they weren't the first 'feminists', a word that wasn't in use at that time. One forerunner that we know about was Tipperary-born Anna Wheeler Doyle who, in the 1820s, had also sought to dispel deeply rooted essentialist beliefs about women's inferiority. She too believed their subordination was socially conditioned and openly endorsed the opinions on women's entitlements to rights that were put forward by Mary Wollstonecraft in *Vindication of the rights of women* (1792), a paper many people regard as the first feminist text. But she went further than the mostly liberal ideas of Wollstonecraft by arguing 'female equality is impossible without socialism'.[2] In the years that followed, Anna Wheeler Doyle's contribution to the historical relationship between socialism and feminism was generally overshadowed by the popularity attained by her co-author William Thompson.[3] Together they argued for reform of the social institutions of education, church, marriage and politics which they presented as 'the engines of oppression' that blocked happiness for all regardless of class, gender and race.[4]

Class prejudice also ran deep. When educated women were allowed to both vote and run as candidates in local elections from 1898 onwards, this was mostly so they could fulfil certain duties as Poor Law Guardians and District Counsellors; roles that were often seen as an act of charity towards poorer women who they rarely saw as equals. Many more suffragette societies had cropped up in towns and cities in the years in between, despite not always being welcomed by other women. Some women were perfectly happy not voting, believing they were much better off left to care for the home and the children. It was considered that they didn't have the time, never mind the intellect, to offer any worthwhile opinions on political issues. Others opposed suffragettes for reasons that are best understood if we accept that their cause was not a homogeneous movement. Suffragists, like the Haslams, backed the continued union of Ireland and Britain. Other societies moved beyond simply not having a vote by also supporting the disruption of Anglo-Irish relations often through the campaign for Home Rule; a political movement that had significant momentum behind it at the time. For other societies, their suffragette struggle went further still by throwing their support behind the struggle for complete independence from British imperialist rule.

These ideological differences translated across tactics too. Pro-union societies mostly sought change through a combination of education and cordial negotiation with those in Westminster whilst republican groups including the militant Irish Women's Franchise League (IWFL) believed this approach would not disrupt a situation that had festered for years. They didn't shy away from a confrontational approach including acts of civil disobedience. In 1912, eight members of the IWFL, including the renowned republican Hanna Sheehy-Skeffington, protested against the absence of votes for women in a Home Rule bill by smashing the windows of government buildings. Their revolt led to Sheehy-Skeffington spending two months in prison where she successfully won political prisoner status by staging a hunger strike in support of the treatment of some English suffragettes.[5] Another division that cut across the British Empire's suffragette movement was its fracture during the outbreak of war across Europe. Some feminists argued that loyalty to the nation-state and support for the war effort should take temporary precedence over equal citizenship, whilst others, including Sylvia Pankhurst, rejected nationalism and extended their campaign to include the equal distribution of food, equal pay for women during the war effort, a moratorium on debts and the extension of welfare to working-class women.[6]

Regardless of their political hue or choice of tactics, the feminists who fought for franchise faced fierce opposition from many men involved in politics. The Irish Home Rule MPs who drafted the aforementioned Home Rule bill, and who held the balance of power between political parties in Westminster, refused to even mention suffrage for women for fear it might jeopardize what they determined was a very separate project.[7] As far as they were concerned, Home Rule represented no break with male rule. In the end, Home Rule was never granted, in part because of opposition from unionists and in part because of the aforementioned Europe-wide war. Instead, the Irish Free State (hereafter Ireland) of twenty-six counties was established following an armed rebellion, war of independence and ultimately a civil war. Many women participated in the struggle for independence. They helped smuggle weapons across Ireland, provided safe houses and actively fought on the front line, most famously as Cumann na mBan (which translates as The Women's Council). When the new state's *Constitution of the Irish Free State* (1922) was drawn up, the more radical perspective on suffrage won through, allowing all citizens of a certain age the right to vote. Only property owners could run and vote in the now partitioned six counties of Northern Ireland which remains part of the UK to this day.[8]

It seems fair enough to presume that, if the suffragettes were around today, they would be disappointed to learn that in the more than one hundred years that followed, just 173 women had served as TDs (Teachta Dála which translates as member of Parliament) by 2025, out of 1,358 TDs overall. An essential part of feminist theory is believing that stereotypical ideas about what good leadership looks like impact women's likelihood to succeed in the political arena. But there are other factors that explain women's capacity to even get involved in politics in the first place. Sue Maguire neatly categorizes these into three core areas: the first is structural and institutional barriers such as an array of sometimes complicated recruitment and selection procedures that disadvantage women. The second is knowledge and information barriers on how things work, and the third is social and cultural barriers including time pressures, the disproportionate care loads many women carry and a fear of online abuse.[9] Women who enter politics definitely face a more difficult working environment than their male counterparts. To illustrate, Neasa Hourigan of the Green Party once described her work as a TD as being marred by a persistent 'dark hum' of online abuse as well as more occasional in-person harassment and even assault.[10] And whilst most political parties claim to support gender equality, they often fail to protect their own members from deeply ingrained sexism within their ranks. For example, when a Limerick-based local councillor was one of many women to be the subject of misogynistic hatred in a WhatsApp group that included the then sitting TD Brian Leddin, he initially refused to admit any wrongdoing despite describing the independent councillor as 'unhinged' and 'craving fame'. He eventually apologized but faced no sanctions from the Green Party, much to the disappointment of some of its female members including Catherine Martin, the former leader of its women's caucus.[11] There has also been reluctance to tackle sexism in Northern Ireland despite equally clear examples. In 2022, Doug Beattie was unanimously backed by his party to remain as leader of the Ulster Unionist Party despite a series of vile racist and misogynistic tweets surfacing.

Even if there were more women in politics, the diverse perspectives of the suffragette movement illuminate how, just like other strata of society, women are not a homogeneous group that share the same political beliefs. This hasn't stopped repeated campaigns by liberal feminists who blanketly appeal to us to vote for women despite knowing that there is no guarantee this will lead to anything other than singular career success for some women. Garnering votes for women is just one aspect of this approach. The group Women for Election was amongst those who changed how electoral politics works in Ireland by successfully campaigning for gender quotas. Since 2012, political parties that don't select at least 30 per cent of female candidates to contest each election face fines. In 2023, that quota rose to 40 per cent. Women who seek to avail of these quotas are sometimes offered training in politics, economics and campaign management by other feminist groups such as that provided by the Longford-based See Her Elected that work with women across the political spectrum, including on the far right, who are contemplating running for public office.

The trouble with politics

Gender quotas and bespoke education programmes that create pathways into politics might seem reasonable at first glance, but they tend to benefit white, middle-class women who haven't had to face the same challenges as many working-class women, women of colour, LGBTQIA+ candidates or women from other marginalized communities. They also don't address some of the structural issues outlined by Maguire nor do these reforms do anything about much-deeper issues with systems of representative democracy and institutions of political power which I will now outline. Although Dáil Éireann (Ireland's lower house) and Seanad Éireann (Ireland's upper house) are mostly presented as fair and transparent, there are many ways in which they are rife with exclusionary processes. There are many examples of how this is the case including how Ireland's neoliberal political parties feel very much at home within a donation-driven model of Western politics where wealthy individuals and corporations often curry political favour.[12] Ireland does have tight limits on the size of political donations and foreign donations are not allowed at all. But this doesn't guarantee governments will act in the spirit of these rules. One stark example was when, much to the dismay of many people, a Fine Gael government appealed against a ruling by a European Commission (EC) watchdog that the multinational tech company Apple was to repay €13 billion in unpaid taxes to compensate for paying as little as 1 per cent on profits. The EC ruling was that Apple received preferential treatment from the Irish government which disadvantaged other countries that also wanted to attract the company to their shores. The government reversed tack in 2024 when Apple lost its latest bid against the order, but indicated the money that must now be repaid to Ireland could not be used for day-to-day spending.

Political parties that support more of the same also undeniably benefit from the capitalist-friendly control of major media outlets, which often fight politics on moral issues or on the likeability of individual candidates, giving much less attention to the incremental fiscal policies politicians pass that global corporations like Apple are most likely to benefit from. At the same time, opponents who expose the flaws in mainstream politics or suggest that we might move beyond capitalism are portrayed as troublemakers who hold naïve, ill-thought-out ideas.

There are other problems with electoral politics too including that some people's trust in government can be so low that they don't bother voting at all, especially when the white, middle-class and cis male-dominated political mainstream is worlds apart from their lives. Other people are denied the right to vote including prisoners, those forced to migrate, some migrants and those whose precarious housing circumstances deny them a suitable postal address. Karl Marx's observation, many years ago, that '[t]he executive of the modern State is but a committee for managing the common affairs of the whole bourgeoisie' would appear to ring true to this day.[13]

The complex role of the state, women and the church in early politics

Of course, the Dáil and Seanad are just one entity within a much broader apparatus of *the state,* something that can be quite difficult to define but is best understood as a convergence of contradictory institutions with different functions and hierarchies. The government's job, at least on paper, is to collect and spend money on behalf of citizens, to formulate the will of the people into laws which they then implement (i.e. their pre-election promises) and to represent the totality of the state in its interactions with other nation-states. However, history reveals how, since the foundation of the Irish state, its actions have frequently strayed beyond these boundaries. Almost immediately after the ink was dry on the aforementioned equality-focused constitution of 1922, the political party Cumann na nGaedheal (predecessor to Fine Gael) and the first to govern a new postcolonial state, formed the first of many alliances with the Catholic Church that proved deeply damaging for women and girls. Part of the reason for this union was that the new state had practically no financial reserves and therefore needed Church support to enable its transition into a stable, independent, capitalist state.[14] Almost immediately, the Catholic Church assumed control of schools, hospitals and just about every other aspect of Irish society, meaning the morals of Catholicism were deeply inculcated in people of all genders who were conditioned to internalize its teachings from a very young age. These were reinforced by Cumann na nGaedheal who introduced a raft of morally driven reforms that brought state laws in line with the teachings of the Catholic Church, including censorship laws, anti-divorce laws and restrictions on women's access to the workforce. As these reforms made their way through the Irish parliament a cultural environment was created where unelected religious clergy assumed significant positions of power.

One of the purposes of this chapter is to illuminate how involving women in electoral politics doesn't necessarily change anything and that being female is a wholly unreliable marker in determining the political decisions a person will make. One early example of this was that there were six women on the executive committee of Fianna Fáil when it was established in 1926 including well-known suffragettes and freedom fighters.[15] But instead of offering an alternative to an already established coalition of church and state when they took power in 1932, their model of *economic nationalism* was wholly dependant on the subordination of women. Fianna Fáil extended the marriage bar, banned contraception and even curtailed socializing through a strict licencing system for dance halls. One of Fianna Fáil's most significant interventions in casting women's role as one of childrearing and homemaking was when they successfully introduced a deeply misogynistic, second *Constitution of Ireland* in 1937. This legislative framework not only afforded a 'special position' for the Catholic Church, it also explicitly stated, in Article 41.2, that a woman's place is in the home without which 'the common good cannot be achieved'.

Pausing this historical narrative for a moment, this is as good a time as ever to point out that Article 41.2 is still *in situ*. In March 2024, a referendum to remove this wording was defeated by a whopping 73 per cent. All government parties and indeed most parties on the political left had supported the proposal as had the membership organization the National Women's Council of Ireland (NWCI) which ran an extensive campaign in support of removing sexist language and essentialized gender roles. Disability groups and some civil rights groups, including the Free Legal Aid Board and the Irish Council for Civil Liberties, campaigned against the amendment because of real concerns that the alternative wording proposed by the coalition government of Fine Gael, Fianna Fáil and the Green Party would enshrine care as an individual responsibility and not a constitutional right. As the disability rights activist Alannah Murray explained in the run up to the vote:

> I welcome the removal of wording that has long been outdated and sexist. Changing the wording, however, will not make a meaningful difference to the view of women. It does have the opportunity to fundamentally set the conversation about disabled rights and justice for disabled people back a considerable amount.[16]

Back in 1937, when the original wording was inserted, there were two female politicians in the Fianna Fáil party in government. These were Helena Concannon, who had previously been vocal about women's right to education, and Margaret Pearse, sister of the renowned republican Pádraig Pearse. The tactic appear to have adopted to stay out of discussions regardless of how they might have felt about their party's position.[17] A third woman, Bridget Redmond, who was the widow of former Fine Gael TD William Redmond, was also a TD in the opposition benches. Being a close family member of a former or sitting TD wasn't uncommon. In fact, of the just twenty-eight women who served as TDs between 1921 and 1980, twenty-one were either widows, mothers, sisters or daughters of a former serving politician. This practice doesn't necessarily undermine liberal perspectives which largely presume that simply getting more women around the political table will bring unique insights into topics that would otherwise be ignored. But keeping it in the family does lead us to assume that certain people are primed for political life, creating a cycle of entitlement that ensures the concentration of power in the same demographic. This makes it even more difficult than it already is for people from different backgrounds to gain a foothold in what sometimes acts as a closed system.

To be fair to the three women in the Dáil, their presence was greatly outnumbered by men and they likely had no say in their exclusion from the all-male working group that crafted the constitution. But there isn't much evidence to suggest that they supported what resistance was there to anti-women reforms, all of which emanated from outside the Dáil. It was the Irish Women Workers' Union (IWWU) that campaigned for and won an amendment to a 1927 law that allowed women to 'opt out' of jury duty rather than be banned altogether,[18] a revision that, in the end, was largely ineffective. The IWWU also resisted the 1937 constitution along with graduate and professional women's groups as part of what Joyce Padbury has described as 'a lively articulation of feminist opinion that surprized the political establishment by its vigour, its persistence and its critical dexterity'.[19] These feminists sought amendments to the constitution in the first instance, and then called for its outright rejection when the reforms they won were insufficient. But they failed to sway the electorate mostly because voting patterns were largely in accordance with civil war politics.[20] A vote against the constitution was considered a vote against Fianna Fáil who promoted the constitution as an expression of Irish sovereignty that would end certain legal and economic obligations to Britain.[21] Many people simply weren't tuned into the consequences for women and a strong nationalist ideology won out. Women would have to wait in line.

The anti-constitution campaign was far from perfect and there are lessons we can learn from it. The IWWU, whose membership included thousands of mostly working-class women across the country, pulled back once minor amendments were agreed to, meaning that the campaign that continued didn't have the potential power of collective action paid workers hold (more on this in Chapter 3). The campaign also failed to connect with the lives of ordinary women which, at that point, were already dominated by high levels of social reproductive labour within patriarchal domestic environments.[22] The sociologist Ronit Lentin also notes that these feminists' failed to depict Irishness as anything other than white-Europeanness and therefore dismissed ethnic diversity, including Traveller identity. According to Lentin, Irish feminists have continued to gloss over this failure when recounting events of the time.[23]

Opposition to the constitution and its consequences continued within the political arena but with little success. This was mostly through the Women's Social and Progressive League (WSPL) which was formed in 1937. One of its founders and former Fianna Fáil member Dorothy McArdle described the need for a new entity as a 'humiliating necessity' given the repression of women's rights.[24] In 1943, the WSPL backed four independent candidates in the general election including the republican and suffragette Hanna Sheehy-Skeffington. All four were unsuccessful. There is no doubt that these and other feminists were operating within a hostile repressive cultural environment and a picture is sometimes painted of zero feminism between the 1940s and the 1970s. However, several feminist historians have rejected this analysis including Linda Connolly, whose extensive research on what she calls the Irish Women's Movement, acknowledges some retreat post-independence, but documents a persistent and oppositional feminist presence throughout the twentieth century.[25] Equally, Liz Kyte's study of socialist feminism reveals strong internationalist connections and a phase in Irish feminism 'as interactive, plural, dynamic, diffuse and exhibiting a persistent presence' where these women's 'self-conscious dissent from the political and social mainstream provided an alternative world-view conducive to creative experiments in fusing feminism with socialism and other radical currents of the day'.[26]

Historians also illuminate the work of the Irish Housewives Association (IHA) which was established by Hilda Tweedy and some friends in the early 1940s and campaigned on the cost of living and the oppression of women for over thirty years. In response to concerns about escalating food and fuel prices and their impact on working-class children in particular, one of the IHA's first actions was to deliver a statement of concerns to members of parliament the day before the 1941 budget.[27] They also collaborated with the Communist Party of Ireland (CPI), the IWWU and some members of the Labour Party in forming an ad hoc pressure group called the 'Lower Price Council' (LPC), borrowing its title from similar state-initiated entities in the UK.[28] Maureen O'Carroll, one of the founders of the LPC, served as a TD for the Labour Party between 1954 and 1957. Despite this long history of protesting against government policy and a pattern of nominating candidates for election, the IHA always claimed to be non-political and non-sectarian and its membership was always a politically mixed bag. Claiming to be non-political remains common today and is somewhat understandable given the way so many people feel let down by politics. However, the IHA's absence of a clear political stance allowed others to dictate where it stood, as happened when, after much internal debate, they sent a message of support to a Paris-based peace congress co-hosted by a communist feminist organization. When this was made public, the IHA failed to stand its ground and lost control of the narrative, leading to sections of the Irish press negatively describing them as communist sympathizers and organizers, leading many members to complain or resign outright.[29] Charles McQuaid, archbishop of Dublin and close confidant to then Taoiseach (Prime Minister) Éamon De Valera, was so troubled by the accusation, he coaxed allies into joining the association so they could report back on its inner workings, forcing the IHA to close its membership for a time.[30]

Feminism from the 1960s onwards

A key argument that I make throughout this book is that, when potential challengers to the capitalist status quo begin to gain ground, one of the central features of its protagonists in government is to co-opt their demands into the capitalist project. This likely influenced the Irish government's engagement with the IHA who, by the 1960s, had rebuilt its reputation and was prepared to negotiate with the government in seeking a better life for women. In 1967, through their connections with the International Alliance of Women, Tweedy learned about a directive from the UN Commission on the Status of Women (est. 1946) inviting non-governmental groups to investigate the status of women in their own countries. This directive didn't appear out of the blue but in the context of significant social unrest and anti-government protests across Europe. The IHA joined forces with the Association of Business and Professional Women who were also aware of the directive and called a meeting of about twenty women's groups including trade unionists but mostly graduates groups, sports clubs and religious groups.[31] Following this initial meeting, negotiations with politicians in power led to the establishment of Ireland's own Commission on the Status of Women in 1970. Never mind that this was the same government that was colluding with the Catholic Church on the routine incarceration of women and girls and the trafficking of their babies, upholding marriage bars that relegated women to the domestic sphere where male violence against women was not seen as an issue at all, and denying access to abortion and contraception. Eventually, this commission evolved into the Council for the Status of Women (CSW) that received their first tranche of government funding in 1975.

The formation of this government-friendly CSW probably drew groups like the IHA away from more radical influences, including the outspoken Irish Women's Liberation Movement (IWLM) which burst onto the scene in 1970. This gathering of around twelve mostly journalists and professional people but also trade unionists, nationalists, civil rights and housing rights activists lit a spark in Irish society by publicly demanding immediate action on equal pay, equality before the law, equality in education, contraception, housing and justice for deserted wives, widows and unmarried mothers. Some of its members weren't afraid to call out politicians, sometimes with mixed results. One example was when the IWLM was invited to appear on, and format, an episode of the popular prime time television show *The Late Late Show*. When one of their members Mary Kenny commented from the floor that politicians didn't give a damn about women, the sitting Fine Gael TD Garret Fitzgerald (who would go on to serve twice as Taoiseach) was so infuriated that he left his home close by and drove to the studio. He was then escorted on set by RTÉ staff and seated amidst the IWLM panellists. Recalling the evening many years later, IWLM member Rosita Sweetman writes:

> The rest of the show didn't turn out to be quite the mature, reasoned, reasonable exposition on the rights of women which we'd hoped and drilled. Once on the panel 'Garret the Good' had a great time telling everyone in his big booming man's voice how brilliant things were going to be for women once he got in. The studio duly exploded. There was lots and lots of screaming. We thought we'd arranged for every eventuality on *The Late Late,* but we'd never foreseen a six-foot-something upper-middle-class politician parachuting in and taking over.[32]

But the IWLM was not united in its political analysis, and it disbanded within eighteen months. One member, Nuala Fennell, went so far as to write an open letter accusing other members of 'using Women's Liberation as a pseudo-respectable front for their own various political ends'.[33]

Characterizing 'being political' as a negative trait is a common tactic in seeking to discredit one's political opponents and Fennell never applied this metric to centre-right parties. Indeed, following an unsuccessful campaign for election as an independent, and with the support of the Women's Political Association (est. 1977), she joined a Fine Gael party that was pivoting strongly towards neoliberalism and entered the Dáil in 1981. She was soon joined by her party colleagues Monica Barnes, co-founder of the CSW and chairwoman of Women Elect, and Gemma

Hussey, founder of the Women's Political Association. These women were undoubtedly the forerunners of the neoliberal lean-in feminism that remains strongly present within Fine Gael to this day and that speaks mainly to middle-class women.

There were other female candidates vying for parliamentary seats at that time whose politics held a strong focus on women's rights. These included Nan Joyce, the first Traveller to ever run for parliament, and Liz Noonan who ran as an independent Lesbian Feminist Candidate in 1981 and 1982. The Northern Irish civil rights activist and former MP in Westminster for People's Democracy from 1969 to 1974 Bernadette Devlin-McAliskey also ran in these elections mostly to highlight the ill-treatment of republican prisoners.[34] All three were unsuccessful, demonstrating just how difficult it was, and still is, to assert a political voice that is diametrically opposed to mainstream conservative politics especially without the infrastructural supports the large political parties have. Back then, the constituents these and other anti-establishment voices sought votes from were still mostly polarized along civil war politics and, it would seem, united against radical republicans, lesbian activists and the housing demands of the Traveller community.

Anti-establishment feminism would continue, including through the Irish Women United (IWU, est. 1975) which was set up following a meeting in Dublin attended by around eighty women including those from the Socialist Workers Movement, Revolutionary Marxist Group, People's Democracy, the Labour Party and Women's Liberation groups within University College Galway and University College Cork as well as other non-affiliated radical feminists. The IWU produced a manifesto called *What We Stand For*, which called for free contraception, abortion and divorce. Writing in the *Socialist Worker* newspaper at the time, M. Mc Adam noted how participating groups 'differed in the emphasis they placed on the different sections', continuing 'it was agreed however, that the Charter was in the nature of a Manifesto, and it was not intended that trade union branches, or tenants' organisations etc. should be asked to accept its totality or reject it'.[35] One of the things the IWU is most remembered for is its publication *Banshee* which outlined its key demands as equal pay, employment, divorce, childcare and reproductive rights, none of which showed any sign of being delivered through parliamentary politics.[36] *Banshee* regularly criticized the Catholic Church and was predictably banned under censorship laws. Brigitte Bastiat's media analysis of *Banshee* concludes that it was 'one the main vehicles for the emancipation of women and the modernization of the country'.[37] The IWU also frequently engaged in direct action including a 1975 picket of the Department of Justice, demanding improvements in women's lives. Writing in *Socialist Republic*, Pat MacDonogh explains that '[p]lacards called for "Women's Right to Choose", "Free, Legal Contraception" and "Women to decide their Fate – Not the Church, Not the State" and several hundred copies of a leaflet were handed out to passers by [sic]'.[38] Although the IWU would fizzle out by 1977, many members remained active across a range of campaigns.

The Communist Party also played an important part in developing feminism in Northern Ireland including through the work of Linda Walker and Madge Davidson who helped create the cross-community Northern Irish Women's Rights Movement (NIWRM, est. 1975) which in turn spawned the Belfast Women's Collective (est. 1977) and Women Against Imperialism whose activism will be discussed in Chapter 5. This was one of three prongs of feminism north of the border – socialist, liberal and republican. Liberals such as those in the Standing Conference of Women's Organizations for Northern Ireland enjoyed close ties with the British establishment and showed no real appetite for political engagement outside of seeking greater representation for women in political, corporate and other leadership spaces. Republican feminists, most of whom were members of the political party Sinn Féin, viewed the principal offender as the British Empire. Theresa O'Keefe uncovers how republican feminists often felt marginalized within republicanism because they were women, and equally marginalized within feminist groups because of the different analysis they brought.[39] Feminists across all three prongs criticized high levels of sexism within republicanism that often enacted interpersonal violence against women including punishment beatings where there was even a hint that they might be fraternizing with British soldiers.[40]

Party loyalty over feminist convictions

Thus far, my brief historical analysis has concentrated on past markers that bring certain patterns to the surface: the restrictive democracy of parliament, the challenges of engagement amidst a highly repressive political environment, the extent to which resistance to regressive reform came from outside of the Dáil, the political nature of a 'non-political' platform and the near-insurmountable task smaller anti-establishment candidates face when standing against the status quo. A further concern yet to be articulated is the extent to which liberal feminists that did join mainstream political parties managed to influence the direction of these parties. The short answer is that they didn't. Instead, Fennell, Barnes and Hussey became part of a Fine-Gael-led government that introduced the first-ever constitutional ban on abortion in the world. Monica Barnes did speak out against the position of her party and even received death threats for doing so. She continued to voice her disapproval after the results were known including publicly predicting the ban would have dire consequences for women.[41] Where her actions differed from McArdle and others who left Fianna Fáil in the 1930s, is that Barnes, and this wider circle of liberal feminists, stayed on board. Barnes continued to serve as a TD for Fine Gael until 1992 as did Fennell. Gemma Hussey intermittently served until 1989, which included a spell as Minister for Education. In this role, she oversaw the government's refusal to honour an agreed pay award for teachers, resulting in a series of one-day strikes by the mostly female workforce and a coordinated campaign across all teachers' unions the likes of which have not been replicated since. For all their hype about feminism, these women legitimized the neoliberal policies of their parties and sent a strong message to political leaders that words are often meaningless and that they had no red line. Practically anything was possible in terms of eroding women's rights.

Conservative politics over feminist struggle would again be the case in 1986 when liberal feminists in the Dáil failed to enthusiastically support a referendum campaign to delete a constitutional ban on divorce. The idea to hold a referendum in the first place wasn't dreamed up in government by these or other supposedly progressive TDs but was foisted on the political establishment because of sustained campaigning by the Divorce Action Group (DAG). When a cross-party committee recommended a referendum, Fine Gael, who were still in government, supported the amendment but adopted what Michelle Dillon describes as a 'soft yes' for fear of losing face with a still-powerful Catholic Church. The CSW also adopted a soft yes approach and did practically nothing to advance the cause. Describing it as 'the sole national representative body of the various women's organizations in Ireland', Dillon explains:

> The CSW did not engage in an activist role during the debate. Although it expressed its endorsement of the amendment, it did not actively campaign in its favour. It did not, for instance, organize a nationwide canvassing campaign or lobby women through advertising or the mass media to endorse the proposals. In short, it adopted a very low profile during the debate.[42]

The only party in government to actively support the motion was the Labour Party. Fianna Fáil, the main opposition, favoured rejecting it – a position that was vociferously embodied by their leader Charles Haughey. This aligned them with the powerful Catholic-led Anti-Divorce Campaign which exploited existing parish structures to preach about the dangers of divorce, including that it was bad for women because of the financial protections they would lose. This was the atmosphere within which the DAG, some Labour Party members, revolutionary-left parties including the Socialist Workers Movement (SWM) and the Workers' Party, civil liberties groups and some smaller feminist organizations began knocking on doors convincing people to vote for change at a time when Ireland was deeply divided on the issue.

I interviewed Mary Ryder, who joined the SWM in the late 1970s when she spotted a sign on a lamp-post in Dublin city centre advertising a public meeting on 'the role of women in the revolutionary movement' which had been organized by Mary Gordon. She canvassed as an SWM member and sets the scene: 'I had a car so I was put out to Ballymun [a suburb in North Dublin] where there was a very active group that had that gutsy approach' by which she means a community-based feminist group that held a political over charitable outlook, '[S]ometimes you got the door slammed in your face or things thrown at you,' she tells me, then recalls one particular example:

> [O]ne door I knocked on. I said 'I am here campaigning for divorce and this is our leaflet' and this hand came from behind the door and said, 'Oh grand', and took the leaflet. He then showed me a bucket of water and said, 'If you were against divorce I was going to throw this at you'. That was the level of division, people on both sides were taking a very strong position.

Sadly, their efforts were not enough and the proposal was rejected by a 63.48 per cent majority. It would be 1995 before divorce was eventually introduced.

Organizing communities for political change

Losing both referenda; the first to prevent a constitutional ban on abortion and the second to introduce divorce, strengthened the Catholic Church's dominance and was a crushing blow for radicals who were subjected to a strong anti-feminist backlash that made it difficult for them to gain public support. Counterattacks to feminist gains are not unique to Ireland nor are they that unusual but are a recurrent feature following hard-fought wins. Where feminism did begin to thrive was at the local, community level, such as through the Ballymun-based group Mary Ryder talked about, when campaigning for divorce. This group was part of a growing grassroots resistance to the status quo that emerged from the 1980s onwards and included dozens of community-based women's groups. In search of funding to ensure salaries for community workers, many of these groups entered Ireland's community development sector, a liberal label that typically avoids political debates. There was a distinctly conservative strand within the community organizations that were emerging at the time but overall, Ireland's community development sector was much more radical and oppositional than what was practised in other European countries.[43] Its philosophy was that collective community effort could influence politics through a combination of lobbying, evidence-based research, meaningful consultation, consciousness-raising education and protest. In its early years, this political grassroots movement was mostly controlled by the people directly affected by the issues it sought to address such as poor housing, high unemployment and the lack of local services, including childcare and even playgrounds. They weren't afraid to point out the flaws in liberal feminism or the ways in which women in positions of power had let them down. One woman I spoke to called Chris explains her reason for starting an education group for women in west Dublin:

> I would have been very critical of the Council for the Status of Women at the time because they were speaking in a way that didn't relate to my life ... we could decide what to learn and it became very political very quickly – we learned the language of analysis ... it was only when you start to talk to other women you could see that it was the way society and patriarchy and [how] the system was working. That is what you were unhappy with.[44]

In a similar vein, the outspoken and well-regarded activist, Rita Fagan, who has managed the St Michael's Estate Family Resource Centre for thirty-five years, locates the origins of her community work in tenants' rights and the rent strikes of the early 1970s organized as part of the National Association Tenants Organisations (NATO) that fought against a blanket rent increase that most families couldn't afford. Women might not have been the face of this campaign, but Rita believes they were its backbone. They sat on tenants' organizations, collected and saved rent for striking tenants, they were the barricades, and they organized the rosters for pickets that were set up to protect tenants issued with eviction orders. She has a different perspective on what being a feminist meant in the 1970s. 'I've been thinking about the women's movement' Rita begins, 'you know, working class women were there as well, they played a very big role. They were marching for their rights, mostly their housing rights.' Regarding the specific focus of campaigns, she alerts us to the fact that 'if you were to ask women at that time what would have been at the top of your priority, it may not have been abortion and it may not have been contraception, it may have been that you hadn't enough to live and pay your rent'.

However, a rapid professionalization process in the 1990s shifted much power once held within community politics and by local people like Chris and Rita into the hands of outsiders from more affluent communities. Many professionals believed their qualifications and middle-class attributes gave them the right to dismiss lived experience as a legitimate source of knowledge and gave them the authority to speak for working-class communities in political spaces.[45] At the same time as these groups were professionalizing, the CSW was somewhat moving in the opposite direction by determining that it would be far better to 'break ties with the Fine Gaelers',[46] as one staff member put it, and align more with these diverse local women's groups. And so, after much internal discussion, it rebranded as the National Women's Council of Ireland (NWCI) in 1996. But the community sector was rapidly losing whatever political clout it once had and had shifted towards a liberal perspective that preferred consensus over disruption and was content to work within existing systems rather than seeking to tear these down. The community sector wasn't completely depoliticized by professionalization process, that would come later and as part of neoliberalism's seemingly endless cuts to public institutions which, from 2008 onwards, deliberately targeted community groups through harsh austerity cuts and forced mergers that resulted in thousands of job losses, the closure of many vital community-based services and the effective silencing of a political opponent.

The ongoing influence of the revolutionary left

If the community sector were perceived as powerless in bringing about social change, the state would not have sought to neuter it, and its reliance on public funding was probably always going to lead to co-option. One of the few remaining authentic spaces for an anti-capitalist feminist articulation was within left-wing revolutionary parties including the SWM which, in 2005, was absorbed into People before Profit (PbP). Bríd Smith, who served as a PbP TD from 2016 to 2024 explains the thinking at the time:

> We [the SWM] were involved in the bin tax movement [which opposed the taxation of household waste removal services], we were in Shell to Sea [an environmental movement that opposed the construction of a natural gas pipeline off the west coast], the anti-war movement [opposing the US invasion of Iraq]. We are building all these movements and working with great people but we had no political platform that they could relate to. We were not electorally oriented, but people do want something to vote for. They hated Fianna Fáil and Fine Gael and they were pissed off at the Labour Party. So, we decided to set up something and register it and it took off from there.

There can be issues with absorbing feminist demands into political parties and movements that principally focus on class struggle. Indeed, some of the activists I spoke to left left-wing revolutionary parties because of sexism including the continued dominance of 'manels' (meaning a panel discussion where all speakers are men) especially on economic issues, and a sense that only lip-service was paid to women's rights which were often seen as a distraction from the real business of the day – class politics. As the historian and former Socialist Party member Mary Muldowney puts it, '[N]obody was saying directly that there was no room for feminism but the feeling was that being too explicit in demands for abortion rights was – getting ahead of the class.' Equally, Marese Hegarty, founder of the South Dublin network *women4women* (est. 2011) shares, '[M]en on the left can be just as bad as right-wing ones – actually sometimes worse because they think/pretend they're not.' Sexism in left-wing spaces is sometimes given as the reason why the Revolutionary Anarcha-Feminist Group (or RAG for short) began meeting in 2005. As one former member put it to me, 'people just found that they weren't being heard and that they didn't necessarily always feel safe in their spaces or events … it felt like the class struggle was the number one priority'. Some anarchists were also uncomfortable with Ireland's male-dominated 'antifa movement' which was mostly organized through Anti-Fascist Action Ireland (AFA, est. 1991) and whose tactic was to use violence against far-right opponents including the anti-abortion group Youth Defence.[47]

Without glossing over these experiences, there is no denying that Irish-based left-wing revolutionary parties and anarchist groups have remained central to organizing and sustaining feminist campaigns including on contraception and abortion, against gender-based violence and for the rights of women workers. Consistently, Ireland's revolutionary feminists turn outwards beyond their membership in an attempt to politicize the general public and either instigate direct actions through campaigns and protests or throw their weight behind existing single-issue campaigns. One example of this united front approach was through the Feminist Open Forum (est. 2009), a left-wing, non-membership collective created by the trade unionist and journalist Therese Caherty who first became politically active in the 1970s when she joined a women's centre in Dublin, then the IWU and the IWWU, and the political activist and scholar Ailbhe Smyth. Smyth has been involved in radical feminism since the early 1980s and is known for spearheading politically infused feminist spaces in universities, campaigning on reproductive rights and her activism on a range of LGBTQIA+ rights. Smyth also helped set up the radical feminist publishing house Attic Press in the 1980s along with the key instigator Roisin Conroy who was the convener of the group Irish Feminist Information. With Caherty, as its assistant editor, Attic Press disseminated radical information to women across the country, published radical feminist texts that were being turned away by mainstream publishers and recorded key moments in feminist development.[48]

During its short existence, the Feminist Open Forum organized several meetings including one against a 2009 referendum that sought permission to ratify the EU Lisbon Treaty,[49] on trade unionism, the impact of austerity on women and one called 'Is feminism necessary?' Speakers came from across the spectrum of left-wing feminism including from RAG and the Labour Party. Orla O'Connor of the NWCI also supported the efforts of the Feminist Open Forum. O'Connor would go on to become the director of the NWCI which has been much more willing to take a public stance against government policy under her stewardship. Outside of Dublin, other left-wing feminist groups were also organizing public meetings including on austerity like Cork Feminista (est. 2010). One of its founders, Linda Kelly describes their work as 'taught activism' and 'a space for people to explore'.

When a left-wing electoral pact called the United Left Alliance (ULA) was initiated by the Socialist Party (est. 1996) in 2011 with the express intention of uniting left-wing parties and independents in seeking election to the Dáil, the Feminist Open Forum publicly backed the ULA and Ailbhe Smyth was one of the speakers at its high-profile launch. By this time, the political landscape had moved on from the civil war-style landscape of the twentieth century in that it now reflected broader European patterns of a dominant neoliberal centre-right (in Ireland's case Fine Gael and Fianna Fáil) whose presence outweighed those that claimed to be on the left (mostly the Labour Party, Social Democrats and Green Party) in terms of voting strength. Repeatedly, these centre-left parties have demonstrated their willingness to pivot to the right and form coalitions with centre-right parties, a tactic that has pushed them to the margins where they offered – and still offer – no meaningful alternative to the neoliberal status quo. Sinn Féin was also growing in popularity at this time, a rise that was undoubtedly linked to a growing desire for a left-wing alternative to Ireland's centre-right dominance. The ULA did better than expected and secured five seats including one for the anti-bin-tax campaigner Joan Collins of PbP (which she left in 2013) and one for Clare Daly, trade unionist and founding member of the Socialist Party (although she too would leave her party the following year). Daly had served time in prison in 2003 for refusing to pay bin charges, was at the fore of uncovering Garda corruption and was a high-profile opponent of the US military's use of Shannon Airport during the US invasion of Iraq. Throughout her term as a member of the European Parliament (MEP) from 2019 to 2024, she consistently spoke out against the militarization of the EU and the ongoing occupation of Palestine by Israel.

Sometimes it is the people behind the scenes who have the most impact. This can be said about the work of the long-time feminist activist Alison Spillane, who was employed as a parliamentary researcher for the independent TD Mick Wallace, who was also elected in 2011. At the time, Spillane was a member of the Irish Feminist Network and also Action on X. She would later become heavily involved with the Abortion Rights Campaign. When I interviewed Alison, she told me how, when she began working in the Dáil, she was determined that she would seek to 'hold the state to account' as she put it to me, on their failures to introduce long-overdue abortion legislation needed to align the statute books with a 1992 Supreme Court ruling (discussed in Chapter 6). Alison believed the December 2010 ruling of the European Court of Human Rights in *A, B and C v Ireland* provided a critical opportunity to shine a spotlight on the abortion issue. So, with the help of the Irish Family Planning Association (IFPA) – who had supported A, B and C to take their case to Europe, she worked with Clare Daly, Joan Collins and Mick Wallace on a plan to bring the abortion issue to the floor of the Dáil and force a response from the new government. In February 2012, to coincide with the twentieth anniversary of the X case, Daly tabled a bill on behalf of herself, Collins and Wallace.

'Fine Gael and the Labour Party had a massive majority at the time,' Alison explains, 'and the bill was crushed.' She attributes this in part to the fact that Ireland's pro-choice movement 'hadn't really kicked off. So, politicians weren't feeling public pressure to act. This completely changed with the death of Savita Halappanavar later that year.' She outlines the hostility of the environment she was working in like this:

> I remember Clare getting all sorts of comments thrown at her about how she really wanted abortion on demand, that this bill was a smokescreen and so on. As if she was trying to conceal the fact that she was pro-choice! She was always clear that she wanted much broader access. The content of the 2012 bill was limited by the Eighth Amendment [Ireland's constitutional ban], it only provided for access to life-saving abortion, and it still got hardly any support in the Dáil. That illustrates how conservative the political environment was at the time.

In 2014, a second Socialist Party TD, Ruth Coppinger, was elected. Again, one of her first actions was to table a bill on abortion, something the Labour Party had repeatedly failed to do despite claiming to be pro-choice since 2003. These interventions might have been unsuccessful, but they were important steps in eventually forcing a referendum in 2018.

The general election of 2016 returned six left-wing TDs who were now collaborating through the united platform of the Anti-Austerity Alliance-People Before Profit (AAA-PbP).[50] Having six TDs brought certain technical advantages including speaking rights. When they nominated Coppinger as Taoiseach, she became the first female nominee in the history of the state. What was different about these politicians was their determination to advance truly anti-neoliberal aspirations in collaboration with grassroots movements beyond their own parties. They were also prepared to break Dáil rules. Soon after their election, all six TDs deliberately broke with the parliamentary dress code and entered the Dáil wearing the black-and-white REPEAL jumpers designed by Anna Cosgrave that were emblematic of the pro-abortion movement. Four days earlier, 40,000 people, including all six of these TDs, had joined the 2016 Annual March for Choice demanding free, safe and legal abortion services. Wearing the REPEAL jumpers ensured media coverage of a question to then Taoiseach Enda Kenny by Coppinger calling for an immediate referendum on the issue. She was also involved in a second stunt when, in 2018, Coppinger sought to explicitly highlight rape myths in Irish courtrooms by holding up a laced thong in the chamber, again during Leaders' Questions. Her actions made worldwide news and helped publicize a rape trial where the seventeen-year-old alleged victim's underwear was used to build a case against the accusation.

Demanding access to abortion and an end to misogyny and rape myths in the judicial system went alongside an emphasis on issues that disproportionately affect women, such as the lack of decent housing or no house at all, poverty wages, childcare and a substandard healthcare system. Their actions were worlds apart from what liberal feminists continued to do which was not much at all aside from prioritizing party loyalty over everything else. One particularly stark example of this was when the Labour Party leader Joan Burton, a regular in liberal feminist circles, served as Tánaiste (Deputy Prime Minister) in a coalition government with Fine Gael from 2014 to 2016. Despite repeatedly stating that she was 'pro-choice', Burton didn't support Alison Spillane's work with the IFPA. 'I mean it was actually Labour Party policy,' Alison recounts, 'but they didn't support it.' Burton also opposed Coppinger's 2014 bill on abortion by vociferously asserting there would be no referendum on the matter in the lifetime of her government. What she did do was introduce some of the harshest austerity measures in the history of the state including cuts to eldercare, healthcare, disability services, fuel allowances, lone-parent benefits, school uniform and footwear allowances. As the socialist feminist Deirdre Cronin put it at the time, 'women have become the main targets of the war on welfare instigated by … Joan Burton, in a disgraceful attempt to deflect blame away from those really responsible – the banks, the developers, the capitalist class and system as a whole – and focus people's minds on the necessity of slashing public spending'.[51] When asked to comment on her former party's performance in an interview in 2016, the outspoken independent TD Catherine Connolly, who has been particularly critical of the state's redress scheme for the survivors of Mother and Baby Homes (see Chapter 1), described the Labour Party as having 'lost its soul'.[52]

Others too have modelled a strategy of using parliamentary structures to advance anti-capitalist agendas. This includes Lynn Ruane, one of several independent senators to serve in the Seanad in the 2020s. I was fortunate enough to interview Lynn during which she explained her approach to politics. Just like those who are members of anti-establishment parties, Lynn seeks strong collaborations with campaigners outside the Dáil, especially community-based campaigners, connections she built up through her previous role as a community worker. Together, they seek to create a less harmful legislative framework within a system she knows will never deliver equality. She painstakingly considers all laws that are brought before the Seanad 'through the lens of a woman and then as a working-class woman' continuing:

> I try to pick up parts of legislation that are actually harmful to women and to class-proof them and gender-proof them and try to create change on those specific aspects. I may disagree with the rest of the bill, and I know that it is going to pass because the numbers are against me, so rather than just go in and fight on the bill and then vote against it, I create a scenario where I can minimize the harm.

She also endeavours to 'tell people the truth about what is happening' referring to the regular occasions when she has openly called out politicians, so they do not get to, in her own words, 'pass laws or make decisions without fully knowing the impact of what they are doing'. In a separate interview, the housing activist Clare O'Connor tells me about the impacts of Ruane's work when she shares, 'there was a particular interview that Lynn gave that reflected back on my own experiences … and I realised for the first time the power of representation … it was not just that she was a woman, it was that she was talking about poverty and not behaving as other women who were going to go in an exclude'.

The re-emergence of a far right

In *Doppelganger* (2023), Naomi Klein outlines how the rise of the right we are currently witnessing cannot be uncoupled from the actions of centrist politics that recklessly create the conditions under which the racist far right is surging ahead in some parts of the globe, especially across Europe. A 'war on meaning' has emerged, Klein surmises, where centrist politicians have normalized the practice of saying one thing to the electorate, then behaving in a way that is anathema to these very words. Consider, for example, how centre-left politicians feign concern about precarious housing circumstances, whilst at the same time passing laws that deepen neoliberal practices that privatize the provision of housing. This disingenuousness, Klein explains, has created fertile ground for populist independents, far-right and fascist activists to tap into people's genuine anger about the impact of these and other neoliberal policies. One of the consequences of this war on meaning is that aspects of anti-capitalist language are just as likely to be used by the far right as they are by anti-capitalists on the left with voters and indeed some political activists switching alliances from left to right at lightning pace and without appreciating the ideological shift this incurs.[53] One way to counter the rise of the right, Klein believes, is a clear articulation of authentic left-wing ideas and the conviction to follow these through.

Perhaps, the presence of left-revolutionary politicians in Ireland's parliament has helped stem parliamentary gains for far-right political parties such as the National Party (est. 2016) and Ireland First (est. 2023) aside from some modest gains in 2024 when a handful of far-right local councillors were elected on a platform of immigration controls, restrictions on sex-education and abortion, and transphobia, all of which sit within broader policies to reduce government spending on welfare, which women are more likely to rely on. Six months later, none of several far-right candidates who ran in the general election secured a seat in the Dáil. But it is important not to be complacent as some openly fascist candidates did garner reasonably high numbers of votes in some communities. These are some of the same people who have been visible at the fore of nasty anti-immigration protests including the burning down of at least thirty-one properties or locations linked, or rumoured to be linked, to the housing of migrants seeking asylum or international protection.

In the 2024 general election, marked by a less than 60% turnout, only three revolutionary left TDs were elected with center-right parties emerging as the clear winners. Feminism that persists with a patriarchal lens only, upholds these centrist politics under the belief that women in politics is always a step forward. This viewpoint strengthens rather than weakens the far right by continuing to create space for its expansion. One stark example of centrist politics is the recent actions of Sinn Féin, a party that has built significant support by expressing left-wing views and is led by two women – Mary Lou McDonald in the south and Michelle O'Neill in the north. In an analysis of their performance in the 2024 local elections, Kieran Allen details how this leadership has persistently 'tried to drag the party to the centre, preparing for a possible SF-FF [Sinn Féin-Fianna Fáil] coalition' therefore moving away from its voter base including by holding meetings with stockbrokers and Silicon Valley capitalists and, most notably, tilting to the right on immigration.[54] Contrastingly, PbP's response to growing anti-immigration sentiment has been to ally with the Movement of Asylum Seekers in Ireland (MASI) in launching a bill to extend the right to work for people seeking asylum whilst their applications are being processed.

Final thoughts

There is no perfect way to engage with the political mainstream and we cannot ignore the ongoing structural barriers to women's participation and their under-representation in politics. Some notable increases in participation have occurred across the globe, and several heads of globally significant countries, have now been women. But these leaders have either been to the political right or centre-left and their behaviours continue to uphold capitalist, imperialist patriarchy. A good example of this is Jacinda Ardern's time as New Zealand Prime Minister from 2017 to 2023 during which she and her Labour Party continuously spoke about social justice and an ambition to reduce poverty but implemented economic policies that maintained neoliberal frameworks and continued support for free-market principles with minimal interventions to lateralize inequality. Alternatively, consider the reality for Palestinian children living through genocide. It doesn't matter to them what the gender of the president selling arms to Israel is. Lessons from Ireland equally indicate that liberal feminism has failed to advance even the most modest of gains for many thousands of poorer women.

It would be naïve of me to suggest that the anti-capitalist feminists I have talked about in this chapter, whatever their gender, can deliver anything near the sort of social transformation that is needed to defeat capitalism through parliament. Today's new political terrain of a rise in right-wing politics should serve as a reminder that seeking to overturn exploitation is only possible with a clear theoretical analysis of how capitalism works. As the Marxist feminist Maryam Jazayeri reminds us, 'the destruction of the present system in practice is not possible without first bringing it down in theory – in the consciousness of people'.[55] Anit-capitalist feminists can and have used their platform to politicize the general public and have used every opportunity to uplift causes whilst keeping their principal focus on building a mass movement that seeks to end the global conditions of capitalism including poverty, imperialist war, ecological destruction and oppression through privatized domestic and care labour. Collective consciousness-raising, solidarity building, campaigning and protesting also need the support of other potential sites for change including the trade union movement. As the next chapter will argue, its capacity to effectively organize labour power requires significant changes to the practices of trade unions today.

I have identified as a socialist feminist since I was a teenager, over 30 years ago. I am a full-time union organizer and campaigner. I organize workers because I believe a strong trade union movement is the best vehicle for the transformation of work and society.

– Anonymous contributor

Chapter 3

FEMINISM, WORK AND TRADE UNIONS

On International Women's Day in 2023, an event was organized at the university where I work that celebrated the appointments of the first female presidents in six Irish universities. Less than three years earlier, there had never been a female president. 'Good morning on this great and glorious day,' the anchor and journalist Kathy Sheridan announced to a packed hall before explaining that the event would begin with a procession. As the women filed in, they were met with rapturous applause. 'My goodness it is joyous, isn't it?' Sheridan interjected, before audaciously relaying apologies from one absent president who was 'too busy meeting with the Taoiseach' (Prime Minister).

When Simon Harris, the government minister then responsible for universities and a future Taoiseach himself, took to the stage, he knew how to please the crowd. He opened with quips about being the 'token male', promised not to 'mansplain' and joked about being able to 'multi-task' – a reference to how he was also managing the state's justice portfolio so that his colleague Helen McEntee could take maternity leave. Harris described the gathering as 'a wonderful turning of the tables after over 400 years' then adopted a self-congratulatory tone sharing how, when he first took office, insiders had resisted what was as obvious to him as the nose on his face – that there simply had to be gender parity at the highest level of the Irish education system. He nostalgically relayed how excited he was when the first female was appointed in 2021, helping to propel others forward. 'The glass ceiling had been shattered,' he remarked, then turned to the presidents and proudly beamed, 'and I think we can really agree today that the glass ceiling hasn't just been shattered, we've all managed to smash it to pieces over the last number of years and congratulations to each and every one of you and thank you for your leadership.' The crowd were euphoric. Harris then assumed a more sombre tone and cautioned listeners not to interpret these successes as 'job done'. Yes, the achievements of these women were significant, they had defied the odds and climbed the academic career ladder to its highest rung. But he reminded the audience that 73 per cent of all professors were still men despite women making up 55 per cent of the total academic workforce. Four years earlier, men had held a whopping 81 per cent of professorships.[1]

Overall, though, Minister Harris's tone was optimistic and suggested that the bad old days of discriminatory bosses and unpleasant anti-women working environments are a thing of the past. Had he been asked to expand on why this is the case, he might have talked about how women enjoy much better maternity care than was the case just a couple of decades ago, how there are options for parental leave, albeit unpaid, and how there is less cultural stigma about leaving children with childminders. He might even have plugged his own government's recently introduced domestic violence leave policies for public sector employees. Whatever examples he might have settled on, it seems fair to presume that the national picture that would have been painted would be one of positivity and low unemployment, which was measured at just 3.9 per cent in the first quarter of 2023, the lowest rate since records began.

This chapter has three functions, the first of which is to refute these wholly progressive narratives on women and work by examining their applicability beyond certain workplace environments. I argue that despite an expanding Irish economy, neoliberalism has brought a decline in many workers' standards of living. To illustrate, Harris never mentioned the dark underbelly of our increasingly neoliberalized universities. Or what, professor of Organizational Studies, Peter Fleming more frankly calls 'factory-style education'. As universities increasingly mimic private sector corporations, Fleming accuses them of hyper-commercializing education and of being governed by authoritarian management structures that are mostly designed to monitor the individualized, measurable outputs of staff.[2] This, Fleming maintains, creates a damaging atmosphere for both staff and students and only works because it relies on the mass casualization of much of its workforce. An eye-watering number of lecturers, tutors and research staff in universities (and indeed Further Education Colleges) are employed on short-term zero hours and pay-by-the-hour measures not just in Ireland but across much of Europe. These working arrangements are more likely to be applied to women for a variety of reasons but mostly because of the additional work they do minding children and older people and managing the domestic sphere.[3] The casual contracts these staff are given deny them many basic rights including maternity leave, sick leave and holiday pay as well as the option to pay into a pension.

My own research on the topic (published more extensively elsewhere) has brought me into contact with university staff who depend on social welfare outside of term time and who have no clarity on how many hours they will work each year, meaning they don't know how much they will earn. Casual employees have talked to me about the challenges of being on constant alert for extra classes and about having no choice but to say yes to everything they are asked to do even when there is no pay attached. Unlike the esteemed presidents who earn somewhere between €140,000 and €190,000 per annum, it is not unusual for their annual earnings to dip below the minimum wage. I've met lecturers, tutors and researchers who have been turned down for mortgages because they don't have the right contract or who have had to rely on sympathetic landlords to retain accommodation. I've spoken to people who have struggled to get car loans, delayed having children or decided not to have children at all because of the uncertainty of their circumstances. Their plight isn't captured in unemployment statistics which shield the fact that across the board, Ireland has much fewer full-time permanent jobs and secure part-time jobs than in the past and much more involuntary part-time work and temporary, pay-by-the-hour work instead.[4]

Unlike these mostly visible workers, there was also no talk whatsoever in Harris's address about the working conditions for the millions of invisible workers worldwide who do the worst jobs for the lowest pay so that the wheels of capitalism keep turning. I'm talking about the mostly female and often migrant workers who clean rooms like the one the esteemed presidents were celebrated in, work in the factories that process the food guests were served and who scrub the toilets that they frequented. And that's before even mentioning the, mostly, women working in crèches and homes so that other women could attend this event.

The second function of this chapter is to demonstrate how historically, any improvements in working conditions have been fought for and won through collective action by workers. When Simon Harris and others who are involved in organizing tertiary education do sometimes acknowledge high levels of precarity and outline steps that have been taken to create permanent pathways, they never link this to the fact that these professions have strong occupational networks, access to legal resources, a better overall understanding of their rights and, perhaps most importantly, high trade union density. These factors have made them better at waging campaigns and legal battles. To illustrate, the modest growth in female professorships is mostly because of legal challenges taken in 2014 by Micheline Sheehy Skeffington and some of her colleagues against their employer, University of Galway. These union-backed gender-discrimination challenges were also supported by sometimes large on-campus student demonstrations.[5] The third function of this chapter is to discuss the often-fraught relationship between trade unions and feminism which is mostly due to the trade union movement's disastrous track record on supporting women in the workplace and in society more broadly. As chosen historical examples will illustrate, mostly male-led unions have turned their backs on and betrayed women so often and so deeply that some feminists, Selma James, argue women should mostly stay away from official trade unions altogether.[6]

This chapter is offered in the context of a changing landscape of paid work. According to the left-wing think tank TASC, almost two-thirds of Irish workers who are paid the minimum wage are women, with 46 per cent of these same workers being the main household earners.[7] Ireland also has an unusually high level of older women trapped in low-paid, low-status jobs when compared to the rest of Europe, many of whom gave up superior jobs so they could better manage their domestic loads.[8] Some of these jobs form part of Ireland's rapidly expanding *gig economy* which is typified by highly exploitative short-term, flexible, bogus self-employment work that strips away some of the most basic workers' rights, rights that have been won through trade-union-organized collective action. One in five of all workers are now classified as non-Irish,[9] many of whom work in these low-paid feminized, essential jobs in retail, customer service, tourism, food processing, as healthcare assistants and as childcare workers, sometimes regardless of the professional qualifications they might hold from other countries. Decades of neglect of our long-term elder care services have also led to some families directly employing migrants, including undocumented migrants who enjoy little or no workplace protections. Overall, non-naturalized migrants earn 22 per cent less per hour than Irish nationals.[10]

Some migrants do work in professional careers such as medicine, nursing or as software engineers, keeping these industries and care sectors afloat. In other high-status occupations that don't have a labour shortage, including academia, migrants and ethnic minorities are less protected from recruitment prejudice. Research by the sociologist Ebun Joseph has detailed how skin colour, having a foreign sounding name and/or speaking with an accent locks many people out of decent work even when they hold better qualifications than their white-Irish counterparts.[11] And although there are policy and cultural advances in addressing interpersonal gender-based violence in the workplace, it remains endemic within some workplaces where there is a high density of female migrant workers. To illustrate, research by Deirdre Curran found that over three-quarters of mostly female hospitality workers regularly endure verbal abuse and more than half experience harassment and bullying – all within an environment where there are significant breaches of basic employment rights and a complete absence of reporting mechanisms.[12] Human trafficking is also endemic under capitalism's profit-driven system where economic gain is often prioritized over human rights. Sixty-seven per cent of all people trafficked into Ireland are female, brought in for the purposes of sexual exploitation, labour exploitation and trafficking for criminal activities.[13]

Liberal perspectives on workplace inequality

Liberal feminists don't have a good track record when it comes to addressing the working conditions of low-paid workers. When Sheryl Sandberg, the author of *Lean in*, visited Harvard Business School in 2014, she declined an invitation to meet with female housekeeping, front desk and service staff at a nearby hotel. These women were in the process of unionizing and had hoped that Sandberg might host one of their 'lean in circles' which they were modelling on her ideas.[14] Even feminists who claim to support workers' rights have failed to protect low-paid workers including when they are in government. In 2015, the Labour Party's first female leader and Tánaiste (Deputy Prime Minister) Joan Burton backed a proposal for a 'no strike' clause in public sector pay negotiations by claiming that strikes simply don't work.[15] In 2024, Minister for Justice Helen McEntee led Ireland's delegation to the UN Commission on the Status of Women in New York where she delivered a national statement on achieving gender equality which included expanding family leave entitlement for working parents, better breastfeeding breaks and more short-time care leave. But where was her concern for the migrants who, two months later, protested outside her office under the banner 'Families Belong Together' calling for radical change to their circumstances particularly on family reunification, which protesters claimed can take up to seven years to process.

Instead of seeking work-based equality, liberals back a host of justifications that explain away occupational discrepancies through the myth of meritocracy which supposes that the jobs we get mostly reflect our intelligence and how hard we are prepared to work. Any account of how middle-class people are afforded enormous advantages in education is minimized, as are a person's proximity to whiteness and the ableist and/or hetero advantages that they might also hold all of which begin from an early age and continue throughout a person's life. Even when people are open to the way a person's circumstances reduce their opportunities, the fixes that are proposed are mostly fresh hiring practices and the eventual elimination of work-based discrimination through better workplace policies then, if all else fails, the legal system. This is without appreciating how carceral measures only work for some people and can cost a lot of money, meaning it is not an option for many working-class women without the fulsome support of their trade unions, if they have a trade union. Moreover, asking vulnerable workers to engage with legal and governance systems mostly brings them into structures that perpetuate white supremacy, violence and silencing where, as Sara Ahmed argues, managing 'the complainant' becomes the focus and not any real attempt to address their grievance by creating safer, better-paid working conditions.[16]

Understanding the trade union movement

In sharp contrast, anti-capitalist feminists are much more likely to interpret the labour landscape as I have described it and to advocate for trade unions as a force for change pointing out how they have won all kinds of improvements for workers including limits to the number of hours employers can demand, maternity and parental leave, holidays and sick pay.

Sometimes it is assumed that everyone understands what a trade union is, but this is not always the case. The best way to understand them is as entities that bring together the collective effort of employees in seeking to ensure their employers create working conditions that are fair and reasonable. Structurally, the American union organizer and researcher Jane McAlevey describes unions as similar to political parties in that they too have branches, are funded through member contributions (or subs) and hold elections to vote people into certain positions. They are distinctly different in two ways, the first of which is their collective bargaining power which McAlevey describes as 'a process through which workers, united through their union, sit down with management and hammer out the terms of their employment'. The second difference is their capacity to initiate strikes, a fundamental principle of trade union activism.[17] Strikes mostly happen because collective bargaining isn't recognized by employers, because negotiations fail to deliver sufficient change, or because bosses renege on promises that are hammered out during the bargaining process. Unions use other tactics too including 'work to rule' – where employees adhere only to tasks outlined in their job description, 'go-slows' where they intentionally decrease productivity, or 'sit-ins' – where workers disrupt operations by occupying their workplaces. When they win better terms and conditions in a particular place of work such as a pay-rise or longer breaks, these apply to all workers and not just union members.

Many people also don't know that the first person to put forward the suggestion that workers associations should unite and collectively resist deplorable working conditions was the feminist Flora Tristan in *The Workers Union* (1843), written five years before Marx and Engels penned *The Communist Manifesto*. Where Marx and Engels paid scant attention to gender, Tristan outlines how working-class women are conditioned into believing that their domestic and care chores should be their primary focus, arguing that women should be 'placed in society on a footing of absolute equality with men to enjoy the legal birth right all beings have' including the right to education and the right to take on the same jobs.[18] Unions, she argued, should also create and fund what she called workers' palaces where children, those who are unwell and the elderly could be cared for amidst a society where people work cooperatively and according to their abilities.

A history of exclusion

However, as is the case across the Global North, there is a long history of Irish-based trade unions excluding women from their ranks. The very first workers' associations were mostly for *skilled workers*, a coveted title that signified a person had completed an apprenticeship, most of which excluded women and poorer sections of the working class.[19] Irish women began joining unions as part of a socialist-influenced mass recruitment drive of unskilled workers in the early 1900s and therefore before independence. But many trade unionists responded by resisting female members including the Irish Transport and General Workers Union (ITGWU), the largest and most influential union.[20] This opposition left working women with little choice but to set up their own unions or separate sections within unions. The most durable of these was the Irish Women Workers' Union (IWWU) which was formed in 1911 with the support of the socialist and general secretary of the ITGWU, Jim Larkin. Its earliest leading members included Delia Larkin (sister of Jim), Hanna Sheehy Skeffington, Louise Bennett, Constance Markievicz and Rosie Hackett.[21] Throughout its seventy-five-year existence, the IWWU would represent tens of thousands of female workers across around two dozen occupations. Speaking about her own first encounter with the IWWU in the 1970s, Therese Caherty says, 'I couldn't believe that such a union existed for women; to look at women's needs in the workplace … that the union had to fight for women to be recognised as workers … It was a real eye opener to me.'

The IWWU might have been one of Ireland's smallest unions, but it was also sometimes amongst its most militant. However, this wasn't always duly recognized by the wider labour movement, as was the case during the Dublin 1912–13 lockout – a dispute that centred on the right to unionize in the first place. In her detailed history of the IWWU, Mary Jones highlights fundraisers, collective food relief initiatives, caregiving and other essential tasks crucial for the success of the lockout. But when the lockout ended in defeat, their reward was a much lower rate of re-instatement compared to male workers, something the broader trade union movement and its male leaders endorsed.[22]

As is still the case to this day, all union members faced considerable opposition from the government including siding with employers during the Dublin lockout and deploying police to sometimes violently suppress striking workers. This anti-union perspective continued post-independence despite Ireland's new identity centring on championing ordinary people.[23] But women workers faced double discrimination as, time and again, the male trade union leadership sided with the state in restricting the rights of women including by supporting marriage bars that forced hundreds of thousands of women to stop work on their wedding day. Such was the depth of patriarchy and the sanctity of the Catholic Irish family that some female trade unionists also supported marriage bars claiming that, when married women worked outside the home, it was bad for society.[24] Marriage bars were common across Europe, but Ireland's ban was deeper and longer than elsewhere, lasting until 1973. It was also blanketly applied across most workplaces and not just when it was a legal requirement thereby greatly reducing women's capacity to work where a second wage was desperately needed or when they were parenting alone for whatever reason. As Myrtle Hill notes, less than 6 per cent of married women in the Republic of Ireland were in paid employment between the 1920s and 1960s compared with 15 per cent of women in Northern Ireland and 21 per cent of women in industrial Belfast.[25] The home environment women laboured in instead was one where men held power as the more esteemed breadwinner. Remember contraception wasn't readily available, especially in poorer and rural households and women had practically no agency over sexual decision-making, it wasn't unusual for women to birth 10–15 children and raise them in often-dire conditions. There were no mod cons, sometimes no electricity and, in many rural areas, no running water aside from an outdoor pump.[26] If there wasn't enough food to go around, the husband would eat first, then the children, with the wife surviving on whatever was left over.[27]

One of the first women's organizations to seek to address these conditions was the Irish Countrywomen's Association (ICA, est. 1910) which, in the 1960s, launched the 'turn on the tap' campaign aimed at educating people on how to take action to bring water into their homes. The Irish Housewives Association (IHA, discussed in more detail in Chapter 2) also campaigned on the cost of living well into the 1970s. Both organizations raised the issue of equal pay but received little support from a trade union movement that was in concert with the government and employers in asserting that equal pay would drag down male wages, a perspective that placed Ireland on a European blacklist of discriminatory laws.[28]

The persistence of female trade unionists

Female trade unionists did seek to have their workplace concerns addressed and a laundry workers strike of 1945 won holiday pay for all workers and was one of several IWWU-backed collective actions. These laundresses went on strike because of a build-up of grievances that were being ignored, including low pay, unsafe working conditions and forced overtime.[29] Their victory emboldened the trade union movement more broadly and contributed to a nationwide growth in confidence and militancy.[30] However, as is often the case following workers' victories, the government's response was to enact anti-union legislation in the form of *The Industrial Relations Act* (1949). This law restricted lightning strikes and, for the first time, imposed compulsory arbitration.

Women also fought for better conditions during the 1960s, a time when one-third of all women were working, most of whom were unmarried.[31] Class was – and is – the biggest determinant in the jobs these women held, be this in domestic service or factory work, as seamstresses, typists, housekeepers, maids or nurses. Whatever their role, the male-led trade union movement had no interest in addressing how it was perfectly legal to pay them less money for performing the same work as men. In 1963, there was an attempt to even further relegate the conditions for local authority female clerical officers by introducing differential pay that would remove the parity with male peers they were fortunate enough to enjoy. It was the Women's Advisory Committee (WAC) in the Irish Congress of Trade Unions (ICTU) who supported these clerical officers' successful industrial action despite being repeatedly sidelined within the trade union movement.[32] Instead, the ICTU continued to conspire with the state and employers in keeping women's pay low. As Margaret Ayres writes more broadly of attitudes at the time:

> It might have been expected that Irish trade unions would have campaigned vigorously in favour of equal pay, as a basic human right, for their female members, but this was not the case. Although resolutions were regularly passed in its favour, action to achieve equal pay was notably lacking especially in the case of private sector unions. Employers, journalists, and government ministers were all aware that the unions often paid only lip service to women's rights.[33]

When pay discrimination was eventually eliminated in the early 1970s, it was because of a convergence of political pressure from the European Union, grassroots pressure from Western civil rights movements and the action of domestic feminists including liberal feminists in the Council for the Status of Women (CSW). The CSW, under instruction from the government which was in turn acting under pressure from Europe to meet conditions for EU membership, engaged with female trade unionists including the IWWU in preparing a report for the government on equal pay. According to Mary Daly, this report 'forced trade unions seriously, to confront the position of women in the labour market for the first time ... [marking] a new era for the Irish trade union movement'.[34]

However, Irish trade unionists, politicians and employers continued to resist even after a National Wage Agreement was reached in 1972. At one stage, radical feminists from Irish Women United (IWU), many of who were trade unionists, occupied the offices of the Federal Union of Employers, because it refused to endorse an anti-discrimination bill that would guarantee equal pay by the end of 1975.[35] These same feminists also grew women's groups in their unions including in the ITGWU where Ann Speed began a women's group that circulated a Working Women's Charter.[36] This was during 'an explosion of industrial militancy that laid the basis for rank-and-file forms of organization ranging from breakaway unions to unofficial shop stewards' committees' mostly because the majority of workers were not experiencing the financial gains of a new influx of multinationals.[37]

More of the same: Sexism and conservativism in unions

According to Yvonne Gilligan, the contribution of feminist groups certainly influenced the enactment of equal pay legislation in Ireland. However, once the relevant legal framework was in place, Gilligan explains, 'the political opportunity for developing a women-centred agenda in employment again retracted matters became restricted once more as traditional relationships among the main interests', the state, a male-led trade union movement and employers 'were reasserted'.[38] Familiar tactics were implemented to exclude women, including organizing meetings and away days at times that were totally unsuitable for mothers caring for young children.[39] On the factory floor and in workplaces more broadly, sexual harassment and sexist micro-aggressions were just as likely to come from union members as non-union members.

Some female trade unionists did manage to interrupt this normalcy, as happened in 1984 when the then popular *Sunday World* newspaper printed a misogynistically toned article about female bus conductors headlined 'Sexy High Jinks in the CIE'. It claimed female bus conductors were having affairs with men they worked with and were performing sexual favours to further their careers. The article, read in thousands of households across the city and beyond, had an immediate negative impact on female conductors who endured a barrage of unwanted verbal, physical and visual advances from both colleagues and passengers. And all in an environment that was already hostile to women. In response, a small group of female workers held a meeting to determine what they might do about these unbearable conditions. One of these trade unionists was the future TD for People before Profit, Bríd Smith. When I interviewed Bríd for this project, she sets the scene: '[T]he men in the union were so dominant and so bossy and not listening to us, I thought if we want to do something here, we will have to lead out on it ourselves.' The conductors began their attempt to effect change by lodging a complaint with the National Union of Journalists. They then mounted a picket that blocked deliveries from the newspaper's headquarters to retailers. 'I will never forget it,' Bríd says, 'it snowed that day ... and I thought the fucking snow, we are not going to get the crowd we wanted. Well, it was brilliant, about 350 workers turned up, men and women, and despite the snow they turned up and we marched up and down outside the Sunday World and we got loads of media attention.' Before long, the newspaper conceded, retracted their claims and made a public apology.

Whilst the example of these CIE workers is a very particular one, it points to the effectiveness of collective action. What can sometimes fly under the radar is the extent to which sexual harassment can be a tipping point for broader industrial action in a way that isn't always obvious. This was the case when, in 1984, a small group of retail workers employed by Dunnes Stores in Henry Street, Dublin, began industrial action against events that were happening thousands of miles away, namely the systematic oppression of South Africa's majority black population under an apartheid regime. On 19 July 1984, a checkout worker named Mary Manning complied with a directive that had been circulated by her union, the Irish Distributive and Administrative Union (IDATU) and refused to handle an Outspan grapefruit imported from South Africa. Both Manning and her shop steward Karen Gearon were immediately suspended. They were instantly supported by eight other workers who went on strike in solidarity. When I spoke to Karen Gearon, she was in no doubt about what initiated their actions. 'That strike would never have happened if there weren't other circumstances surrounding the way we were treated as female workers in Dunnes,' she told me. 'We were all very young workers. Even though Dunnes Stores workers were better paid than some of the other supermarkets, the conditions were much worse.' Sexism was undoubtedly behind much of their treatment and Karen recalls a lot of harassment from male managers. 'When your bag was searched going out every evening, if there were sanitary towels or Tampax, there would be a big joke and women were made to feel very embarrassed,' Karen explains, 'and we were young girls, I was 20 at the time, ... we were all very young women working in Dunnes and the conditions were so bad.' Certainly, the reason for the strike action was a union directive 'but that union instruction from IDATU could have been anything' Karen says, 'it was because of the way we were treated. Like we could only go to the toilet twice a day, those toilet breaks were timed by managers, male managers would follow you to the toilets and go in to see what you were doing. So, all of that was going on. Then the union instruction happened, and it was kind of the straw that broke the camel's back.' Very quickly, the strikers educated themselves about apartheid and immediately resolved to never handle South African goods again. Their two years on the picket-line was supported by left-wing political parties, the Irish Anti-Apartheid Movement and, in time, the public. This was despite an initial absence of support from the ICTU.

> Karen: We didn't have their support at all. We had to fight for an all-out picket, we actually had to fight Congress to give us that and that took a while, probably six weeks.
> Camilla: But it came in the end?
> Karen: In the end, out of embarrassment. The first couple of weeks it was … 'this is wonderful' and all that sort of thing. And then after that it was 'how do we get rid of these?' Because it embarrassed the trade union movement.

On several occasions, the state deployed the police against these young strikers. Gardaí linked arms across the doors of the store to prevent striking workers from picketing and, as Karen recalls 'used to drag us off the place. One of us nearly got our finger torn off and got seven stitches. I mean they absolutely battered us, and I mean battered us'.

The era of social partnership

The state response after the Dunnes strike was again to seek to limit union power, this time through the *Industrial Relations Act* (1990) which banned both industrial action beyond the conditions of a worker's own job and flash strikes such as this. There was some resistance, especially from rank-and-file members on the left who continue to campaign against a law that bears all the hallmarks of Thatcherite anti-union laws in the UK. But not from the leadership of the trade union movement who were in unison with the government in claiming that a more stable industrial relations landscape would help lift Ireland out of recession by attracting foreign investment. By this stage, they had already helped craft the first of several social partnership agreements that were formally negotiated between the state, trade unions and employers. These agreements became a defining feature of the Irish political landscape from 1987 to 2006 and are said to have contributed to Ireland's economic growth and development. Conversely, in his extensive analysis of social partnership, Kieran Allen demonstrates how, rather than financially benefitting ordinary workers and creating a more equal society, the fiscal reforms and corporate deregulation social partnership enabled a massive transfer of wealth upwards away from wages and social welfare payments towards tax breaks and even more profits for people who were already rich.[40]

Social partnership also coincided with women entering the workforce in greater numbers than before, helping many to gain important financial and other freedoms. But there were challenges too including the absence of childcare (discussed in Chapter 6) and an atmosphere where the logic of the family wage remained strong. In 1996, the National Women's Council of Ireland (NWCI) was formally invited into social partnership negotiations and became a key component of its 'community pillar'. The NWCI's principal ambitions were to inject recognition for unpaid work and to ensure a commitment to the provision of childcare. Importantly, this invitation and decision to participate, coincided with what Joe Larraghy describes as a 'leftist trajectory' within the NWCI meaning their focus shifted towards seeking to address working conditions for all women, including those with lower earning power and especially women who were parenting alone. He describes this shift as 'paradoxical ... in the context of more active engagement with partnership-style institutions that the new [NWCI] echelon viewed with suspicion' and within which they held 'a defensive role' within a structure where they were mostly invited in because 'it would not look too good internationally, especially in a European context, if the NWCI were not in'.[41]

The NWCI walked out of social partnership when it refused to accept the terms of *Sustaining Progress* (2003), believing it was at odds with its own newly agreed internal commitment to supporting the redistribution of wealth and to meaningful political representation. In 2006, the NWCI sought to re-enter social partnership; a request that was not granted. Two years later, social partnership collapsed as did the Irish Celtic Tiger economy. Reflecting on their involvement in the process today, their current director, Orla O'Connor, told me how they continue to work with the government but seek to be 'realistic' about what this can achieve 'because there is a danger of absolutely getting so co-opted that that is where all your energies go'.

Trade unionism and feminism today

One of the lasting impacts of social partnership, Adrian Kane argues, is that it dramatically transformed the culture within trade unions by sanitizing the once revered notion of collective struggle.[42] Unions also moved towards a model of professionalization where they were more likely to be staffed by legal and public relations strategists and experts than campaign managers or grassroots organizers as participation and consultation within formal structures prevailed. Meanwhile, the gulf between union officials and rank-and-file workers remained pronounced as many trade unionists, including those who are anti-capitalists, began losing faith in the movement as a force for change.

Indifference towards trade unionism has also played a significant role in a steep decline in membership. In the 1980s, 60 per cent of the workforce were members of a trade union. By the 2020s, this was just 25 per cent.[43] This apathy didn't spring from nowhere. First, many people, especially young people, have never heard of trade unions or don't fully understand what they do; a situation that isn't helped by the absence of any account of the labour movement within capitalist-friendly school curricula. Secondly, people can be influenced by the mainstream media's depiction of trade unionists as troublemakers and of all industrial action as unreasonable and unnecessarily disruptive. Thirdly, a growing number of private sector employers actively impede employee attempts to unionize. Fourthly, there have been serious failures within trade unions which include an overriding gap between the theoretical visions of what trade unions can and should do, and the actuality of their day-to-day practice. Union effectiveness greatly varies with some unions struggling to deliver on even the most basic supports. Many continue to be characterized by old-fashioned rules and regulations and can be slow to adapt to the diversity of our workforce and the normalcy of people moving between jobs and across borders.

The union movement also failed to sufficiently support wider feminist struggles including the fight for abortion access which, as Chapter 6 details, was the largest feminist uprising in decades. This was despite extensive efforts by some rank-and-file members to illuminate how abortion is a workplace issue. There was a Trade Union Campaign to Repeal the Eighth whose leadership included Therese Caherty, and which was funded by Unite the Union, but these activists didn't get the fulsome support they should have from the movement's leadership. This influenced the Trade Union Campaign to Repeal the Eighth's failure to back a successful 2016 Strike4Repeal which took place in around thirty locations and involved thousands of people. Caherty did meet with the Strike4Repeal organizers in a personal show of solidarity and remembers how 'they were amazing, so full of energy and so committed ... and it worked, it worked brilliantly'. But she explained how their action sent 'a ripple of panic through the trade union campaign because they were talking about Strike for Repeal without any regard for the legislation, about the fact that you can't call a strike'.

There are other ways unions are not feminist, including how they are still not always welcoming or indeed safe spaces for women. In 2020, a report into GMB, one of Britain's largest unions, uncovered high levels of institutional sexism and described the organization as in dire need of fundamental change.[44] Although no such study exists in Ireland, some union members I spoke to shared examples of both conscious and unconscious sexism from rank-and-file members, committee members and union staff alike including rape-jokes and other derogatory comments at committee meetings, male comrades taking credit for their contributions, ongoing out-of-hours expectations that can be difficult for people with care responsibilities to attend and a general sense of not being listened to.

Trade unionists have also experienced some heavy defeats, including protracted industrial action taken by the mostly female ex-employees of the British-owned department store Debenhams who, in 2020, were sacked without redundancy pay. This sudden action breached terms Debenhams had agreed with the trade union, Mandate, four years earlier. In response, workers launched pickets outside the once vibrant stores and blockaded depots, preventing the corporate giant KPMG from retrieving thousands of euros worth of stock. The wholly appropriate demand of the blockaders was that the sale of this stock should be diverted to the redundancy payments they were due. Despite early overtures from the government that appeared to support these workers, it wasn't long before the full force of the state was used against them, in a similar way to how they had been deployed against the Dunnes workers and indeed to strikers throughout history. In 2021 and during coronavirus public health restrictions, up to 60 Gardaí manhandled the former Debenhams workers and their supporters, many of whom were in their sixties and seventies, at one of these blockades. Their industrial action eventually ended when 76 per cent of the former Debenhams workers voted to accept a settlement of a training fund, an offer they had previously rejected. Shop steward Valerie Conlon described the result as 'disappointing' explaining it had been backed 'not because we were happy with it' but because 'we can't be on the picket lines this time next year'.[45]

Other heavy defeats outside of Ireland include the 2023 ruling by the UK Supreme Court, which dealt a devastating blow to Deliveroo workers by deciding they were not entitled to collective bargaining because they were not covered by the right to join a trade union under the European Convention on Human Rights (ECHR).[46] Irish-based Deliveroo workers have also sought better terms and conditions and have unionized through the English Language Students' Union, a subsidiary of SIPTU (which is the acronym for the Services Industrial Professional and Technical Union). The lacklustre attitude from some of the trade union leadership once reserved for female workers has now passed on to these workers. It was telling that, on the same day these Deliveroo drivers initiated strike action for the second time in two years, ICTU's launch of 'trade union week' failed to platform their cause or express even the most minimal gesture of solidarity in any of their media broadcasts that day.

Defeats, the ongoing weakening of trade union power through anti-union laws, falling union membership and the absence of solidarity for those most disenfranchised have all contributed to a situation where trade unions are increasingly adopting what Jane McAlevey describes as a 'defensive position' where most of the movement's work is about protecting workplaces that are already well organized instead of building union membership in places of work where the most exploitative practices are to be found. This in turn helps fuel a sometimes-powerful narrative that trade unions will inevitably just fade away. But there have also been important victories, often by female workers. These include the actions of workers at Ireland's largest pharmaceutical chain, Lloyds, which is owned by the multinational, McKesson Corporation. In 2018, it took just seven days of strike action to win better pay and an end to zero-hours contracts. Before this, Lloyds had adopted several commonly used tactics in an attempt to break the workers' resolve. They ignored or delayed responding to letters from the workers union Mandate, repeatedly portrayed Mandate as irresponsible and claimed most workers didn't want to be part of a union. When the Labour Court ordered them to talk to workers, Lloyds tried to sideline Mandate, insisting they were already talking to workers through internal forums they had set up. Mandate remained focused, resilient and undeterred by bad faith negotiations and attempts by employers at sabotage and had no option but to initiate a strike which had strong support from the public.

Other tactics have also brought some success. In June 2023, mostly female employees of the British-owned Iceland supermarket chain staged a sit-in when their employment ended abruptly and unfairly after receiving an email informing them the store would be closing immediately. They didn't save their jobs, but their union – the Independent Workers Union – did manage to secure better redundancy conditions. There has also been a growth in labour organizing outside of trade unions. One example is the work of FairPlé, a collective of female musicians who helped address sexual harassment and gender-based discrimination in the traditional Irish music industry through their 'Safe to Create' dignity in the workplace programme, the publication of workers' rights, legal aid, counselling, awareness training on sexual harassment and assault, and collaborative high-visibility interventions at music events. This work is to be welcomed; its limitation is expansion beyond the boundaries of a very particular workplace.

There are also examples where unions have shown solidarity with migrant workers. For example, SIPTU has led campaigns to improve working conditions, wages and safety standards in meat factories where many workers have signed overseas contracts that deny them basic welfare protections and a minimum working week.[47] SIPTU has also backed the 'Right to Work Campaign' led by the Movement for Asylum Seekers' (MASI), which helped secure permission for asylum seekers to take up paid work six months following their first application for international protection. This was introduced by the Supreme Court ruling that found the Irish state was breaching people's constitutional rights as protected under the *Refugee Act* 1996.

And there have been victories through the labour courts and the Workplace Relations Commission. In 2016, with the support of the civil society organization the Migrant Rights Centre of Ireland (MRCI), the Workplace Relations Commission ordered one Irish-based family to pay their former Spanish au pair over €9,000 in back-pay by determining they had breached the National Minimum Wage Act. The case ended decades of discriminatory practices by mostly wealthy families who had moulded what was designed as a language exchange programme into a way to access domestic and care labour at a rock-bottom price.

Some progress has equally been made in expanding trade union membership beyond its traditional public sector base. In 2017, the notoriously anti-union airline Ryanair was forced into recognizing several pilot unions. One year later, there was a marked uptick in members of the Financial Services Union in response to Google announcing mass redundancies in 2018.[48] But pilots and software engineers fall into the higher paid category of workers, some of whom have probably been exposed to unions in other jobs. A bigger challenge is to flex the muscle of collective bargaining for the most marginal of workers, something that is more difficult to imagine since the right to strike in solidarity with others was banned. But unions can support workers to self-determine, as happened with the London-based 'Justice for Cleaners' campaign which created an important sense of collective identity for cleaners working across the city and secured an industry-wide agreement with several multinationals, the city of London and at the Canary Wharf financial district.[49]

There are also examples of Irish activists unionizing previously non-unionized workers including the work of staff employed by the trade union Fórsa who continue to invest significant time in educating and organizing Ireland's female Special Needs Assistants (SNAs) workforce. These mostly female workers provide essential support and assistance to children with diverse learning needs. They are underappreciated and poorly paid with a starting salary of 41 per cent below the average industrial wage.[50] Over several years, Fórsa has worked at the grassroots, unionizing members and building a campaign for professional training, better pay and decent contracts. They publicly launched their #RespectForSNAs campaign in 2021, which was the culmination of years of effort by staff and members alike. I spoke to Linda Kelly, Fórsa's national secretary and long-time feminist activist who is especially proud of this work and her early career involvement in it. She told me about 'such a gender dynamic' of resistance from their public sector employer, the Department of Education (DOE), explaining 'you know, the image pushed was that SNAs were just out earning pin money, that they didn't really rely on the wage either for their own income or their own independence'. The workers Linda has supported

> have gone from asking 'what's a trade union' and 'why would I want to get involved' to now being one of the most active, most political areas within the union, constantly growing, really challenging around professionalization, standards, pay-scales, and in a short space of time.

So far, the #RespectforSNAs campaign has secured a higher salary rate through an additional pay point. The work of the campaign continues.

What is to be done?

The work of Fórsa, the actions of the Lloyds workers and the international examples of some success demonstrate how our unions are as relevant as they have ever been. Overall declines in union density have also plateaued and there is a particular growth in female participation with Irish-based working women now outnumber their male counterparts.[51] Certainly the collapse of capitalism that Karl Marx and Friedrich Engels believed was inevitable, even automatic hasn't happened but this doesn't render the theory of collective action by waged workers completely defunct. Organized labour can deliver social change so long as we are willing to build a politicized, vibrant, relevant and non-discriminatory trade union movement. This involves expanding our understanding of trade unionism to align with ideas first expressed by the Marxist theorist, Rosa Luxemburg who asks us to swell our efforts beyond workplace grievances. Writing in 1906, Luxemburg describes strikes as 'the living pulse-beat of the revolution and at the same time its most powerful driving wheel' and takes aim at trade union leaders who 'feared the mass strike as something that could spiral out of their control and jeopardise all their careful work of winning small concessions through governments and courts'.[52] These ideas remain relevant today especially because modern labour movements continue to be characterized by a gulf between their establishment leadership that continue to model a professionalized, somewhat-masculine, business-like union with critical rank-and-file members being the ones more likely to push forward a social justice agenda.

Learning from our mistakes and pushing forward a membership-led model creates the best opportunity possible for aligning trade unionism with feminism. Our challenge is to transform our unions into flexible, responsive and relevant entities that can meaningfully collaborate with like-minded civil society organizations and social movements, not only in improving conditions for all workers but in exposing the relationship between paid and unpaid labour, in overturning anti-union laws, and in expressing tangible solidarity with non-unionized workers. These aren't new ideas and there are examples of political campaigning beyond the workplace. Miriam Hamilton, assistant general secretary of the Irish Federation of University Teachers (IFUT), explains, 'I have campaigned for repeal of the eighth, marriage equality, a better, fairer way to respond to austerity, the need for publicly-funded higher education or better local health services etc' believing 'the trade union movement, as the largest group in civil society, has an important role in shaping and influencing social change and social policy.' Realizing this vision involves labouring to create healthy, democratic membership-led environments where political and practical education is prioritized.

Advocating for and strengthening union coalitions and collaborations is also extremely important if we are to prevent employers and governments from using divide-and-rule tactics. Imagine the impact that would be created if teachers, a more prestigious profession with strong union density, were to work in solidarity with the Special Needs Assistants I talked about earlier in addressing the full extent of their grievances? Or if our trade union leadership put any real effort behind its own social and affordable housing campaign, which was launched in 2018 under the banner Raise the Roof. The trade union leadership could, for example, launch a national strike for housing which would not only draw significant focus on the issue, but it could also pressure policymakers into substantial reforms.

I hope this chapter has illustrated how trade unionism isn't separate from feminism but is integral to it. Uniting workers has historically amplified women's voices in the workplace, pushed for equal pay and gone some way in introducing fairer conditions, and more robust protections against discrimination. Looking ahead involves ensuring a continued synergy of actions towards lasting structural change. As Jane McAlevey maintains, '[T]he point of unions isn't their buildings or bureaucracy; it's political education, solidarity, and confidence building among the many that comes from people acting collectively, including strikes, for their own betterment.'[53]

I love spending time with other feminists to hear their stories and experiences and share mine. I have laughed, cried and ranted with amazing people who know what it is like to live in this world as a woman. Dialogue and discussion with kindred feminist spirits feeds my soul. It breaks my heart that we are still such a long way from achieving gender justice.

– Anonymous survey respondent, 2023

Chapter 4

FEMINISM AND TRANS LIBERATION

On 16 March 2023, Kellie-Jay Keen, also known as Posie Parker, appeared at a 'Let Women Speak' rally in the Donegall Quay area of Belfast city centre. The exact location of the rally had been kept under wraps until the last minute because its organizers had claimed that there were credible threats to Parker's safety and to the safety of some of the other scheduled speakers. These included Jolene Bunting, a former candidate for the far-right political party Britain First and former independent unionist councillor in Northern Ireland. There was supposed to be a similar rally in Dublin around the same time but it was cancelled when the scale of opposition it would attract became obvious. Parker is no stranger to controversy. Just a few weeks earlier, her tour of New Zealand had attracted large counter-protests and public objections to her transphobic rhetoric. At one event, she was pelted with eggs and tomatoes by her challengers. There was also controversy during a tour of Australia when some of her supporters performed the Nazi salute outside Victoria's state parliament building. Back in Belfast, Parker warmed up her few hundred supporters gathered at the landmark Big Fish that overlooks the harbour, by claiming that the sheer act of women speaking out was, in today's world, somehow dangerous.

A few metres away, a much larger, livelier and more celebratory counter-demonstration took place. It was organized by the group Songs for Solidarity Belfast – a collective of LGBTQIA+ activists whose modus operandi is to challenge hate through music. People of all genders were at that gathering. Some had travelled many miles to be there, including Andrea Murray, a member of the socialist-feminist group ROSA who came by bus from Dublin. 'I couldn't not be there', Andrea told me, 'punching down on trans people does not elevate the lives of women … there was a banner there yesterday with KEEP MALES OUT OF WOMEN'S JAILS. When have these "feminists" ever cared about women's cruel incarceration or fought for better conditions for women in prison?' Andrea told me about a heavy police presence and shared how, at one stage, she was pushed over by one police officer, landing flat on her back. 'The only animosity was from the other crowd,' she told me, 'yet we were the ones who were heavily policed.'

Parker is one of several people gaining notoriety for their public attacks on the lives of transgender people, but mostly, the lives of trans women, sometimes in the name of feminism. The goal of this chapter is twofold. First, to counter this anti-trans diatribe by articulating a clear trans-affirming stance that defends the concept of *gender* (which can mean different things to different people) amidst attacks by right-wing forces and others. This task is especially urgent given how centre-right governments are currently pandering to anti-trans discourse, partly to shore-up conservative-leaning voters and partly to distract from other issues. Secondly, this chapter seeks to move beyond simply seeing feminism as something that should seek to secure rights for this tiny minority of people in a largely unchanged world, but as something that locates discussions on gender and the struggle for trans rights amidst the capitalist asymmetries of power and privilege we live within. As Marxists Jules Joanne Gleeson and Elle O'Rourke explain:

> [W]e cannot set capitalism on one side, as a fixed and dependable feature, with gender on the other as a 'cultural' set of norms and identifications. The two admix at every turn, developing and shifting more quickly than we can easily keep track. Our gendered experiences are dominated by capital, yes, but capitalism's relation to gender is one of mutual dependence.[1]

Sometimes feminists shy away from writing about trans liberation. Trans feminists can be understandably afraid of discriminatory retaliation, including physical harm and harassment. Cis feminists may also worry about negative repercussions of taking a trans-affirming stance, or they buy into the notion that this is somehow a complicated arena and worry they might absentmindedly say the wrong thing. Cis writers can also be deterred by the fact that much harm has been done by non-trans scientists and scholars, when they uphold cisnormativity as the most natural and normal way to be and treat trans people as 'subjects' that are to be made sense of and controlled instead of as ordinary members of society.

Before going any further, it is no harm to clearly explain the language I am using. Taking my lead from Professor of Women and Gender Studies Susan Stryker, and writer, performer and activist Julia Serano, I use the word *trans* as an umbrella expression that signals moving beyond, or crossing over, from the 'female' or 'male' gender binaries each of us is assigned at birth. This broad spectrum approach works well in terms of inclusivity. But as Serano explains in *Whipping Girl* (first published in 2007), it is less effective in illuminating the different issues experienced by different groupings. For example, trans women often face significant pressure to 'pass', meaning pressure to conform with contemporary gender norms in how women should behave and present themselves. Passing can be tied to ensuring one's trans identity is not 'discovered' by others, which, in turn can't be decoupled from the extent to which trans women endure violent assaults much more often than other people. For trans men, part of their struggle can be visibility and representation whilst non-binary people can face the complete erasure of their gender including within Ireland's *Gender Recognition Act* (2015). The expression 'trans' also glosses over diversity within different groupings and is blind to intersectional discriminations including racism, homophobia, ableism, classism and citizenship status. For these reasons, I adopt the meaning proposed by Julia Serano who suggests we use 'trans' as a political expression that focuses our attention on one common goal – to end discrimination based on sex/gender variation.[2] *Transmisogyny*, also from the scholarship of Serano, describes the obsession some transphobes have with the very existence of trans women, a hatred inspired by their relinquishing of male privilege. This, Serano explains, casts 'a shadow of doubt over the supposed supremacy of maleness and masculinity'.[3] Regarding the expression *cisgender* or simply *cis*, this describes people (myself included) who have kept the original gender assignment given at birth, and signals an awareness of the privileges this brings.

As for *LGBTQIA+*, this is an acronym (where the T stands for trans) that brings together everyone who is not heterosexual or cis. There are debates about this additive model which, broadly speaking, relates to the process of identity labelling. Some people prefer a less prescriptive umbrella model of using *queer*, in a way that doesn't delineate any one identity category, or insist on identity categories at all. Setting these debates aside, most people agree that the undertones of this 'rainbow flag' are positivity, acceptance and inclusion, believing that people who face discrimination are stronger together in the struggle for equality. This doesn't mean that its adoption is universally welcomed and not just by homophobes. For example, LGB Alliance Ireland, an offshoot of the UK organization of the same name, is founded on transphobia and rejects LGBTQIA+ framings claiming that trans rights are in conflict with LGB rights and that lesbian identity is being erased, despite the fact that nothing has changed for them personally. Who exactly is erasing lesbians?

The suggestion that gender is not fixed along certain biological lines, that is, because of our genitals, chromosomes and hormones, can be a difficult idea for some people to get their heads around. But this is mostly because current differentials of primary characteristics, e.g. genitalia and chromosomes and secondary characteristics, e.g. facial and body hair, muscle mass and voice are hardwired into our thinking at a deep level. Some people can find it almost impossible to imagine things any other way. But there are many ways we could stratify physical differences that sit outside of these parameters like hair colour or height. Many people also choose to ignore, minimize or disguise aspects of our physicality that don't fit the gender-binary. Think of the great lengths many women go to removing body hair, sometimes spending thousands of euros over their lifetime. Surely a much better approach would be to embrace it as just another aspect of our bodies. This is just one of many examples. As the biologist Anne Fausto-Sterling points out, it is when we unite our collective bodies that they reveal to us a myriad of differences.[4]

Perhaps the best example of the lengths that our cis-heteronormative society is prepared to go to in order to maintain a biological male–female binary is to consider Western medicine's treatment of intersex variation, something that impacts around 2 per cent of the population. This is where a person doesn't neatly fit as either male or female because they hold a combination of traditional sex traits. If intersex variations are obvious at birth, Western medicine often forces people into the binary including through surgical interventions often without the full and informed consent of a child's guardians and with zero consideration for the rights of the child to non-interference with their body's normal way of being. If differences are detected later in life, which is more common today because of medical advances and greater awareness of sex variation, a battle with the medical profession can ensue. By way of example, Hil Malatino describes his own experience of being 'diagnosed' and pathologized as intersex as one where he 'was supposed to heed the rhetoric of the medical professionals who focused on the notion that I was an "unfinished" woman. One who needed a bit of help along the path to full-blown ladyhood. I was meant to construe the diagnosis as a congenital disorder that *didn't* trouble me at the most basic ontological level.'[5]

These insights, and much of what is to come in this chapter, is drawn from my reading into, and where possible drawing from, mostly trans scholars, including the aforementioned Malatino, Serano, Stryker, Gleeson and O'Rourke, and also Tila Mae Bettcher, Judith Butler, Vivian Namaste, M. E. O'Brien, Julian Gill Peterson and more. These writers, and their different points of view, have helped me to think differently about gender and in ways that sometimes challenged me. But overall, they have strengthened my belief that any feminism that is worth its salt must be clearly and unequivocally trans liberationary. I'm also more aware now of important historiographical accounts of gender variance and trans histories, including within Leah DeVun's *The Shape of Sex: Nonbinary Gender from Genesis to the Renaissance* (2010), which draws from a broad range of thinkers to chart a history of people who do not neatly fit the binary genders that dominate today. DeVun infuses debates about nature, race and religion to reveal a deep history that challenges suppositions that gender variance is a modern phenomenon. Equally, Eilis O'Keefe outlines several instances of gender fluidity and transitioning in Irish folklore, something British colonialism sought to eradicate.[6]

Increased visibility amidst ongoing discrimination

Twenty-first-century Ireland undoubtedly contains greater trans visibility, especially across social and other media, but also because queer presenting people mingle more openly than was the case just a couple of decades ago. The confidence more people are finding to live openly, instead of clandestinely, is helped by the presence of openly trans international celebrities such as Chaz Bono, Laverne Cox, Suzy Izzard, Elliot Page, Sara Ramirez and Hunter Schafer to name just a few. Television is also better at depicting trans experiences, including in Ireland. Jack Murphy, a trans man, recently played a character in the soap opera *Fair City*. The storyline followed his struggles to overcome barriers to healthcare. Rebecca Tallon De Havilland, who is credited with being Ireland's first publicly out trans woman, is now a regular TV presenter. The profile given to these entertainers is a far cry from the recent past when trans personalities were sensationalized and trans characters were there to be made fun of and portrayed as deceptive. Aoife Martin, a regular columnist for *The Journal.ie* who openly transitioned in her workplace, also contributes positively to visibility and awareness. Her public transition was a largely positive experience, she tells me, with most people seeing her as just a regular person with a diversity of experiences. But Aoife is open about the middle-class and white privileges that helped her through, and is concerned about a future reality where the Irish media, in particular, are increasingly giving a voice to transphobes. In her own words, '[W]e are living in a society that is generally antagonistic at best towards trans people. Where somehow, it's seen that we are "an ideology," that we're doing this on purpose. But we're not, you know, all we want is acceptance, some dignity and equality.'

Another development is that more people than before are seeking to medically transition, which can include hormonal therapy, mental health care and gender-affirming surgeries, which date back as far as the 1910s.[7] One recent American-based study of over 3,000 people found significant positives from medical transitioning, including improved mental health, less self-harm and less alcohol and drug misuse than before transitioning.[8] This growth in demand has placed significant pressure on trans healthcare services. Around 2010, Ireland's only National Gender Service (NGS), which is based in Dublin, received about ten referrals each year. By 2022, that had risen to over 3,000,[9] a tiny number that amounts to around 0.007 per cent of Ireland's adult population. Sometimes transphobes spread disinformation about high levels of regret following gender-affirming surgeries. Experts put this figure as low as 1 per cent.[10]

As I write, there is no dedicated trans healthcare in Ireland for people under eighteen years of age and no plans to introduce any. This is despite numerous peer-reviewed scientific studies that have identified particular benefits for young people, including better mental health outcomes, a significant decrease in suicidality and marked improvements in well-being amongst this demographic.[11] Instead, in 2023, access to care was publicly undermined by two leading doctors (both white cis men) who worked at the NGS, when they openly lodged a complaint against the Health Service Executive (HSE) for referring children to overseas services where the model is trans affirming. One cannot be sure what motivated these doctors. Typically, the justification for limiting or banning healthcare for children rests on the transphobic claims of a presumed and untrustworthy 'trans community' determined to recruit and groom younger people. Noah Zazanis explains how proponents of this moral panic claim 'youth transition is a harmful coping mechanism akin to self-harm or alcohol/drug abuse' but express no concern for the way trans children are repeatedly and often vociferously pressured into conforming with their assigned gender, with transitioning presented as the worst possible outcome to their struggles.[12] These ideas fan the flames of those in favour of conversion therapy; a highly controversial practice that seeks to psychologically push people into cis heteronormativity and which is still practised in Ireland to this day.[13] Never mind that one large-scale study in the United States found that trans people who undergo conversion therapy are twice as likely to attempt suicide than their trans counterparts who take part in other forms of therapy.[14]

As these examples illustrate, James Vernon contends that any history of gender variance should principally focus on the profoundly discriminatory impacts of cis privilege on trans people's lives via ideological and social barriers that, for decades, have restricted and controlled trans people's lives.[15] When the Irish-based doctors and the NGS lodged their complaint, it wasn't out of step with a lengthy history of doctors holding a near monopoly on what constitutes healthcare for trans people since modern medicine took shape in the latter half of the nineteenth century. Some trans people came into contact with supportive doctors who pioneered trans-affirming care. But the more dominant model was for doctors to view gender variance as an illness to be eradicated. Their role was to cure people in the first instance. When this failed, they took on the role of gatekeeper, where their job was to regulate and limit the availability of hormone therapy and gender-confirming surgeries. Throughout much of the twentieth century, doctors actively encouraged trans people to segregate themselves from their own communities. Serano describes the principal motivation behind this approach as 'to protect the cissexual public from their own gender anxiety by ensuring that most cissexuals would never come face-to-face with someone that they knew to be transsexual'.[16]

Doctors didn't act alone but with the backing of a legal landscape of stigmatization and discrimination in just about every facet of our society. Some of the earliest Western decrees, that seek to force cis heteronormativity, date back to the 1600s. Ireland's later enforced *Criminal Law Amendment Act* (1885), best known for causing the imprisonment of Oscar Wilde, criminalized anything outside of a straight family kinship and was mostly introduced because of religious pressures.

More recently, many medics, especially those who have specialized in trans care, acknowledge everyone's right to bodily autonomy, support severing ties with diagnostics and uphold values that reflect how no one way of being has legitimacy over another. However, gatekeeping, where doctors, and not the person themselves, ultimately determine whether the criteria have been met for being 'truly trans' does persist. Some of the people I spoke to who have first-hand experience of Ireland's NGS describe being micro-managed and judged in a system that retains a pathologizing approach, despite recommendations to the contrary by the World Health Organization (WHO) and against the grain of many clinicians internationally. Many people wait years simply to get an initial assessment, then navigate the service with a personal aim of getting out the other end with as little trauma as possible. Similar to the way bodily autonomy was denied in Ireland throughout its abortion ban, people are left with no choice but to seek hormone therapy through online forums or word of mouth connections and fly overseas for surgical procedures that are often expensive. And that's without considering other barriers, including the cost of travel and the luxury of having the time to step away from whatever responsibilities a person holds. As is the case when abortion bans are in place, barriers such as these disproportionately impact poorer people, disabled people, migrants, people with care loads and/or people in coercive relationships where it is difficult to get away. Beyond specialist services, people seeking gender-confirming care can face prejudicial attitudes from GPs who are reluctant to prescribe hormone therapy despite regularly prescribing these to cis people for all sorts of reasons including delayed puberty, menopause and when treating some cancers. Some doctors also neglect people's basic right to healthcare by falsely presuming that any issue a trans person presents with somehow links back to their gender identity. As Aoife Martin explains, 'I am aware of at least one trans woman who had neurological problems but the doctor wouldn't treat her because they said it was "too complicated". Why didn't they just treat her like a woman?'

On a more positive note, there have been some legislative advances. Ireland now has a *Gender Recognition Act* (2015) which, like laws in Norway, Argentina and Malta, accepts self-determination as the only required criterion. This wasn't introduced because of enlightened legislators but because of a decades-long legal battle by Dr Lydia Foy, which began in 1992 when she first wrote to the registrar's office seeking to have her birth certificate reflect her true gender but was turned down. In 1997, with the support of the Free Legal Aid Board, Foy initiated legal action. Her case was first heard in 2000 but was rejected due to the absence of an existing law and in the shadow of the need to await the resolution of a European Court of Human Rights (ECHR) ruling about a separate British legal battle which came down in favour of the right to gender recognition leading to the UK's own more limited gender recognition act. When Irish courts eventually ruled in Foy's favour in 2007, the state appealed the ruling, only to withdraw their appeal three years later. In a media interview at the time, Foy described being 'battered' by the ordeal and revealed that she nearly quit several times.[17] By this stage, the Transgender Equality Network of Ireland (TENI, est. 2004) was also backing Foy. TENI also supported the actions of Louise Hannon who successfully took a discrimination case against her employers, First Direct Logistics, who insisted she assume a male identity when meeting clients.[18] And TENI was amongst those to roundly criticize highly restrictive recommendations published by a government-established Gender Recognition Advisory Group (est. 2010) which was created solely to respond to the Foy ruling.[19] The inadequacy of this advisory group's recommendations led to more delays, which were eventually overcome when, in 2013, two private members' bills,[20] written in collaboration with trans activists, forced the issue by spurring the government into creating their own legislative framework allowing them to ensure it was their law that was introduced rather than one that came from the opposition benches. This law was crafted in consultation with trans advisors and advocacy groups and Sam Blanckensee was one of those consulted. 'There wasn't a big pushback within the Oireachtas [parliament],' Sam tells me, explaining some politicians spoke openly about having favourably consulted with members of the public in their own constituencies. Overall, Sam Blanckensee believes simply by talking to trans people, politicians quickly understood the logic of a legal framework based on self-determination. 'Between December 2014, and when it passed in July 2015, the bill changed entirely,' Sam explains, going from a document that proposed a medical assessment, an insistence applicants could not be married and a higher age restriction to one where, 'by the time we passed it, those three had changed quite significantly'. This, he continues, is because 'most of the work was around people becoming more open to a more progressive set of legislation, not whether or not the legislation should happen ... In the press, it was more just informing people ... what it meant to be trans'.

A global surge in violence and the further erosion of trans rights

When the *Gender Recognition Act* (2015) became law, there was no significant public objection. Maybe this was because it coincided with Ireland becoming the first country in the world to introduce same-sex marriage by popular vote, which underscored a broad societal embrace of LGBTQIA+ diversity and a break from Ireland's history of discrimination and division. It seems fair to suggest that if the act were to be introduced today, the internationally polarized climate surrounding gender identity and trans rights would result in at least some public debate. Though more trans people are managing to live in the open and access gender-confirming care, albeit with limitations, we cannot deny a significant rise in transphobia and transmisogynistic violence, including homicide. In 2023, the murder of the British teenager Brianna Ghey – killed by people she thought were her friends, helped humanize the ongoing risks to trans women's safety. In the United States, the death by suicide of Nex Benedict in 2024 after enduring severe bullying over a long period, and the day after an assault in a school restroom, has equally taken the dangers to trans people's lives out of the abstract, as did the suicide of the US-based Saudi Arabian teenager Eden Knight after she was forced to detransition. These are not just terrible events that happen in other countries, the same risks exist in Ireland where trans children are more likely to be bullied and excluded, which impacts their health, well-being and academic attainment.[21] The effects are not insignificant. Eighty per cent of Irish-based trans people have considered suicide at some stage and nearly 45 per cent have engaged in some type of self-harm.[22] The threat of interpersonal violence remains a constant reality, especially for trans women most of which is never reported.[23] Overall, there has been a 29 per cent increase in hate crimes captured in 2022 Gardaí statistics, with crimes against LGBTQIA+ people second only to race-related assaults.[24] Crimes against trans people are specifically captured in UK statistics. Figures from 2023 show a marked rise in reported assaults. In an unusual but welcome intervention, the UK's Home Office blamed the increase on an unwelcoming social environment perpetuated by the way 'transgender issues have been heavily discussed by politicians, the media and on social media over the last year'.[25] Connections to public discourse also surely apply in Ireland given that the independent non-governmental organization ILGA-Europe has identified 'hostile media reporting' that perpetuates negative stereotypes and fuels misinformation.[26]

Beyond the Irish experience, there has been a marked increase in transphobic laws in some parts of the world, especially in the United States, much of which can be interpreted as a conservative backlash to positive change. Several states had introduced progressive laws throughout the 1990s and 2000s, and many people embraced trans identities, influenced by what Susan Stryker describes as 'the new political concept of queerness, the AIDS epidemic, the rapid development of the internet, the end of the Cold War, the maturation of the first post-Baby-Boomer generation, and the calendrical millennial turn'.[27] One particular trigger that set a backlash in motion was when, in

2013, six-year-old Coy Mathis won the right to use the school bathroom of her choice against the wishes of the overseeing district. The counter-attack has been vicious. A range of so-called 'health and safety bills' have now been passed that restrict people's access to mostly bathrooms and sports competitions, and that decrees custodial sentences should be served in segregations that match their assigned gender and not their true gender. In 2024 alone, forty-three anti-LGBTQIA+ national bills were under consideration, an increase on the previously unprecedented thirty-seven bills that were introduced at federal level in 2023.[28] As anti-trans hatred spreads, new challenges are emerging, such as protests outside trans-affirming healthcare providers, some of which have led to some hospital providers cancelling gender-affirming care both for adults and children.[29]

Many of these anti-LGBTQIA+ laws also limit or ban trans even participating in sport including in Ireland. Invasive 'sex testing' in sports, which began in the 1920s,[30] is increasingly under the spotlight. In 2022, the Irish Rugby Football Union (IRFU) followed the lead of World Rugby which, one year earlier, had become the first international sports governing body to institute a ban on trans women participating in global competitions like the Olympics or World Cup. The IRFU's blanket ban on all trans women and children over the age of twelve replaced an existing policy that rigidly tested testosterone levels to ensure these had sufficiently dropped to levels more typical in cis women. The logic behind these bans is that allowing trans women to participate distorts an otherwise level playing field because of the supposed physical advantages they bring from their previous gender identity. But if banning trans athletes is about competitive fairness, why are trans men and boys often also not allowed to compete? Moreover, practically nothing is ever said about the already present and never-ending rules and guidelines trans athletes must comply with to be allowed to compete including testosterone testing but also physical assessments and sometimes even psychological evaluations. According to the academic and sports specialist Lindsay Parks Pieper, gender verification testing has mostly become a tool to control women in sport as part of 'the construction of the ideal western white athlete who is always expected to display femininity over strength and musculinity'.[31] This analysis rings true for the experiences of the cis female Olympic boxer and gold medallist Imane Khelif who, in 2024 faced relentless online bullying including by the author J. K. Rowling, US President Donald Trump and Italian premier Giorgia Meloni when they learned she had been disqualified from the world championships one year earlier because of naturally occurring, elevated testosterone levels. Meanwhile, male athletes' bodies are never policed despite some men having obvious physical advantages over their competitors. At the same time, those imposing bans in the name of protecting women's sports do nothing to address deep-seated problems such as ongoing pay differentials between men and women that make it practically impossible for female athletes to devote their careers to sport, uneven media coverage which impacts investment and sponsorship, representation at the leadership level and the ongoing prevalence of sexual harassment within many sports.

Church and TERFs

Broadly speaking, the two principal sources of discontent have been number one, the Christian right, within which I include Evangelical Christianity that is popular in the United States and also the Catholic Church that is popular in Ireland and, number two, a self-titled 'gender critical' movement which claims to be part of feminism. Dealing with the former first, and with an emphasis on Catholicism, it is worth pointing out that, unlike other religions like Buddhism, Islam or Hinduism, the Catholic Church positions itself as 'the one, holy, universal, and apostolic church, not only concerned with the well-being and salvation of its members but of the entire world'.[32] Catholicism may root itself in the historical text of the Bible when ascribing its beliefs, but its strongly held claims that anything outside cis-normativity is against 'God's will' is relatively new. One recognizable starting point was in 1994 when the church objected to the word 'gender' in documents presented at the United Nations (UN) Fourth World Conference on Women claiming the word was 'anti-family' and therefore 'anti-woman'.[33] Three years later, the high-profile US Catholic journalist Dale O'Leary published *The Gender Agenda: Redefining Equality* (1997), which claimed the UN was at war with marriage, motherhood and the family.

A more powerful and direct attack on gender would follow in 2004 when the Pope's Council (under the Papacy of Joseph Ratzinger) warned that 'gender theorists were imperilling the family by challenging the proposition that Christian family roles could and should be derived from biological sex' and that a return to essentialist gender roles, determined by biology would stave off the dangers of 'gender ideology'.[34] Before this, church teachings had not commented on biological sex and, by extension, trans identities except in passing when upholding gender essentialism and the sanctity of straight marriage when discussing family life, young people and creation.[35] This new perspective was most clearly articulated some years later in 2019 when the Vatican published *Male and Female He Created Them: Towards a Path of Dialogue on the Question of Gender Theory in Education*. This document, circulated to the 90 per cent of Irish schools which remain under the patronage of the Catholic Church, determines we are facing 'an educational crisis' and provides guidance for teachers working with children. It claims 'the process of identifying sexual identity' is being made difficult by 'the fictitious construct known as "gender neutral" or "third gender"', which obscures the fixed nature of a person's sex and where supposed theories of 'transgender' are 'aim[ing] to annihilate the concept of "nature" (that is, everything we have been given as a pre-existing foundation of our being and action in the world), while at the same time implicitly reaffirming its existence' (brackets in original).[36] Ask a trans person if their life is fictitious. With zero consideration for the rights of intersex people to consent, the document insists anyone born with intersex variation require 'a therapeutic intervention' by 'medical professionals' to ensure they are immediately categorized into one or other of the gender binaries.

The Vatican's perspective directly contradicts, on several occasions, Ireland's recently developed Relationships and Sexuality Education (RSE) curricula for schools. Its senior cycle sets out to 'examine how harmful attitudes around gender are perpetuated in the media, online and in society and discuss strategies for challenging these attitudes and narratives', describing gender identity as 'a person's felt internal and individual experience of gender, which may or may not correspond with the sex registered at birth'.[37] In March 2023, and against established trans-affirming practices in some schools, the Catholic Primary Schools Management Association wrote to the government stating 'gender identity' would not be taught in their schools. Later that same year, a Christian fundamentalist group called All Nations Church held a meeting at the National Stadium in Dublin which was attended by around 300 people. One school principal at the event anonymously told a reporter, 'I will be advising parents to withdraw their children from the new curriculum ... If an inspector is standing over me, telling me that I have to teach this, I will still refuse.'[38] This isn't the first time Christian influences have exercised muscle over RSE in Irish schools. In the late 1990s, a pilot programme called 'Exploring Masculinities' was dropped despite positive evaluations from teachers and students because of pressure from the Congress of Catholic Schools Parent Association (CSAP) and a handful of high-profile journalists. They claimed the programme was too heavily influenced by feminism, that it negatively stereotyped men by claiming they are more violent and that it undermined boys by asking them to open up in front of their peers.[39]

Given the Catholic Church's long history of discrimination and destruction, its view on gender is unsurprising. A more complicating influence is when people calling themselves feminists oppose the concept of 'gender' or claim to be 'gender critical'. In a break from radical feminism's long-standing willingness to include intersecting factors, and challenge to rigid gender categorizations, a new breed of 'gender-critical feminists' has emerged. They argue, vociferously and above all other feminist concerns, that we should favour 'sex' as a biologically substantive material reality over 'gender', an apparently subjective experience. Although unflatteringly labelled TERFs (short for trans-exclusionary radical feminists) in the UK, part of the origin story is some corners of US feminism. In particular, *The Transsexual Empire* ... (1979) written by Janice Raymond, with a revised edition republished in 1994 argued, without evidence, that trans women were actually men who were seeking to 'wrest from women those powers inherent in female biology', and therefore a clear and present danger to cis women and a threat to feminism.[40] Doctors who supported their transition, she claimed, were colluding in a 'male fantasy' and trans men were nothing but confused victims of patriarchy. Raymond's ideas helped embolden anti-trans legislators, as did several court rulings at the time that ignored the increased visibility and acceptance of trans people as they continued to legislate against trans people's existence.[41]

By 2013, forty-eight 'radical feminists' had signed an open declaration against 'gender studies' and in favour of the rights of feminist spaces to exclude trans women.[42] This 'gender-critical feminism' gathered pace in the UK following a 2016 announcement that their *Gender Recognition Act* (2004) would be revised to allow self-identification. In response, British-based TERFs injected an unsubstantiated discourse that claimed this change would cause danger to cis women. Gender-critical feminists focused much of their energies on preserving women only spaces, especially bathrooms, gyms and prisons, by which they mean cis-women only spaces. They mostly did this by upholding rare and terrible cases perpetrated by a tiny minority of people, as evidence that all trans women are dangerous. Meanwhile they completely disregarded the fact that the people most at risk from gender-based violence, both in public and in private, are trans women, especially ethnic minorities and people with precarious economic lives.[43]

Seeking to define womanhood isn't new within white Western feminism. For example, it was a central focus of Simone de Beauvoir's revered *The Second Sex* (1949), within which the opening line of Book II maintains, 'one is not born, but rather becomes, a woman'.[44] The lead up to this famous assertion was lengthy discussions on biological differences between men and women, with de Beauvoir maintaining that physical differences between women and men are the foundations upon which gender is socially constructed, with women's autonomy beyond her biological function almost completely eroded. What transpires, de Beauvoir asserted, is an unequal environment where 'humanity is male and man defines woman not in herself, but as relative to him; she is not regarded as an autonomous being'.[45] Context matters and a fair reading of de Beauvoir's existentialism is to appreciate it within a timeframe where the dominant ideas of the time were shaped by Freudian psychosexual theory which determined that the differences between 'male' and 'female' were fixed and forever, with the former superior to the latter. De Beauvoir made mistakes in universalizing patriarchy and in her blindness to white privilege. But she usefully and appropriately interprets criticality as an analytical tool that reveals new ways of understanding the world so we might improve it something the philosopher and gender studies scholar Judith Butler sees as absent from TERFs' misuse of the word 'critique'. Butler argues TERFs weaponize criticality so that they can stand in blind opposition to what is essentially a positivist truth.[46]

Not all trans scholars have been supportive of Butler's theories on gender as first articulated in both *Gender Trouble* (1990) and *Bodies That Matter* (1993), where they contend (amongst other things) that both gender and the sexed body are temporal and malleable and that the distinction between sex and gender 'turns out to be no distinction at all'.[47] Vivian Namaste takes exception to Butler's eagerness to interrupt the male–female binary and any suggestion that gender is free-floating and performed, thereby implying choice over gender being a deeply integral part of one's identity.[48] But as is the case with de Beauvoir, there are important contextual factors we should bear in mind especially that Butler's immense 1990s contributions coincided with a now well-documented 'linguistic turn' that depoliticized many left-wing and Marxist ideas. This is the context within which both Nancy Fraser and Cinzia Arruzza criticized aspects of Butler's theories, arguing that they insufficiently focused on the social and material relations we exist within, where gender is a central organizing principle of capitalism.[49] Contrastingly, trans scholars Tilia Mae Bettcher and Rosa Lee are amongst those who welcome perspectives that break away from conservative individualist views on transitioning, therefore allowing a more malleable reconceptualization that moves beyond pathology and better aligns with the actual experiences and struggles that trans people face.[50]

In *Who's Afraid of Gender* (2024) Butler accuses gender-critical feminists Holly Lawford-Smith, Kathleen Stock and J.K. Rowling of inflicting great harm by associating trans women with heinous acts of violence against women, with no regard for how these women have disidentified from traditional masculinity and are much more likely to be at the receiving end of male violence, including in prisons.[51] Elsewhere, Deborah Shaw asks why, despite many academics' finding Stock's ideas to be theoretically unfounded and openly discriminatory, Stock continues to be given a national media platform from which she claims to speak for all feminists with no such visibility afforded to trans feminists.[52] This, Shaw contends, has given gender-critical feminists a disproportionate influence over government policy in an environment where British politicians have been only too happy to oblige. In February 2024, then Prime Minister Rishi Sunak went as far as to make a dangerous transphobic jibe during a parliamentary exchange, despite knowing that the mother of Brianna Ghey was an invitee to the chamber and was watching on in person. Keir Starmer, the Labour Party leader and Prime Minister at the time of writing, hasn't offered an alternative, rather he has openly expressed transphobic opinions including that trans women should be banned from female-designated bathrooms.

Although slower to emerge and with less obvious support from centre-right political parties, gender-critical feminism has taken root in Ireland. One of its first manifestations was a 'We Need to Talk' event that was planned for Dublin in 2018, the same year as Ireland's abortion referendum (also known as the 'repeal referendum') and at a time when feminist activism was at an all-time high. An initial thirty-six feminists signed an open letter objecting to the event, then posted this on the *Feminist Ire Blog,* from which point signatories grew to over 1,000 overnight.[53] It would be 2021 before home-grown TERF activism would gather any level of pace, arguably beginning with *The Irish Times* publication of an opinion piece that backed conversion therapy for trans children, of which one author was Stella O'Malley (along with Jacky Grainger and Madeleine Ní Dhálaigh).[54] This article resulted in a boycott of the newspaper by the Trans Writers Union. That same year, O'Malley spoke at a conference held on International Women's Day called 'Speak Up for Women's Rights' which was organized by a group called The Irish Women's Lobby. She used this platform to claim that trans identities are a new phenomenon, and that trans women are impostors disrupting an otherwise-harmonious sisterhood. O'Malley was, by this stage, becoming a go-to contributor for mainstream media outlets who seemed less inclined to invite representatives from TENI or Belong To; a national services and advocacy organization for LGBTQIA+ children and young people. She was even chosen, above both of these groups, to address a gathering of non-denominational school providers on the topic 'managing gender issues'.[55]

The main speaker at the 'Speak Up for Women's Rights' conference was Stock whose 2021 publication *Material Girls* argues that choosing 'gender identity' over 'biological sex' is damaging feminism and undermining women's rights. In her address, delivered online because of coronavirus public health restrictions, Stock dismissed decades of rigorous gender studies scholarship when she accused academics of reaching the 'stunning conclusion that there is no such thing as women and girls as a genuine group'. This, she claimed is because academics are too busy chasing a new 'hot-take' as they search for kudos by researching 'queer bodies'.[56] Assuming I am included in this mix, please show me where I claim that there is no such thing as women and girls. Stock further accused academics of duping ordinary feminists by creating an atmosphere in which people are afraid to speak up about any discomfort they might feel. Since then, a handful of small trans-exclusionary organizations have taken root. Most visible amongst these is The Countess (taking their name from the feminist activist Countess Constance Georgine Markievicz) led by Laoise De Brún and also the less visible Radicailín. For their 2024 conference called 'Resisting Ideology', the keynote speaker was none other than Posie Parker who, just six months earlier, had organized a second 'Let Women Speak' event, this time in Dublin where attendees were outnumbered by anti-Parker demonstrators by at least five to one. As was the case in Belfast one year earlier, the tone of the counter-protest was celebratory with protesters objecting to the fascist sympathizer and self-proclaimed anti-feminist speaker by gathering under the banner 'turf out the terfs'.

Despite being very much on the margins of Irish-feminism, these tiny numbers, bolstered by international support, repeatedly claim to speak for all women in Ireland, by which they mean cis women. In particular, The Countess has taken aim at the NWCI, mostly because Sara Phillips sits on their board; a former chair of TENI and a trans feminist and activist. This has been an important alliance.[57] As Sam Blanckensee explains, '[T]he fact that the National Women's Council has been so strong has been a huge plus for Irish feminism. It is really important that our feminist organizations are trans inclusive.' Their Director Orla O'Connor describes how transphobic trolling has taken a particular toll on people working and volunteering with NWCI. 'The anti-trans abuse towards trans inclusive feminists at the moment is really shocking,' she told me, 'dreadful abuse on our social media, really bad'. Orla also explained how a lot of the online abuse they received originated from outside of Ireland. 'We have had to do significant work trying to protect staff and Board members. And we've had some legal threats as well so it is a huge piece at the minute.'

TERFs and the far right

A more comfortable alliance to emerge has been how transphobes obsession with biological essentialism and corresponding disregard for the safety of trans women has increasingly aligned their overall objectives with those of the far right. The far right's motivation might be different, but they too are focused on adhering to traditional gender roles when interpreting masculinity and femininity. But they are also soft on gender-based violence and strongly support bans on abortion. 'They are coming for women's bodily autonomy and I can't understand why the TERFs don't see that,' Aoife Martin points out, continuing 'or maybe they do see that and they don't care. They are so obsessed with their hatred, and it is hatred, no doubt about it, of trans people, and particularly trans women, that they are just prepared to accept that.'

In the context of book bans in the United States, one particular tactic of the far right in Ireland has been the targeting of public libraries by small groups of highly organized, mostly male, often-intimidating protesters some of who have travelled from Britain. These protesters have now entered libraries in Cork, Donegal, Dublin, Leitrim, Kerry, Mayo and likely other counties too in an attempt to remove books including *This Book Is Gay*, a young adult, non-fiction book by the trans activist Juno Dawson. These same faces have also shown up at daytime Drag Story events and intimidated attendees, many of whom are children. Ireland's centre-right government has condemned these actions, especially when agitators intimidated library workers. But in 2023, this condemnation was accompanied by a directive to libraries that they were to change long-established borrowing rules by seeking parental permission when teenagers wanted to borrow books. This change was criticized in the Dáil by the People before Profit TD Paul Murphy, as was the behaviour of Gardaí who, during one of the library attacks, escorted far-right activists inside, then guarded the door to prevent counter demonstrators from getting in.[58]

Feminism and queer activism working together

As was the case with Sunak and Starmer in the United Kingdom, Trump in the United States and Meloni in Italy, it would be naïve to rule out some appetite within Irish politics to pander to populist trends so that they can hold onto voters being swayed in that direction but also because they share the goal of maintaining the family structure albeit for economic and not cultural reasons. Remember using trans people as cultural scapegoats averts people's gaze from much broader symptoms of capitalism, like not having a home or earning less money than you need to get by. In other words, it is much easier to go soft on those who blame trans people for the ills of society and hard on those who encourage an analysis of structural economics.

Establishment politicians and the wider apparatus of the neoliberal state have certainly become expert at pinkwashing – a practice where companies, organizations and the state promote themselves as LGBTQIA+ friendly to distract from or downplay negative aspects of their own behaviours that are the very opposite. Pinkwashing is a particular feature of Pride – an annual global celebration that immortalizes the Stonewall riots of 1969 which began when two trans women, Marsha P. Johnson and Sylvia Rivera, led the successful prevention of a police raid at the Stonewall Inn in New York. Today's Pride is increasingly underpinned by corporate donations and political performativity and not any real attempt to address the genuine concerns of LGBTQIA+ communities including barriers to trans healthcare and the constant threat of violence. There is equally no political appetite to address financial inequality where, in the context of the growing casualization of labour, trans people are less likely to wind up in a stable job where they have at least some sort of workplace protections against prejudice.[59]

Because of pinkwashing, Trans and Intersex Pride (est. 2018) now organize an anti-fascist block at Pride and run a separate annual march which has grown in number from a few hundred in 2018 to several thousand in 2024. Their convener Ollie Bell described its origins as a response to the growing frustrations within the LGBTQIA+ community towards mainstream Prides where ordinary people and grassroots community groups were being pushed to the sidelines to make room for big corporations like Amazon and Google. 'We are anti-rainbow capitalism,' Ollie explains:

> [W]e are against companies that wrap themselves in a rainbow flag for one day a year while actively working against our community the rest of the year, they have no right to march with us at Pride ... we're about bringing Pride back to its radical roots of protest. This is about building a mass movement to push forward the fight for trans liberation.

Trans and intersex pride, which is actively and proudly supported by feminist groups including ROSA and the NWCI is just one example of queer and feminist movements working together. In 2015, feminist groups fulsomely backed Marriage Equality. Two years later, queer allies rallied behind the call for legal abortion with the Abortion Rights Campaign (ARC) consistently using their platform to equally advance trans rights through blog posts and press releases. In 2021, ARC voted to join the Trans Writers' Union boycott of *The Irish Times* meaning they no longer share, read, purchase or write for this newspaper.

Some years on, some of those I spoke to believe more can be done to silence trans-exclusionary ideas and re-invigorate alliances of solidarity. One activist (who preferred to remain anonymous) echoed a wider sentiment when they told me, 'bodily autonomy pertaining to the trans community is not prioritized ... the issues of a marginalized and minoritized group are taking second place to the issues faced by white cis women'. This, they contend, has allowed for 'the growth of gender critical elements ... particularly since repeal'. This comment cuts to the heart of Judith Butler's call for unity across struggles that 'keeps the source of oppression the focus, testing our theories about the other by listening and reading, remaining open to having one's traditional suppositions challenged, and finding ways to build alliances that allow our antagonisms not to replicate the destructive cycles we oppose'.[60]

Feminists cannot oppose discrimination by way of the denial of abortion rights, then not support the same right to bodily autonomy for others. And we cannot ally with political forces who amplify hatred in other directions. The feminist fight must be an alliance for gender freedoms and rights in the context of a critique of capitalism and a broader struggle for a more equal world for everyone. Aoife Martin agrees:

> We should be united in fighting the common enemy, which is patriarchy, it is the far right, it is capitalism, it is all those things. What really worries me is that we have a certain branch of feminism that just seems to be completely concerned with trans people and trans rights or 'trans ideology', ... that is all they seem to talk about. We would probably see eye to eye on a lot of points outside of the trans issues and that is where we should be focusing our attention because that is where all the issues are.

A similar desire is expressed by Sam Blanckensee: '[I]t is all one fight ... we might be looking at it from a slightly different perspective, but it is all one fight'. And from Ollie Bell:

> The feminist movement is nothing if it's not trans inclusive and actively fights for trans liberation. Likewise, Trans & Intersex Pride Dublin knows how integral women's liberation is to the struggle for trans people. Both cisgender women and trans people are negatively affected by capitalism.

Foregrounding solidarity over separation takes work, but it is essential if we are to move forward together and challenge the root cause of inequality – a neoliberal capitalist, imperialist system that thrives on division to maintain its power and that will never deliver respect for difference, never mind justice and equality. This task is especially urgent given that, at the time of writing and just 21 days into his second term as US President, Donald Trump has targeted trans people through a wave of brutal, discriminatory executive orders. As many trans people are fearful of what lies ahead, we must unite in our battle for trans liberation and remind ourselves that attacks on minorities rarely end there.

We're very aware of the constant barrage, the constant patriarchal, sexist, misogynistic surge to weaponize the very means we try to generate to protect ourselves … and the broader question of carceral feminism, the issue of just where crime and justice and punishment should come in? … The issue of domestic violence cannot be reduced to justice, to crime and punishment. It's a caricature, it creates traps, and, in fact, you could argue that it offers new ground for patriarchy. Creating local, effective pathways out of oppressive homes, for example, needs to balance this crime and punishment model.

– Author interview with Mary McDermott,
CEO of Safe Ireland, 4 May 2022

Chapter 5

CONFRONTING GENDER-BASED VIOLENCE

'I suppose I've always been a feminist' answered Rita (a pseudonym) when I asked her why she volunteers with a twenty-four-hour helpline for victims of domestic violence. Her own words, she says, remind her of her mother, who she describes as 'a very independent thinker, very feminist' and a formative influence on her life. 'She blamed the structures of the state and the church, which colluded to deny women agency and to dehumanise them,' Rita explains, before telling me about being brought along on protests about male violence against women in the 1980s when she was just a child. Despite having feminist values instilled in her from an early age, Rita ended up in an abusive relationship herself. 'It was with the help of domestic violence organisations like this one that I succeeded in leaving that relationship and keeping my children safe,' she told me, 'and since then I've always financially supported women's organisations and continued going on marches, all the usual stuff.' Rita's paid job involves working with teenagers and is also a motivating factor for her volunteer work especially what she describes as 'attitudes of toxic masculinity'. She tells me how 'it just became more important … seeing the attitudes that were prevalent and unchallenged in children, and it all kind of coalesced in my head and I just thought that I really want to do something more'. She isn't imagining sexist attitudes amongst young people. One recent report by Safe Ireland found that 'lad culture' is 'alive and well' in Ireland and a big issue for young women who 'often just put up with it'.[1]

'There isn't a typical [volunteer] shift,' Rita explains. The people who ring up 'could be older women, or women who experience a lot of barriers to accessing services, for instance, where their residency status isn't regularized, or very young women who aren't sure what is going on'. Sometimes she answers calls where it might be the person's first time expressing out loud what is going on. Admitting to themselves that they are in a violent relationship can be extremely challenging. There are all sorts of pressures to minimize or deny that abuse is happening including high levels of shame and stigma, the social pressures of being in a relationship and the practical weight of imagining alternative living arrangements, especially in the context of Ireland's decades-long shortage of social and affordable housing. Rita finds it particularly challenging when, in the thick of often-dangerous situations, some women blame themselves believing they somehow made the wrong choices or simply didn't have the skills to properly manage their relationship. She views these often-deep-seated emotions as 'part of the perpetrator's handbook, to make the victim feel responsible'.

Other callers to the helpline have been in touch before. They might need a listening ear or some help getting through a particularly bad bout of abuse. Sometimes this means encouraging them to approach a family member or friend to see if they can stay with them for a bit, but not everyone has this option. So, Rita does her best to put them in touch with one of Ireland's twenty or so domestic violence shelters that are scattered across the country. This can be a stressful endeavour, especially when she knows that the nearest shelter could be up to 100 kilometres away from where the person lives, therefore far from their job and, for mothers, the schools or crèches their children attend. Nearly one-third of Ireland's twenty-six counties have no emergency residential services at all. 'And we wouldn't even know whether the ones that are open would be full or not,' she tells me, 'so I'm referring them on without actually knowing whether or not there'll be a place set for them.' This is a reasonable worry. According to media reports from 2024, over half of Ireland's shelters are already full. This is because many families are staying for longer than usual, unable to find anywhere else to live.[2] Even when there is space to put people up, domestic violence shelters face a constant struggle to stay open because of a lack of adequate funding. Or, as Mary McDermott, the CEO of Safe Ireland, told me, 'we always have our begging bowl out anywhere we can go to stay afloat – lack of multi-annual funding forces the NGO sector into short-term survival, optics and competition – it is most certainly not the way to work towards sustainable change'. McDermott doesn't just reserve her words for researchers like me. In 2021, she told a joint Oireachtas (government) committee on justice that nine families each day were being turned away from emergency accommodation and described the national provision of services as 'Dickensian', accusing the government of knowingly 'placing women, and children, at very real risk of grievous trauma, injury or fatality'.[3]

As of 2025, there are around forty domestic violence services like the one Rita volunteers for, thirty-seven of which are members of the umbrella organization Safe Ireland, mentioned above. Collectively, they offer emergency shelter, crisis hotlines, outreach services, court accompaniment services, legal advice and counselling for victims of domestic violence, a term that is still recognized and commonly used to signal harm within intimate relationships. They also engage in varying degrees of advocacy and activism as signalled by Mary McDermott's political lobbying above. These services offer a lifeline to many thousands of mostly women and their children and help keep the issue of gender-based violence on the national agenda. Sadly, not everyone's experiences with these services are wholly positive. According to Neira Belacy, a community worker with the Muslim-women-led association Amal, many Muslims 'don't feel safe in most shelters'. This, she tells me, 'prevents many women from moving out of very toxic relationships' because they are unwilling to endure micro-aggressions and stereotyping by some staff. Travellers seeking refuge in domestic violence shelters also often face discrimination including a highly discriminatory 'one at a time' policy where some shelters will only house one Traveller family at a time. This unacceptable practice compounds the very particular challenges women living on halting sites can face where their options to seek shelter are already limited because staying with extended family might mean moving only metres away from the abuser.

Setting these discriminatory practices aside, this continued demand for domestic violence services might come as a surprise to some people given the recent shift in outlook towards domestic, sexual and gender-based violence. Much of this stems from the 2017 global Me Too movement which focused on sexual violence in the corporate and entertainment world then rapidly spread beyond a workplace dispute. The Me Too phenomenon created a global momentum where many women felt brave enough to share their own stories across the spectrum of violence and in all aspects of their lives. Suddenly, certain behaviours including the everyday sexual harassment many women endure and the victim blaming that shapes public discourse, began to be routinely called out.

The nature and frequency of gender-based violence

Not everyone shares the same understanding of the expression *gender-based violence*. The European Commission (EC) define it as 'violence directed against a person because of that person's gender or violence that affects persons of a particular gender disproportionately' continuing 'violence against women is understood as a violation of human rights and a form of discrimination against women and shall mean all acts of gender-based violence that result in, or are likely to result in: physical harm, sexual harm, psychological, or economic harm or suffering to women'.[4] The EC thus acknowledges that, although gender-based violence can be visited upon anyone, most victims are women and girls and most perpetrators are men. The spectrum of harm isn't linear; it involves shifting boundaries across different forms of intrusion where each can coexist and compound each other. If we downplay some acts over others, we can accidentally reinforce the idea that certain behaviours *really* constitute gender-based violence and certain behaviours do not.

This EC definition is a useful description of interpersonal gender-based violence, a phenomenon that has become more of a talking point in recent years. In seeking to address the problem, a range of mostly legal reforms have been introduced as well as specialist education programmes and public awareness campaigns, the likes of which are hard to imagine just ten years ago. One recent example is the Department of Justice-led 'Always Here' campaign which was launched in 2024 with the backing of feminist organizations including the National Women's Council of Ireland (NWCI), the Dublin Rape Crisis Centre (DRCC) and Women's Aid as well as Men's Aid Ireland and Male Advice Line.[5] Ironically, given the picture Rita paints, its aim is to let victims know about the state and voluntary sector support services that are there to help them.

To say that these measures show any signs of eradicating interpersonal gender-based violence would be grossly misleading. Instead, we continue to live in communities where male violence, against women in particular, continues at endemic levels. According to the WHO, one in three women has at some point in their lives been denied safety, security or financial and psychological independence, usually by someone they know. There are also the millions of women and girls who, throughout history and across the globe, have fallen victim to femicide, by which I mean their intentional murder because of their gender. Since Women's Aid began collecting data on cases of femicide in 1996, nearly 300 women have been killed in Ireland, mostly in their own homes and mostly by a partner or ex-partner.[6] Femicide isn't limited to interpersonal relationships. One of the first names recorded on Women's Aid's list is that of forty-one-year-old Marilyn Rynn who was abducted and murdered by a stranger whilst she made her way from a bus stop to her house following a Christmas party. More recently, in 2021, one case shook Ireland to the core when twenty-three-year-old Ashling Murphy was randomly murdered in broad daylight whilst out jogging on a busy canal walkway. Thousands took part in vigils that expressed sincere and heartfelt solidarity with her family and friends. Before long, the national mood turned into a collective roar about how male violence against women is anything but random. As researcher and activist Lorraine Grimes puts it, 'it all just started to come out. And once it did, it exploded, you know, it really did ... even my family who wouldn't be political, everybody was talking about how there needed to be more done around domestic violence and just misogyny in general'. There was much less of a public reaction following the death of Urantsetseg Tserendorj one year earlier almost to the day. Ms Tserendorj worked as a cleaner and was originally from Mongolia. She was stabbed in the neck by a teenage boy she didn't know whilst walking home from work and died in hospital nine days later. Some people blame the more muted outpouring of support for her family and anger about her death on the fact that strict Covid-related public health restrictions were in place at the time. But the truth of the matter is that major differences have been recorded in the levels of shock and surprise at the killing of white women over the killing of migrants and women whose ethnicities are minoritized across much of the Western world.[7]

The violent nature of capitalism

Absent from the aforementioned EC definition is any expansion beyond the interpersonal that addresses structural violence including institutional violence, the exploitation of labour (described in Chapter 3), barriers to healthcare such as prolonged waiting lists and unequal access to healthcare professionals, the ongoing erosion of social bonds and community supports that exacerbate poor mental health and the impact of poverty, imperialism and environmental degradation. Dealing with the latter first, constant drilling for raw materials and expansive clearing of land for industrial farming have caused irreparable damage to our ecosystem and habitats. The consequences are particularly devastating for communities that live close by, especially those living in the worst housing and with the lowest incomes. These same people are the first to lose their jobs making them less able to cope with food shortages and are the first to be denied clean water and sanitation leaving them at greater risk of infectious diseases and premature death. When they need a doctor, they are most likely to be locked out of increasingly privatized healthcare systems. If they seek to escape the many negative impacts of globalization by relocating to other countries, they face another form of violence when they are blamed for the actions of neoliberal policymakers that create housing shortages,[8] or erode other basic social supports. And that is if they survive the journey. As the International Organization for Migration noted in 2024, up to 100 people drown in the Mediterranean each month because they are denied the right to regular, safe pathways.[9] Although clearly nobody should be drowning at all, this figure does not have to be this high. In 2019, three female politicians; Mairéad McGuinness, Maria Walsh and Frances Fitzgerald, who all align themselves with feminist values, were amongst four Irish MEPs who voted against increasing search-and-rescue missions in the Mediterranean, a motion that was lost by two votes.

Another form of violence that continues to grow is a burgeoning military industrial complex and imperialist expansion which creates perpetual wars that often target civilian populations. In research published in *The Lancet*, women and children were shown to bear extensive morbidity and mortality within armed conflicts both because of direct violence and because of indirect health effects, including malnutrition, infectious diseases, poor mental health and poor sexual and reproductive health.[10] In the four-month period between October 2023 and January 2024, 70 per cent of the more than 24,000 Palestinian civilians killed by the state of Israel were women and children.[11] And this is before comprehending the loss of life from preventable illnesses like diabetes, cancers or kidney failure, or the impact on maternal care because of hospitals being reduced to rubble. By late 2024, the human rights group Amnesty International were amongst those labelling Israel's crimes against the Palestinian people an act of genocide under international law. They write:

> The tens of thousands of air strikes that Israel has launched on Gaza have resulted in unprecedented numbers of killings and injuries among the Palestinian population. Of the 40,717 fatalities that the Gaza-based Ministry of Health fully identified by 7 October 2024, children, women and older people constituted just under 60%. The remaining 40% were men under 60, with no independent source able to establish how many of those were fighters and how many were civilians[12].

Their report came just weeks after the International Criminal Court issued arrest warrants for alleged war crimes for the Israeli Prime

Minister, Benjamin Netanyahu and his former Defence Minister Yoav Gallant as well as the Hamas military leader Mohammed Deif.

Ireland has its own legacy of British imperialism and, to this day, the six counties of Northern Ireland remain part of the UK. 'The troubles' escalated in 1969, when the British army arrived on the streets of Northern Ireland and then maintained a regular and menacing presence until the mid-1990s, only fully withdrawing in 2007. This was at a time when communities were harshly divided along religious lines of either Catholic or Protestant and where unionists maintained political rule in the Northern Ireland Assembly through gerrymandering. This instilled a sense of privilege in many ordinary Protestants when compared to their Catholic neighbours despite similar and sometimes-dire economic situations.[13] The British army colluded with a unionist police force in targeting mostly working-class Catholic families who endured high levels of house raids, street interrogations, arrests, strip-searches and internments. Catholic mothers were most likely to be left raising families alone when men were forced on the run or interned. According to extensive research by Sharon Pickering, women engaged in a myriad of resistance tactics to coercive policing including physically fighting back and non-cooperation methods. Pickering details how the collective action of women represented 'defiance, distaste, and annoyance' and how 'it was women's tongues that proved their greatest weapon in defying the authorities: through their speech, their yelling, their argument, their silence'.[14]

These examples all highlight the structural nature of violence and locate the imperialist-neoliberal state as a key perpetrator. Including structural violence in discussions about gender-based violence does not minimize the harm of interpersonal violence but simply provides a more comprehensive context for feminist interventions. As the political scientist Françoise Vergès argues:

> [F]eminism cannot conceivably separate 'violence against women' or against 'minorities' from a global state of violence: the children who commit suicide in refugee camps, the police and military's massive recourse to rape in armed conflict, systemic racism, the exile of millions of people due to the multiplication of war zones and to economic and climactic conditions that have rendered zones of living uninhabitable, femicide, and the relentless increase in precarity. Can we imagine addressing only part of this violence without considering the rest? Can we continue to feign not to see that all of these forms of violence mutually reinforce one another, and that those which more directly affect women are the result of an extremely violent society?[15]

Looking back to look forwards: The predominance of an interpersonal focus

The resistance shown by women in the North of Ireland is just one way to draw lessons from the past that help us understand the trajectory of Irish feminist activism to this point, most of which has neglected the state violence these and other women endure to concentrate on interpersonal violence. One starting point in the foundation of the services Rita and Mary McDermott talk about at the beginning of this chapter is the actions of Nuala Fennell, a qualified solicitor and member of the Irish Women's Liberation Movement (IWLM), who established the legal advocacy group Action, Information, Motivation, or AIM for short in 1972. AIM principally lobbied for legal reforms at a time when there was widespread oppression of women within patriarchal households. Fennell was also a freelance journalist, and she received hundreds of letters from women describing their 'living hell', some of which she published in the book *Irish Marriage: How Are You?* (1974). This groundbreaking publication, written at a time when there was no escape for women, cut through a deep silence on the issue for many decades by detailing brutal accounts of beatings, financial control and collusion with psychiatric services in 'gaslighting' women. AIM did essential work to introduce barring and protection orders, to legally ban the sale of a family home without the consent of both parties and to protect a mother's right to collect children's allowance, which had been given to the father up to that point. Fennell also led the opening of Ireland's first domestic violence centre in 1974, in Harcourt Street, Dublin, and this vital work should not be underestimated. However, AIM was staunchly pro-family and pro-Catholic. As Cara Diver puts it, '[A]lthough the group campaigned for marriage reform, it took care to present these reforms as measures to protect the family rather than destroy it.'[16] In doing so, they erased same-sex unions and lone-parent families and perpetuated the preferential legal and financial treatment that heteronormative, two-parent families enjoyed – and still enjoy – to this day.

AIM, whose work mostly dissolved into the work of the Council for the Status of Women (CSW) when it was established in 1975, also failed to shine a light on egregious levels of institutional abuse within Mother and Baby Homes. These centres, the last of which only closed in 1996, purported to be places of care and compassion but were actually the polar opposite. Whether forcibly held or voluntarily admitted because of the shame and stigma associated with unwed pregnancy, the tens of thousands of women and girls who were sent to these places endured gruelling conditions and high levels of cruelty including forced labour, denial of pain medication during childbirth, humiliation and physical assault. Many of the children born into these homes died prematurely, endured unsanctioned vaccination trials and were trafficked through illegal adoptions, including to the United States. The middle-class white couples who took them in rarely fixed their gaze on black[17] or brown babies born into Mother and Baby Homes who were instead shipped out to a network of industrial schools, also run by religious congregations. Academic and author Emma Dabiri writes about how 'shocking official references regarding attitudes to "coloured children", show that institutional racism did very much assert itself whenever the opportunity arose'.[18] Industrial schools also housed thousands of working-class children who were often there because of petty crime or because of a perceived absence of guardianship. Typically, the family's biggest problem was poverty, which remains a subject of monitoring and scrutiny for child protection services to this day. The nuns and priests running these establishments didn't act alone but were regularly supported by the institutions of the state. We now know that one of the few voices of dissent was Alice Litster a local government inspector, who repeatedly went to great efforts to expose the horrors at Bessborough Mother and Baby Home in Cork during the 1940s. But her concerns were basically ignored. There was also silence about the treatment of women incarcerated in 10 Magdalene Laundries, the conditions of which have also been well documented. We do know that, on at least one occasion in the 1940s, the trade union the Irish Women Workers' Union, met with the religious order responsible for one laundry, but this wasn't to raise concerns about conditions inside but to ask the laundries not to undercut the established pricing other laundries were adhering to when tendering for business.[19]

It is hard to know why feminists active in the 1970s paid so little attention to institutional violence. There is no denying that the religious orders responsible were held in high esteem at the time and survivors rarely talked about the conditions they endured. If they did, nobody listened or did anything much to address what was going on, including feminists. The IWLM's manifesto *Chains and Change* (1970) did reference Mother and Baby homes but only amidst discussion on the care of unmarried women presenting to maternity hospitals late in their pregnancies, describing these as 'the girls who shied away from entering

Mother and Baby Homes'. The manifesto acknowledged a growth in the 'numbers of girls entering Mother and Baby Homes' but made no comments on the conditions inside.[20]

The growth of the anti-violence movement

In the years following the publication of *Chains and Change*, radical feminists continued to find spaces to organize against male violence against women including through the Campaign Against Rape (CAR, est. c. 1977) which was formed within the socialist-leaning Irish Women United. CAR sought many of the same legal reforms as AIM did, but combined these with a broader social analysis that demanded a wider demand for social reform. In 1978, representatives from CAR travelled to Belfast to join the campaign for the release of Noreen Winchester, a twenty-year-old woman who had been jailed for the manslaughter of her father. His passing ended years of imprisonment, degradation and assault for Noreen and her siblings. When sentencing her, the judge commented that Noreen 'had been a willing partner for years' and that 'she had had plenty of occasion to tell the police about the incest'.[21] His words revealed a complete disregard for the dangers of even contemplating exposing an abuser or the likelihood that the police would have done nothing to help her, a topic that will be explored in more detail later on. Susan McKay describes this visit as 'enormously educational for the women in CAR' who learned first-hand about 'the class prejudice displayed by the lawyers, judges and social workers'.[22] McKay reports how one social worker had even voiced the view that incest was an accepted way of life within working-class Catholic families.

When news broke in 1979 that a teenage girl was recovering in hospital following a kidnap and gang rape in a derelict flat complex in Dublin, activists within CAR were amongst those involved in organizing Ireland's first 'Reclaim the Night' march – a slogan that had been popularized on similar marches in other European countries especially in the North of England in response to the murder or attempted murder of twenty women by one serial killer. Feminists from across the ideological divide lent their support to the march as did many politicians, journalists and some celebrities. In the end, five thousand people took part in an emotionally charged event the likes of which had not been seen in Ireland before. The message of the march was anti-authoritarian and anti-patriarchal. Its aftermath was marred by public disagreements in a way that brought divergences within feminism to the surface. Some liberal feminists and their supporters believed that the march had gone too far. To illustrate, *Sunday World* columnist and an initial advocate, Micheline McCormack, wrote a scathing article that accused the organizers of being 'extremists who … are neurotic about women being the downtrodden race' and suggested 99 per cent of those on the march agreed with her, not them, 'the typical pro-contraception, pro-abortion type women that men automatically dismiss as "women's libbers".'[23] The march organizers defended the evening's strong patriarchal analysis across the letters pages of the country's main newspapers.

One of the consequences of these clashes was that some activists made the strategic decision to prioritize service delivery over advocacy work, folding most of this into the Dublin Rape Crisis Centre (DRCC) which was also central to the reclaim the night event. Its volunteers took on essential work including running an emergency helpline, often in their own homes and meeting women in public places such as hotels, offering them emotional, practical and legal supports. They also expended great energy securing, and maintaining, small amounts of government funding which was never enough to keep up with the demands for their services. Much the same was the case for rape crisis centres that opened in Limerick, Galway, Cork and Tipperary, which also relied on volunteers and shoe-string budgets. Over the next ten years, many more services emerged, not because of top-down policy-led interventions concerned with protecting women, but because of feminist and survivor groups who sought to create safe havens for people who were enduring abusive and often-dangerous situations. Rita Fagan, a community worker in Dublin, describes the origins of their community response – the Inchicore Domestic Violence Centre which was founded in 1991 following the killing of a community worker who 'went to help a woman and was knocked to the ground. Her skull was cracked, and she died there and then' continuing, 'we at the centre realised that men can kill women, some men do kill women and we needed to have some response within the community. So, we got a small bit of funding from Allen Lane [UK Philanthropy] and set up a part-time confidential service where women could disclose'. It was initiatives like these that led to the emergence of an ad hoc nationwide network of supports and advocacy groups that was (and still is) sometimes called the Anti-Violence Movement.

Divergent strategies and approaches

These examples from the past illustrate that, from the outset, feminist activism against gender-based violence diverged along two distinct strategies that, in today's language would be identified as either carceral, or abolitionist. The former individualizes gender-based violence and sees the criminal justice system as our main defensive and preventative tool and advocates a zero-tolerance approach with tougher laws, more policing and longer prison sentences. Along with public awareness campaigns and targeted education that emphasizes consent and healthy relationships, these measures are thought to minimize future assaults mostly by deterring potential perpetrators. Abolitionist feminism is critical of this standpoint, not least because most victims will never report their assaults. In Ireland, this figure has been estimated to be as high as 80 per cent.[24] Abolitionist feminism collectivizes our responses by focusing on the need to dismantle oppressive systems. Its origins are often linked to the philosopher Angela Davis's analysis of the prison industrial complex as racist, patriarchal and pro-capitalist, and also the wider work of INCITE, a US women-of-colour collective, which shone a light on the failures of the anti-violence movement to respond to disproportionate levels of violence perpetrated upon women of colour.[25] Theories of abolitionist feminism focus beyond prison abolition to include the criminal justice system in totality; an apparatus of the state that reinforces an unequal status quo to the benefit of capitalism. Abolitionism also helps us to challenge carceral responses more broadly like in the workplace where increasingly, transgressions are managed through often complex, individualized complaints structures rather than by addressing wider social and cultural norms. Typically, abolitionists seek alternative solutions including radical education, restorative justice and community supports all amidst a commitment to address systemic oppression that dismantle all forms of structural and institutional violence.

Divergence in addressing imperialist violence

In reality, most Irish-based responses to gender-based violence existed – and still exist – on a continuum advocating for some level of punitive-oriented state intervention whilst also emphasizing community-based solutions and a focus on root causes, especially the power of patriarchies. However, there were times, in the past, when these different perspectives vied for the right to articulate the problem and determine the approach to be taken. One difference was on how best to respond, if at all, to the ongoing imperialist violence endured by citizens north of the border. Some Southern feminists were active in, or sympathetic to the Republican and civil rights movements that were growing in

Northern Ireland, whilst others were vociferously anti-Republican and also offered no active support for civil rights mass demonstrations. One example that illustrates division centres on responses to the treatment of female prisoners in Armagh prison, the only women's prison in Northern Ireland where the vast majority of detainees had been charged with 'terrorist type offences'.[26] In 1980, Women Against Imperialism (WAI, est. 1978) had escalated pickets outside the prison when inmates began a 'no wash' protest which sought to call attention to appalling conditions inside where women were regularly humiliated, were denied medical care and sanitary protection, and were often beaten by mostly male guards.[27] Several socialist feminists including Linda Walker from the Communist Party raised concerns about these pickets arguing for city centre protests also that would highlight the mistreatment of all prisoners and not just republican prisoners.[28]

Some southern feminists became involved in these pickets. One avenue was through the work of the Feminist Forum, a left-wing feminist group that formed from a discussion group in the offices of Ailbhe Smyth, who was an academic at University College Dublin (UCD). In 1980, the Feminist Forum organized a conference at Trinity College Dublin which attracted around 120 predominantly female attendees. About three-quarters of the way through the event, a group of women walked in who had come straight from a prison picket. Mary Ryder, a member of the Feminist Forum and an attendee at the conference, told me that the new arrivals implored attendees to join their protests claiming, '[I]f you are into feminism and you are into protecting women, these women are being treated so badly there, all the publicity is about the men'. One week later, Mary was one of about a dozen women on a bus pointing north to join the picket, one of several such trips that happened during 1980 and 1981. Therese Caherty also remembers travelling to Armagh several times. On one occasion she recalls 'being petrified' when an army vehicle travelled in front of them with soldiers brandishing rifles, another time she recalls their bus being boarded by armed loyalist paramilitaries. However, support for Northern Irish political prisoners created deep fissures in some groups including the Women's Right to Choose Group. One central organizer described a 'poisonous' environment within a group that was 'politically incredibly mixed'. She details how support for political prisoners especially the H-Block campaign created 'a rift down the middle which at times was quite hurtful for people like me who were also involved in the fight for political status' believing this 'probably reflected a class divide'.[29]

Divergence in addressing interpersonal violence

Although there was less obvious division regarding the urgent need to address male violence against women, philosophical divisions across feminist groups sometimes prevented them from collaborating on nearly identical campaigns as happened around 1980 when both the CSW and the DRCC launched campaigns seeking to criminalize rape within marriage. According to research by Yvonne Galligan, the CSW's principal motivation for non-cooperation was to maintain strong relationships with conservative politicians who viewed the DRCC as untrustworthy radicals who operated outside of mainstream politics.[30] In the end, the *Criminal Justice Bill* (1981) didn't outlaw marital rape because the then Minister for Justice believed what happened inside a marriage was a private matter.[31] It would take nine more years of campaigning for this to be overturned with the first conviction not occurring until 2002.

Differing feminist perspectives also played out within service provision. This included the Rathmines Women's Refuge, one of the first purpose-built shelters in Europe and a replacement for the Harcourt Street refuge. It was one of twelve that, by the mid-1980s, was in receipt of state funding. As well as transferring its services from Harcourt Street, the shelter's voluntary board of management also transferred its Catholic ethos. In 1989, and somewhat out of the blue, the board sacked its director over political differences. This sparked strike action by staff and the dissolution of the board, which had no qualms about consenting to the shelter being absorbed into the Irish healthcare system meaning little or no advocacy work would be carried out and no political statements on gender-based violence would be forthcoming. In response, a breakaway group of staff and some board members opened an alternative organization which, following some legal wrangling over ownership of the name, became the Women's Aid organization that remains operational to this day. Niamh Wilson, a striker and member of this breakaway group recalls, 'we were really overtly feminist, we were clearly feminist, strongly feminist and we were at the forefront … anyone who wasn't strongly grounded in feminism really backed away because of that'.

By the late 1990s, Women's Aid had emerged as the leading campaign and advocacy organization in Ireland. However, they were lured by assurances from policymakers that they could be trusted as partners and invested a lot of energy into ensuring that the Irish government adopted the United Nations General Assembly's *Declaration on the Elimination of Violence against Women*, which contained a strong patriarchal analysis.[32] Women's Aid and other anti-violence advocacy groups also sought carceral solutions and collaborated on the introduction of a more comprehensive scheme of safety, protection and barring orders. They also partnered with the government in producing the *Task Force Report on Violence Against Women* (1997) which acknowledged the piecemeal and haphazard way that services had been developed and promised to address the gaps in these services citing an urgent need for substantial, multi-annual funding.[33] 'While it wasn't perfect, we felt very hopeful at the time', Niamh explains, 'we felt that this would make a difference.' Putting their faith in government responses would eventually prove to be a tactical error. With reference to the Task Force Report, Niamh is clear that 'nothing came out of it'. This wasn't for the want of trying and a true analysis of Women's Aid's inability to influence radical change rests with its dependence on state funding, meaning its long wait for a guaranteed financial future that never arrived. Here's Niamh again:

> We were so vulnerable, because we were so dependent, because there was such a clear power dynamic ... some of them [funders] were impressive, some were really overtly wielding the funding stick and had no care or concern for the quality of the work. They didn't understand it, they were dismissive of our knowledge and expertise and so we had a huge power dynamic to deal with where you were basically covering your back because you knew they could pull the funding at any time.

This practice – of having little option but to engage with a state apparatus that said one thing but then did something else – seeded the ground for the co-option of the anti-violence sector and whatever radical goals and principles it once held began to fade. As new public managerialist practices of accountability and measurability took hold, a tunnel vision focus on providing services took over, leaving many of the original frontline workers feeling disillusioned and let down.[34] The professionalization and depoliticization of domestic violence services have been documented by other feminist historians including Niamh Wilson's own research on the topic and also Susan McKay's detailed account of the work of the DRCC. At one stage, McKay describes how 'the feminist vision of the DRCC began to change' after they hired a PR company to re-brand. 'From then on', she writes, 'DRCC annual reports were large and glossy and featured photographs of staff, volunteers and board members. The stark feminist symbol that used to be the DRCC logo became a soft, Celtic-looking swirl.'[35]

Ireland's carceral turn

There is little doubt that the people who work in these non-profits aim to do good, and they typically support an equality agenda. But this dependence on state funding makes them part of what Angela Davis, Gina Dent, Erica R. Meiners and Beth E. Ritchie describe as a 'nonprofit industrial complex' where, instead of producing long-term structural changes, their work has mostly become about data collection and individualized care.[36] This neutering of potential opponents was just one step in a sharp carceral turn Ireland took which included the establishment of the state-led Cosc (formerly the National Office for the Prevention of Domestic, Sexual and Gender-based Violence) in 2007 housed within the Department of Justice. One of Cosc's first actions was to strengthen an already growing 'gender neutral' philosophy, meaning their focus would ignore patriarchies and male privilege, something that angered many activists. To date, Cosc has published three successive strategies on domestic, sexual and gender-based violence.[37] Each one involved consultation with non-profit service providers, claimed to enhance protections for victims and accountability for perpetrators, and reasserted support for the Istanbul Convention, a Europe-wide treaty that aims to prevent and combat violence against women. But little has changed from that first Task Force Report. Lorraine Grimes, who has connections with Domestic Violence Response Galway, shares much the same sense of futility as Niamh Wilson:

> Printing another strategy and putting it up there online, what difference is it actually going to make? You can have a nice glossy thing, 'we will do this, that and the other' but will it be actually implemented? And I don't know if it will make any real difference on the ground. You get tired of these government strategies, don't you?

Some of you might be thinking that a more accurate benchmark would be to examine the impact of some of the new laws that have been passed rather than focusing solely on policy. And there are several new laws to talk about including the *Criminal Law (Sexual Offences) Act* (2017) which created a definition of consent, and protections for children from abuse and exploitation, the *Criminal Justice (Victims of*

Crime) Act (2017) which provides a framework for protecting victims as they traverse through the criminal justice process, and the *Domestic Violence Act* (2018) which is best known for criminalizing coercive control. For some people, these laws have made a difference. They have helped people to self-assess their own circumstances, have taken away some shame about speaking out and have resulted in the imprisonment of some perpetrators, particularly in high-profile cases. But these are the minority and a central argument within abolitionist feminism is that these carceral responses mostly legitimize and strengthen a criminal justice system that cements racist and sexist narratives of crime, oversimplifies victim–perpetrator dynamics, and gives enormous power to policing and judicial systems.

One of the first problems with these laws is that none of them address how the legal system first and foremost treats intimate partner violence as a private matter where the first line of defence is to obtain protective and barring orders from the family law courts. These don't criminalize abuse; an offence is only committed when an order is breached. There are other problems with family courts including how, until 2024, they entertained 'parental alienation syndrome' meaning the deliberate act of one parent turning a child against the other parent, but which is mostly used by perpetrators to inflict more harm on their victims and ignore the very real fears of leaving children unsupervised with a violent parent. Ireland was admonished for allowing this practice by the Council of Europe Group of Experts on Action against Violence against Women and Domestic Violence (GREVIO) when, in 2023, they assessed our performance against the Istanbul Convention.[38] This likely influenced its exclusion as did a sustained campaign by the group Survivors Informing Services and Institutions (SISI). 'A lot of our members have had their children forcibly removed through the lens of parental alienation,' SISI's founder Mary-Louise Lynch told me. 'We consider this to be one of the greatest threats to women.' There are other broader issues with family law court systems including how these structures uphold the family as natural and normal and repeatedly prioritize biological and marital ties above all else. Nobody talks about how the family is a social construct and one where it is perfectly normal to present a healthy group dynamic to the world then reserve a very different, often unhealthy dynamic for behind closed doors. This, the family abolitionist M. E. O'Brien maintains, normalizes various forms of violence that would be completely unacceptable in any other situation.[39]

There are also significant issues within criminal courts, whose function is to deal with offences against the state, i.e. when a person breaks the law. Issues include how alleged abusers are arrested regardless of the victim's wishes, but only brought to trial if the same victim agrees to their prosecution. This can be very dangerous because, as Safe Ireland put it, they are 'at a risk of increased violence if the abuser is informed that there will be no prosecution without the victim's consent and the victim is statistically at a greater risk of further abuse having entered into a legal process'.[40] When charges are filed and a case goes to court, our courtrooms continuously maintain victim blaming in a variety of ways. Defence councils are allowed cross-examine victims about their sexual history, can enter the clothes victims were wearing as evidence and, until 2024 could use notes from therapy sessions to discredit people. Irish courts also entertain misogynistic myths about the nature of rape, i.e. that a 'real rape' involves a stranger, that there must be evidence of physical assault and that there is an 'ideal victim', i.e. a certain way a person should behave before, during and after an assault. In the case of violent gang rapes, the often-grotesque idea that someone actually consents is still commonly presented as a legitimate point of view.

Conviction rates are also abysmal. Susan Leahy brings our attention to the English experience of coercive control where convictions remain 'disappointingly low'.[41] As we await a comprehensive study on the investigation and prosecution of coercive control in Ireland, we do know that there were only twenty-one convictions in the first two years of its criminalization. On occasions when a person is found guilty of sexual or domestic violence, courts still allow character references as mitigation against sentencing where the reputational damage to the perpetrator is weighed against the harm they caused to their victim(s). In 2022, twenty-three separate character references were entertained before sentencing a man found guilty of sexually assaulting three children, all friends of his daughter, who were on a sleepover in his home. The variances in sentencing can also be alarming, something that directly affects people's confidence to come forward and seek support. In June 2024, a serving member of the Irish Defence Forces named Cathal Crotty had the full three years of his sentence suspended, meaning he walked free despite pleading guilty to beating Natasha O'Brien unconscious on a busy Limerick Street then boasting about the assault on social media later that day. Crotty had never met her before. She came to his attention because she and a friend had asked him to stop shouting homophobic abuse at another couple. On this occasion, the judge rejected Ireland's supposed zero-tolerance approach claiming a jail sentence would jeopardize the army career of someone presented as of exemplary character despite this one transgression. I wonder had the judge hadn't educated himself about the Women of Honour, a group of former female members of the Defence Forces whose stories of sexual harassment, bullying and abuse within the military were broadcast in a television documentary in 2021 leading to widespread public outcry and promises of change from the political establishment and senior military personnel. The judge's minimization of the severity of Crotty's crime and his disregard for the victim resulted in thousands of people joining protests organized by the socialist-feminist group ROSA in Dublin, Cork and Limerick. When Natasha O'Brien addressed the large crowd in Limerick, she told the hundreds of onlookers:

> It is one thing to be subjected to a violent assault at the hands of a man that has pledged to protect the citizens of Ireland, but it is another thing when the Department of Justice and the Defence Forces push me away ... I was retraumatised at the hands of the courts. To be a victim of a violent crime is bad enough, but to be a victim of the state – they need to change now.[42]

In January 2025, Crotty was jailed after an appeal court ruling.

It is important to point out that carceral solutions have gained significant traction because they act as tangible evidence that progress is being made. Many legal reforms have been advanced because of feminist-sounding campaigns with good intentions and where survivors are at the helm. This includes the criminalization of image-based sexual abuse in 2020 which was the result of a campaign spearheaded by Megan Fox because of her own traumatic experience of image-based abuse. It then gained wider traction after hundreds of thousands of sensitive videos were released online.[43] However, in-depth research by Antoinette Raffaela Huber of the British experience of a similar law identified fundamental failures in criminal justice and policing responses with victims being repeatedly let down by the system.[44]

State violence as policing

A legitimate question to ask ourselves is why feminists and survivors alike seek out criminal justice solutions when their track record is so abysmal and when even the best laws in the world will never cancel out the harm that is done or succeed in making the problem go away. The main reason, Lola Olufemi writes, is because 'everything about the world we live in tells us that the police are there to protect us and prisons force the criminal to reflect on their actions, deter them from committing other crimes and remind them that nobody is above the law'.[45] A central tenet of abolitionist feminism is to dispel this myth including by highlighting how you cannot separate the laws that are passed from the violence of policing, an institution that regularly uses force and coercion, especially against certain populations, including women, even when they are not resisting or fighting back. Many studies have uncovered an international policing culture that is homophobic, misogynistic, racist and sexist, including a 2023 independent report into the UK's Metropolitan Police which highlighted significant shortfalls in responding to domestic and sexual violence.[46] It would be naïve to think Irish policing is radically different. In 2022, I interviewed the academic and policing expert Vicky Conway who has studied behaviours and practices within An Garda Síochána over many years. Vicky described domestic and sexual violence as something that is traditionally dismissed by police forces all over the globe. 'It's literally referred to as rubbish work,' she tells me blaming this in part on the 'machismo nature of the organization and suspicions of quite high levels of domestic violence within the forces themselves'. She does see some difference in Ireland where people often join the Gardaí with more community-oriented intentions than other police forces, but surmises 'the research is clear, people might join the Gardaí because they want to do good, but they fall into this global "police culture" that's incredibly difficult to change'. An Garda Síochána has a poor track record when it comes to responding to sexual, domestic and gender-based violence. Gardaí have ignored 999 calls, including in cases of domestic violence,[47] inaccurately recording information then done nothing to rectify this when it becomes evident,[48] and have dismissed victims to the extent that they are often re-traumatized and left with no protection from further abuse.[49]

In the wake of the murder of London-based Sarah Everard by a serving police officer, police services across the Western world came under scrutiny regarding disproportionately high numbers of perpetrators within their ranks.[50] An Garda Síochána responded by promising to ensure Gardaí accused of domestic or sexual violence were investigated properly. Twenty-one Gardaí came forward when invited to self-declare family court orders with more expected to have since come forward.[51] The most serious Garda conviction for intimate partner violence would come in 2022 when Paul Moody was sentenced to over three years in prison for coercive control of his terminally ill partner. Since his imprisonment, further allegations have surfaced including reports that there were several complaints of inappropriate and coercive behaviour from women he met on dating apps which were not properly investigated. His sentence didn't deter others as carceral feminists maintain would be the case. In 2024, a former Garda called Mark Doyle was jailed for six years after pleading guilty to years of torturous abuse over a twelve-year period against his former wife and stepsons.

There have also been abuses captured whilst Gardaí are on duty including the 'rape tapes' controversy when a conversation between five Gardaí was accidentally recorded. According to the Garda Ombudsman's own investigation, Gardaí were joking about raping two climate change activists they were transporting into custody and about enlisting the support of immigration authorities to deport the activists, one of whom was American and one of whom was Canadian.[52] Another particularly upsetting case was of image-based sexual abuse by a Garda, who deliberately video recorded and then shared compromising CCTV footage of a young woman called Dara Quigley who was in the midst of a mental health crisis. Not long after the video went viral, she died by suicide. No criminal case was pursued against any of these Gardaí. Even our police stations are not safe. In 2020, a serving Garda sexually assaulted and falsely imprisoned a woman who had called in seeking Garda assistance. He was convicted four years later.

Police practices have also been universally criticized for systemic racism and the disproportionate targeting of marginalized communities. Ireland is again no different. In 2024, extensive research within racialized communities uncovered some helpful interventions by Gardaí, but many more negative experiences including being racially profiled, unsupported or dismissed when making a complaint or reporting a crime including domestic violence, and disproportionate uses of force.[53] For Irish Travellers, they have endured a long history of over-policing including wrongful arrests and excessive uses of force, wrongful convictions and imprisonment, and disproportionately high sentences.[54] With reference to domestic violence, Megan Berry describes the Gardaí as 'the last service that Traveller women will contact when they are in crisis' because of highly discriminatory perceptions that violence against women is 'part of Traveller culture'. When Gardaí do respond to calls from Traveller halting sites, Megan explains how they are often more interested in checking insurance and tax plates on cars, than responding to a call for help. Megan further explains 'when they don't arrest the man and just walk away, the risk that woman is put under not just by the perpetrator but by the rest of the site is an immense issue.'

Carceral feminism and militarization

As well as not doing enough at all to address systemic failures within our criminal justice system, neoliberal feminists have also become active supporters of military conflicts. Rafia Zakaria has written in depth about what she coins *feminist wars* or imperialist incursions into mostly Muslim and often-oil-rich countries that are justified through claims that the motivation is to free women from sexism. These same Western saviours rarely consider the opinions of feminists within the countries they interfere with. Using Afghanistan as an example, Ireland played a role when, in 2021, the Taliban regained power after twenty years of US occupation. Specifically, the former Fine Gael minister Josepha Madigan, who describes herself as 'a dedicated feminist',[55] co-chaired a special sitting of the UN Security Council during which members were urged to vindicate women's rights in all actions they took on Afghanistan's future.[56] This was without enough support for Afghan women to self-determine because, to do so, Zakaria maintains, would quickly expose how most Afghan feminists would prioritize ending repeated imperialist occupations before anything else and would abhor their own weaponization against Afghan men.[57]

Despite Ireland being a neutral state, largely because of its past experiences of being colonized, there is increasing pressure to drag the country towards NATO membership (short for North Atlantic Treaty Organization), especially since the Russian invasion of Ukraine in 2022. Pro-establishment politicians, including Jennifer Carroll MacNeill, then Minister of State with responsibility for EU Affairs and Defence, and a regular advocate of feminism, want to ramp up Ireland's support for the militarization of Europe. In 2024, she proposed Ireland should double its defence expenditure to €3bn, claiming this would protect our territory and our people.[58] These sorts of actions demonstrate the extent to which pro-establishment feminism can pull liberal feminism away from a once strong anti-war strand within all Western feminism,[59] towards an alignment with militarism that interprets equality as the equal right for women to fight as soldiers within the armies of invading nations that expand colonial rule and strengthen global military alliances.

Beyond carceral feminism

Feminism that is serious about addressing gender-based violence advocates for a peaceful world. It seeks the divestment and shrinkage of policing and an end to the production of arms, believing militarization makes our world a more dangerous place. And whilst activists working against sexual and domestic violence have made some gains in terms of the wider recognition of the problem, theories of abolitionist feminism help us recognize and avoid carceral approaches and become aware of the dangers of collaborating with a penal state when, as Aya Gruber argues, 'sometimes the best thing to do is nothing – to live with the problem rather than invoking a state solution ... [that] generally punishes the poor and the powerless and is particularly impotent to dismantle entrenched power structures'.[60]

Typically, abolitionist feminists (not all of whom are anti-capitalist) propose alternatives like restorative justice, holistic and community-centred responses, investment in social services, better educational interventions and community support networks. Abolitionists also interrogate a reluctance within feminism to legitimately question why structural patriarchies create a world where so many men are violent in the first place. The work of Lynn Ruane, an independent senator and former community worker, who passionately challenges the imprisonment of mostly working-class people is inspiring in this regard. Lynn's work, which includes engaging with men who have been violent, involves exploring their behaviours in relation to 'drug use, poverty, trauma, unemployment, and low levels of educational attainment', Lynn explains 'and men's inability to respond appropriately to volatile or emotional situations'.

Abolitionists also focus on how law-and-order responses successfully detract from chronic underfunding of vital domestic violence services. What of Rita, and the dozens of others who volunteer on helplines and other domestic violence services across the country? When I asked her about how she, and other volunteers, keep going she answered, 'there is a lot of support from the organisation, which is good, and people would volunteer on a very prolonged basis because of this, but ... I look at how long feminists have been working to try and make situations better for other women. And I suppose I feel a sort of sadness that we are still here'. CEO of Safe Ireland, Mary McDermott's vision is to create 'a very clear overground railway that stops in every town and every village in the country' providing 'everything to people who want to flee' including welfare and legal supports, housing, counselling and whatever else a person requires. This, she tells me, 'is potentially a big political hot ticket' given the generosity and goodwill the general public hold. She even tells me about individuals and businesses offering all sorts of supports including land and buildings that could be transformed into more services. Her ask is for an equal response from government, specifically 'a coherent national response, not another burst of ad hoc responses'. Instead of getting behind this call for a significant and sustained injection of funding, pro-establishment feminists present these shortfalls as regrettable but a result of wider more complicated budget constraints that are beyond our control. At the same time, many collude with state violence by overlooking ongoing institutional abuses caused by neoliberal policies. Not nearly enough is done to prevent the heightened risks of sexual violence that endure in Direct Provision[61] assaults within residential centres that house disabled and elderly individuals, and revelations of the state knowingly placing children in hazardous foster care situations. There is predictable condemnation when these stories break through the news cycle but never the radical reforms that would prevent their reoccurrence.

There is a lot to digest in this chapter, especially if the division of anti-violence activism along these very distinct lines is new to you. One thing that is for sure is that increased militarization that perpetuates violence and contradicts core feminist values of equality, peace and social justice will not lead to a safer world for women and girls. Equally policing, the courts and our prisons are part of a much wider oppressive system that is authoritarian, racist and classist. These structures will never deliver gender justice. It is our collective imagination, and the praxis that can follow that has the best chance of offering solutions to all forms of violence. As Davis and colleagues remind us, nothing is possible in the real world unless it can be imagined in our heads first,[62] recognizing the state as a key perpetrator, helps reverse a tendency to segregate interpersonal violence from all other forms including the violence of denying reproductive rights. This will be the focus of the next chapter.

As I've become more involved in activism over the years, I've started to see issues around reproductive rights, sexism, domestic violence, medical misogyny etc as being interconnected ... I've become informed and engaged with intersecting systems of injustice. Learning about reproductive justice, for example, and seeing the unequal treatment of women of colour and their reproductive rights at the hands of the Irish State and healthcare system has made me more aware of my responsibility to think about and practice my activism in a more intersectional way.

– Canvasser with Together for Yes in 2018
and survey respondent, 2023

Chapter 6

REFRAMING REPRODUCTIVE RIGHTS

If you have read other chapters of this book, you will know that each topic draws from in-depth conversations with Irish-based anti-capitalist feminists and left-wing activists. Halfway through this field work, I received an email from a volunteer within a campaign and advocacy group called Abolish Direct Provision, asking if I would be interested in talking to some of their volunteers living in Direct Provision (DP), Ireland's for-profit system of housing asylum seekers whilst their international protection applications are being processed. Residents of these centres are fast becoming one of the most researched populations in Ireland with most studies criticizing DP as being unfit for purpose for a variety of reasons. Back in 2020, the government agreed with this assessment and promised to phase these centres out.[1] Instead, the opposite has happened as more, not fewer, contracts have been signed, each one guaranteeing private providers a generous income for accommodating the 20,000 or so people living in these congregated settings. It's hard to believe that these are the lucky ones when compared to the hundreds of asylum seekers the state houses in tented accommodation or who see no option but to pitch tents themselves in city centre locations.

I readily agreed to the offer of an interview and a Zoom call was scheduled for the following week during which six women generously shared the circumstances of their lives. Their stories included difficult journeys to Ireland, sometimes to escape sexual violence, being separated from loved ones, the shock of acclimatizing to extremely cramped living conditions and the persistent racism they endured since arriving in Ireland. Much of our conversation centred on their experiences of pregnancy, birth and parenting. Kaya (a pseudonym) talked about giving birth to her second child soon after arriving in Ireland and during the coronavirus pandemic of 2020–2, meaning she birthed alone because of strict hospital restrictions. This practice, of denying a birthing partner, was replicated across all Irish maternity settings despite contravening a directive from the WHO that the risk of Covid-19 did not negate a person's right to have a birth companion.[2] Even if there hadn't been a pandemic, the maternity system Kaya entered into was one where established patterns of care repeatedly privilege white bodies. She wasn't the only woman to share negative experiences. Gaby (again not her real name) remembers being 'spoken to like absolute trash' by a healthcare worker who threatened her with deportation continuing 'I mean, how do you do that to people that are vulnerable?' Sadly, these experiences chime with findings uncovered by other researchers who exposed several issues residents of DP face, including women's care being disrupted when they are suddenly moved to different reception centres, poor channels of communication, and negative and resentful attitudes from some midwives.[3]

Substandard maternity care is by no means unique to people in DP. Rather, black and brown women face significant discrimination in a system that is rife with a 'them' and 'us' mentality and a sense amongst staff that racialized women must adapt to the system, rather than the system adapting to them.[4] A typical stay in hospital includes general negative attitudes, harmful stereotyping, erroneous assumptions about pain tolerance and sometimes individual acts of racism and bigotry.[5] Shockingly, but not surprisingly when compared with figures across the Western world, black and brown women are more likely to die during childbirth relative to the maternal deaths of white women. Ireland's most recent *Confidential Maternity Death Enquiry*, published in 2023, found nearly one third of all deaths occurred in migrant women amounting to 'an over-representation of non-Irish women among maternal deaths in Ireland'.[6] For African women like Kaya, there is a higher perinatal mortality rate and double the number of stillbirths that white women endure.[7] In the last nine years alone, inquests into the deaths of seven migrant women – Bimbo Onanuga, Savita Halappanavar, Dhara Kivlehan, Nora Hyland, Malak Thawley, Nayyab Tariq and Tatenda Mukwata have all returned verdicts of medical misadventure. In 2019, a law was passed that mandated inquests in all maternal deaths. But it seems this *Coroners (Amendment) Act 2019* was ignored following the death of Geraldine Yankeu, a resident of DP, who died in 2021, eleven days after the stillbirth of her daughter. At the time of writing, we await the outcome of a judicial review granted to the family who claim that the coroner who handled the case exercised extreme prejudice in not ordering an inquest.

Returning to the Zoom call, the women I conversed with also talked about violations to their right to parent in a safe and suitable environment including, for some, the impossible challenge of surviving on just €38.80 per adult and €29.80 per child per week as they wait for their asylum application to be processed. Two women had been granted permission to stay. But they hadn't managed to move out because of a combination of factors including the absence of social and affordable housing and the structural racism they endure when seeking to rent in the private market.[8] So they stay in substandard, cramped accommodation where there are numerous rules and regulations, many of which make very little sense. Thembeka (again a pseudonym) isn't allowed to have a kettle in the hotel room where she lives with her two sons despite this being standard practice when the exact same room is used for tourists. And she has no cooking facilities, something that is again common. Instead, residents must eat the canteen food provided despite its poor quality and unsuitability for weaning small children. Little wonder that people break the rules and hide electric plates, microwaves and rice cookers so they can prepare food themselves. If they are caught, they could be moved to another location meaning losing important connections with schools as well as other community supports. Mostly though, Thembeka worries about being caught with the nappies, breast pads, baby food and other essentials she hides for Abolish Direct Provision's Pregnancy Kits Project which is funded by public donations. She outlines the importance of these kits and of reaching out to new parents with this simple statement – 'The mothers keep crying, begging for help ... they have a lot of needs but realise that they can't complain.'

In *Undivided Rights: Women of Color Organize for Reproductive Justice* (2004), Jael Silliman, Marlene Gerber Fried, Loretta Ross and Elena Gutiérrez outline a Reproductive Justice Framework that merges 'reproductive rights' with 'social justice' to articulate three fundamental rights:

- the right *not* to have children through birth control, abortion or abstinence;
- the right to *have* children under the conditions a person chooses;
- and the right to *parent* in safe, healthy environments.

The analytical tool these feminists articulate draws our attention to the structural oppressions women in DP endure including racism, poverty, precarious citizenship, and the absence of considerations for cultural and geographical differences. Its origins are mostly attributed to the US feminist group Women of African Descent for Reproductive Justice (est. 1994) which opposed then president Bill Clinton's approach to reproductive healthcare and criticized mainstream feminism's failure to challenge the racist, neoliberal state his presidency upheld. Other feminists had been expressing similar ideas before this, including Ireland's Women's Right to Choose Group (WRCG) who met for the first time in 1979 mostly to campaign for abortion access but whose pamphlets and public meetings consistently demanded action on social and economic factors including housing, childcare, decent jobs for women and proper social welfare payments.

When the history of Ireland's struggle for reproductive rights is penned, this focus is often outweighed by the emphasis on a constitutional ban on abortion that was introduced in 1983, four years after WRCG first came together. The willingness of Irish politicians to support this ban 'took feminist activists by surprise and forced them into a reactive position from which arguably they never managed to escape'.[9] The feminist struggle that led to the archaic ban's eventual repeal will be discussed in this chapter and it is understandable why it often gets so much attention. Free, safe, accessible and legal abortion is an urgent and central feminist demand. When it is in place it enables millions of people to decide when and with whom to have children, if at all. It allows women in particular to pursue life goals otherwise denied to them, to counter decades of discrimination in terms of their social and economic progress, and to manage their care burden. Banning abortions doesn't stop them from happening, it just moves them outside of the healthcare system, leaving abortion seekers and activists with no choice but to break the law to make sure people get the information, medication and sometimes surgical interventions that they need. These can be dangerous. Worldwide, the WHO estimates that there are 23,000 annual deaths from unsafe abortions.[10] Banning or restricting abortion also denies people critical care during obstetric emergencies, putting their health and lives at risk.

This chapter will contextualize abortion within a reproductive justice framework which expands our concerns to include menstrual care, access to contraception, fertility treatment, appropriate birthing conditions and health and social care for children but also to much broader social determinants by which I mean factors that exist outside of ourselves that fundamentally shape our capacity to exercise our reproductive rights. A reproductive justice framework is concerned

6. Reframing Reproductive Rights

with everything that impacts our capacity to not have, have and raise children, including the quality of the air that we breathe, the type of education we are afforded if any, the social supports that we have and the environments within which we are housed. I will refer to specific events that reveal a persistent pattern of historical and ongoing interference in our capacity to exercise reproductive rights by governments, religious groups and medical professionals each of whom repeatedly impose restrictions and controls over people's bodies which they vociferously uphold in the face of feminist opposition. But I will also challenge liberal, individualist approaches to reproductive rights which, I argue, solely emphasize personal choice and bodily autonomy as the most sensible position to hold. This seems logical at first glance. After all, our bodies are our own and the right to exercise personal sovereignty should surely trump everything else. But whether we are talking about contraception, abortion, childbirth or parenting, there are problems with this singular approach including that, in practice, it ascribes substantial authority to the medical, legal and welfare professions, forgetting that their involvement in debates about abortion access is relatively recent.[11] As I will illustrate, liberal approaches to reproductive rights also ignore the intersectional nature of oppression, and the challenges millions of people face in securing their human rights and well-being.

Struggles and successes: *The fight for contraception and abortion*

Despite what some people think, one of the most persistent and longest reproductive rights campaigns in Ireland wasn't the eventual securing of abortion on demand (albeit with restrictions that I will return to), it was the fight for contraception. The advertisement, sale and distribution of contraceptives were banned in 1935, and the struggle to overturn these lasted for decades. One of the earlier efforts to reverse the denial of contraception was led by the politician Noel Browne who served as minster for health from 1948 to 1951. When Browne sought to introduce a free healthcare scheme for mothers and children, he included family planning and free, hospital-based maternity care. This was at a time when most births were occurring in highly feminized community settings and in the company of midwives, not medical doctors. There were fatalities, but these often happened because of poor public health standards and the effects of poverty more broadly. Hospitals were mostly for privileged women or in emergencies where labouring at home was not progressing in line with expectations.

As inpatients, some women were subjected to the barbaric action of symphysiotomy and often without consent. This surgical procedure involves cutting the fibrous cartilage of the symphysis pubis to widen the pelvis and had been abandoned in most other European countries by the 1940s in favour of caesarean section. But it continued in Ireland because the Catholic Church, who controlled our hospitals, falsely believed it was less likely to prevent future pregnancies. Symphysiotomy left many women with significant trauma and often catastrophic long-term disability. In 2014, the United Nations Committee on Human Rights instructed the Irish government to open an independent enquiry into this practice, citing concern at the state's failure to initiate its own enquiry. Marie O'Connor, a spokesperson for survivors, has described its eventual redress scheme as 'an official whitewash'.[12] This criticism is hardly surprising given that the scheme does not accept that survivors' bodies and words are evidence of what was done to them. Instead, the redress scheme demands documentary evidence that the procedure was performed and that it resulted in disability.

Had Noel Browne's efforts been successful, maybe they would have protected some women from this procedure. His Mother and Child Scheme definitely had women's best interests in mind and was part of a wider attempt to introduce a public health service similar to Britain's National Health Service (NHS). Brown's vision was to create access to healthcare without the need for a means test. This would have opened the doors for large portions of the population who were denied many services that were available to people who were financially better-off. Class difference also played a part in fierce opposition to Browne's proposals both by the medical profession and by the Catholic Church. For the former, they viewed it as a step towards socializing healthcare. Rhona McCord explains, 'The Irish Medical Association would never accept the socialization of medicine, as it would have impacted negatively on their privileged position within Irish society.'[13] McCord also describes the Catholic Church's objections as threefold: that the state had no right to discuss family planning with women because this was the church's role; that the scheme interfered with individual freedoms which was 'a step towards totalitarianism'; and again that it didn't include a means test. The church's campaign against a national health service was led by the then archbishop of Dublin, Charles McQuaid, who was much more used to politicians acting in accordance with the moral teachings of Catholicism. Browne's willingness to take on the Catholic Church interrupted this well-established pattern and resulted in significant opposition, including from his own government allies. This proved to be too much and he was eventually forced to resign over the issue. A watered-down health bill was introduced two years later which had no reference to family planning.

Browne's failure solidified the authority of the Catholic Church and the willingness of the state to conform and it would be the 1970s before feminists began to substantively challenge this tight-knit relationship. Contraception wasn't completely absent at this time, there was a steady flow of illegal condoms and contraceptives circulating and many doctors were beginning to prescribe the pill under the guise of regulating people's periods. Women were also travelling to the UK for abortions once the procedure was legalized in 1968 and without much controversy. However, contraception was more difficult to access outside of large urban areas and not everyone had the money or freedom to travel meaning multiple births were the norm. As is to be expected, many women resorted to dangerous methods to end pregnancies including using contraband remedies, back street abortions or self-harm in the hope of inducing a miscarriage.[14]

When the Irish Women's Liberation Movement (IWLM) took a public stand on the absence of contraception in their manifesto *Chains and Change* (1970), they were staunchly opposed by the church, again led by McQuaid who wrote a strongly worded letter condemning contraception that was read from church pulpits across the capital city. Using Sunday sermons might sound trivial today, but they were a powerful medium for shaping public opinion and behaviours at the time. In response, the IWLM orchestrated walkouts of Dublin churches and even demonstrated outside the Archbishop's church-owned residence with thirty picketers forming a 40-foot chain across the entrance to McQuaid's house.[15] In her comprehensive oral history account of the time, Laura Kelly details further actions by the IWLM including when, in 1971, fifteen members and a dozen or so children,

> marched outside Leinster House, the home of the Irish parliament, before bursting through the entrance, to the surprise of army and police security, who refused to allow them entry to the building. The women began singing 'We shall not be moved', later changing the lyrics to 'We shall not conceive'.[16]

Not long after this demonstration, the IWLM embarked on the action they are possibly best remembered for when they took the train to Belfast to openly smuggle condoms into the south under the glare of the awaiting media. The journalist June Levine, who was on the train, explains the thinking behind the action: 'The point was that the Contraceptive Law affected those who most needed contraceptives, the poor and women who could not take or get the pill. Anyone who could take the train to Belfast could have all the contraceptives they wanted.'[17] Their stunt made headline news and is regularly used as an exemplar of Irish feminism. But not everyone supported the actions of the IWLM. In fact, the campaign for contraception was a polarizing one. Radio stations regularly debated the issue with many callers condemning what they saw as a weakening of Catholic values. A number of anti-contraception campaign groups were also active at the time including the League of Decency, Parent Concern, the Irish Family League and the feminist-sounding Women of Ireland.

One of the pro-contraception movement's earliest and most significant steps forward was a 1973 Supreme Court ruling under a privacy ruling which was granted to twenty-seven-year-old Mary McGee, a mother of four, who had been advised not to become pregnant as this could induce a stroke or even lead to her death. The ruling, which only applied to married couples, didn't automatically lead to the legalization of contraception – feminists had to keep fighting for this in a hostile environment. When future president and then senator Mary Robinson introduced a Private Members Bill in the Seanad (the upper house in parliament) she was roundly criticized in many quarters. Two years later, the socialist-leaning Irish Women United (IWU, est. 1975 and discussed in Chapter 2) began running rallies and workshops on the issue. In 1976, IWU launched a campaign for contraception called the Contraceptive Action Programme (CAP), with the express intention of ensuring a strong class analysis that would centralize access to contraception for working-class women. As Laura Kelly surmises, 'CAP members regarded the Catholic Church and the "capitalist state" as being a "double barrier" in the campaign for the right to control one's own fertility.'[18]

The persistence of CAP/IWU and an increasing public awareness of how the Irish experience was out of step with rights being won across Europe eventually led to government action mostly because they were bound by the McGee ruling which five years on, had still not been legislated on. In what has become known as an Irish solution to an Irish problem, a Fianna Fáil government eventually passed the *Health (Family Planning) Act* (1979) which only allowed contraception for married couples and only by prescription. CAP campaigned against this restriction including by distributing a poster that superimposed the heads of leading politicians and senior clerics on pregnant bodies with the slogan 'If they got pregnant would we have this bill?'

The Eighth Amendment

The McGee ruling had another lasting mark because of its similarity with an earlier US Supreme Court (SCOTUS) ruling from 1965 called *Griswold v. Connecticut*. This had also overturned bans on contraception on a privacy ruling and it became the basis for the inclusion of the right to abortion in the 1973 *Roe v. Wade* ruling. The likelihood that the very same thing could happen in Ireland, i.e., that the McGee ruling could be expanded, aroused concern amongst conservatives and a small but dedicated anti-abortion movement was convened as the Pro-Life Amendment Campaign (PLAC). Its membership included some of the same people who, as the League of Decency, had opposed contraception. PLAC successfully convinced politicians that the best course of action was to introduce a constitutional ban on abortion, something that would require approval from the electorate. And so, the political establishment became willing partners in crafting an *Eighth Amendment* to the Irish constitution which, if passed, would equate the life of a woman to the life of a foetus. An Anti-Amendment Campaign (AAC) was quickly established initially from within the WRCG but with much wider membership from across the spectrum of feminism. The AAC was never a united group. As Sinéad Kennedy writes when reflecting on its creation, 'there were, from the beginning, clear divisions between "radicals" who advocated for a pro-abortion perspective and "moderates" who favoured a more liberal position with the latter's position coming to dominate'.[19]

This domination wasn't immediately apparent as attempts to foist a liberal leader on the group failed when the socialist Goretti Horgan was appointed coordinator.[20] Where liberal feminists did succeed was in shaping the tone of the campaign which mostly stressed moral and legal arguments relating to the wording of the amendment. This was at a time when even the most disruptive feminists simply weren't used to talking about abortion. With reference to the IWLM and writing in 1983, June Levine notes, '[F]or all the radical image of that first group, they never got around to discussing abortion, not even in consciousness raising.'[21] Such were the contradictions at the time, including within feminism, Levine made this comment whilst sharing her own story of abortion, writing, 'I am anti-abortion but I had to have one for myself.'

This was the social and political climate that AAC sought to influence; one of hostility and where support for the amendment was repeated across media, in decrees from the pulpit and even within our schools and colleges, something I remember first-hand. There was practically no debate on why abortion was necessary in the first place and no talk about the conditions of women's lives more broadly. Canvassing against the amendment was an uphill battle. The historian Mary Muldowney, a young mother at the time, sets the scene:

> My daughter was about five or six at the time and I literally pushed her around in a buggy delivering leaflets and being rather appalled by the reaction I got on some doorsteps. I thought that the Eighth Amendment was such an obvious thing women should stand against, and I was very taken aback that so many people fell for the propaganda.

As the date of the referendum approached, the AAC sought to break through this seemingly impenetrable wall of opinion by focusing on the fact that women would die if the amendment was introduced. But this wasn't enough to sway the electorate who voted by a two-thirds majority to insert a constitutional ban on abortion with a turnout of 53.6 per cent.

In the immediate aftermath of this significant defeat, anti-abortion activists targeted two voluntary, feminist-led services – Open Door Counselling and the Well Woman Centre whose counselling model included helping often desperate women to book flights and appointments in overseas clinics. To prevent this, the Society for the Protection of the Unborn Child (SPUC) initiated legal action. In 1986, the attorney general joined SPUC's action, and a High Court injunction was secured, prohibiting both organizations from operating. Campaigners weren't perturbed and continued to operate and promote a telephone helpline. Its number was distributed on posters, stickers and by gathering in urban areas where it was chanted out loud. In the years that followed, bans on information would extend to student union publications and even the *Cosmopolitan* magazine, which was forced to black out advertisements in the copies sold in Ireland.

It would be 1992 before the national conversation was again dominated by the Eighth Amendment when a High Court injunction prevented a fourteen-year-old rape victim, Miss X, from travelling for an abortion despite being suicidal. When newspapers broke the story, thousands of people took part in street protests that were mostly organized by anti-capitalist activists, especially the anarchist group Workers Solidarity and the Socialist Workers Party. The Supreme Court reversed the ban determining that 'risk to life' included the 'risk of suicide'. A second referendum followed this time on the right to travel and information (in essence a reversal of SPUC's injunction) and the option of reversing the Supreme Court decision on suicide. As would be the case in all referenda that followed,[22] the electorate voted as liberally as they possibly could, meaning yes to travel and information and no to removing the risk of suicide. Note the change in mood Mary Muldowney captures when she tells me, 'It was clear from talking to people as I was handing out leaflets that there were an awful lot of people saying, "I didn't really think it would end like this".' In the years that followed, Muldowney would help organize the Dublin Abortion Rights Group (DARG) which formed following the case of Miss C, which was essentially a re-run of the X case, the difference being that the teenager was in the care of the state.

By the late 1990s and 2000s, the abortion debate was in some ways becoming less important for liberal feminists. The cost of flying overseas had come down and pills could now be sourced online or through feminist circles. Contraception was also no longer controversial, in large part because of a global change in attitude towards condoms amidst the AIDS pandemic but also because the Catholic Church in Ireland was fast losing its moral monopoly. DARG, which overlapped with student unions, the revolutionary left and anarchist groups, was amongst those who kept the dangers of denying abortion access on the agenda at a time when it was sometimes difficult to get any national coverage for the issue. Sometimes, the simplest actions, like writing a letter, can be impactful. When Rebecca Gomperts, founder of the Dutch group Women on Waves, appeared as a guest on a popular TV show, Mary Muldowney contacted Gomperts on behalf of DARG and invited her to visit Ireland. In 2001, their ship, *The Aurora* docked in Dublin and Cork (organized with Cork for Choice) in a stunt that was designed to kickstart a near-dormant pro-abortion movement.

Childcare and the rights of migrant children

There are lots of reasons why people choose abortion, many of which overlap. One reason is concern about future childcare, something one UK study found influenced 60 per cent of decisions.[23] Childcare, or the absence thereof, was a major issue for women in Ireland when they began joining the Irish workforce in large numbers from the 1990s onwards. But the impossible situation its absence can create was often overlooked by liberal feminists whose own socio-economic positioning allowed them to hire in care, which was usually provided by poorer women, to stay at home until their children were in school or to work in professional careers that afforded more flexibility.

A good way to demonstrate this neglect of childcare is to look at the second *Commission on the Status of Women* (1990) whose membership included trade unionists and strong representation from the membership organization the CSW. This didn't prevent the commission's report from completely overlooking childcare,[24] therefore seeding the ground for a continued narrative that minding children was a private matter and not something the state had any business interfering with. One new law was passed at this time namely *The Child Care Act* (1991). But this was mostly about child welfare, and it gave significant powers to state agencies to intervene where they determined there was neglect or abuse. It did set standards for childcare facilities but said nothing about childminding in people's homes despite this being a major area of provision.[25] Standards in childcare are important, especially when the concern is keeping children safe, but a negative side effect of this and other future regulatory laws was to make it impossible for many local groups to continue informal childminding arrangements where women took turns to mind children so other women could participate in consciousness-raising education. And so, a once-widespread 'no class without crèche' policy within women's community education became impossible to implement. The community sector's capacity to provide supports was also greatly diminished by the actions of Mary Harney, the first woman to lead a political party (the Progressive Democrats) in Ireland and someone who is sometimes dubbed Ireland's Thatcher. Harney was in government for much of the 1990s including as Tánaiste (Deputy Prime Minister). In 1996, she sought to axe over 10,000 community employment (CE) jobs that were mostly held by lone parents living in working-class areas, claiming these posts were making it difficult for employers to fill low-paid posts in retail and service industries. The fact that CE provided re-training, and subsidized childcare was, for Harney, irrelevant.

The 1990s also saw a notable rise in migration. People from around the world joined the Irish workforce and there was a sharp rise in international protection applicants just like the women volunteering with Abolish Direct Provision who opened this chapter. These migrants would, and continue to, fill significant labour shortages in both high- and low-skilled professions. Their reasons for leaving their own countries were anchored in push–pull factors in terms of safety and opportunity, political and cultural difficulties, and the daily inequalities people encountered.[26] When these migrants had children, who were Irish citizens by birth right, they too were impacted by a lack of affordable childcare in a system that was often hidden and where they didn't have the same family and community supports. Migrant mothers, in particular, were less able to take on paid work as their labour was needed to care for their children at home.

The Twenty-seventh Amendment

A notable shift in circumstances for migrant parents happened in 2003 when the Supreme Court changed tack on an established pattern of granting leave to remain to so that people could raise their children. Instead, they began ruling against parental entitlement as a reason for staying in Ireland. Soon after, the government announced that no further applications for residency based on parentage would be accepted, claiming this was to protect the integrity of the asylum and immigration processes.[27] What transpired as a result of this announcement was an environment where migrant women were openly accused of 'citizenship tourism', meaning deliberately arriving in Ireland whilst pregnant so they could circumvent a supposedly impartial immigration system. In July 2003, a campaign group called the Coalition Against the Deportation of Irish Children (CADIC) was convened whose members included the migrant-led women's group AkiDwA (est. 1999), the Irish Council for Civil Liberties and the National Women's Council of Ireland (NWCI, formally the CSW). CADIC came together on the heels of a slew of deportation orders including those to women parenting alone whose applications to stay were at risk because they were not in paid employment. Zero consideration was given for the near impossibility of working and parenting alone given Ireland's abysmal childcare supports. In an archived interview, the founder of AkiDwA Samone Imbugna recalls:

> I remember very well, I was training in Edenderry and five women called me when I was in that meeting, to tell me that they had received deportation letters … some of them had pulled out of or cancelled the application for asylum, and actually just stayed with

their children because they had the right, to be with their children in the country, because their children were Irish citizens. But the Irish Government wanted to remove that right.[28]

With the support of the academic Ronit Lentin, Imbugna organized a meeting in the offices of the trade union SIPTU calling for an end to these deportations which, if executed would lead to almost 17,000 women and their children being deported. 'We ended up having more than three hundred people coming for those meetings' Imbugna recalls, 'with buggies, with children, people were in fear, they were panicking about these deportations happening'. This action worked and, with support from the NWCI, the government agreed to allow women who had children to that point apply for residency.

But things would soon take a turn for the worse when a referendum was announced for 2004 that, if passed, would abolish citizenship as a birth right and only grant automatic citizenship to babies where at least one parent was already a citizen. The referendum was championed by the right-wing then Minister for Justice, Equality and Law Reform, Michael McDowell (also of the Progressive Democrats), who justified the need for a constitutional amendment by stating that migrant women were creating an unsustainable strain on Ireland's maternity system. He even claimed that the chief obstetricians at Dublin's maternity hospitals had 'pleaded with him to change the law', something the doctors collectively refuted.[29] His comments helped fuel high levels of misinformation and disinformation including false claims about benefits pregnant women were accruing. CADIC campaigned for a no vote but were competing against a media frenzy and hostile public discourse. There was some support from feminist organizations especially the NWCI, who convened a meeting of its members to take a position on the referendum. Its membership opted to reject the amendment and to campaign against it. The NWCI organized a conference on the issue and produced a leaflet which they distributed nationally, but it was a very difficult campaign and showed that anti-migrant sentiment was a feature of Irish society in 2004. Their actions did not gain the same level of support that other issues managed to attract. And so, on 11 June 2004, and with a turnout of almost 60 per cent, the Irish electorate took a step backwards when 79 per cent of voters backed the Twenty-seventh Amendment to the Constitution of Ireland which removed automatic birth right to citizenship. The NWCI received criticism for the position they took particularly as the referendum was rejected by such a majority In the years that followed, schools, community groups and individual

TDs would go on to campaign against the deportation orders that stemmed from this decision when young Irish-born children were issued orders that sought to send them to countries that they had often never set foot in and where they knew no one.

The growth of Irish feminism through the 'Repeal Movement'

Had the 2004 referendum happened a few years later, maybe there would have been more support for the reproductive rights of migrant parents as it might have been picked up as part of a surge in feminist activism in response to growing awareness of the heartache, trauma and even deaths that were occurring because of ongoing restrictions on abortion. One driving force for this surge was the regularity with which more alphabetized tragedies of human suffering were brought to the public's attention through the work of investigative journalists including Justine McCarthy and Kitty Holland. Miss D was a seventeen-year-old who, in 2007, was initially denied the right to travel despite the foetus having no chance of surviving. The ABC case, in 2010, was a landmark European Court of Human Rights ruling against the Irish government for violating the human rights of three women – A, B and C. Miss P was a woman who died whilst pregnant in 2014 and whose family was forced into the High Court to secure the right to terminate her life support because there was a foetal heartbeat. That same year, Miss Y, a young asylum seeker and the victim of rape, was force fed and endured a caesarean section against her will when she was twenty-five-weeks pregnant. Take a moment to think about the cruelty of these actions. Any of the governments in power at the time could have called a referendum but didn't. Instead, they went to great lengths to actively uphold the Eighth Amendment's stringent restrictions.

The year 2012 was a turning point for several reasons. In February, over two hundred people turned up to a meeting in Dublin to address how twenty years had passed since the X Case and the government had still not legislated on the matter. Its organizers included Action on X which was led by socialists Ailbhe Smyth and Sinéad Kennedy. Goretti Horgan was one of its speakers. Around the same time, the voluntary organization, Termination for Medical Reasons (TFMR), broke an established taboo by publicly talking about their own abortions. Self-proclaimed 'pro-life' opponents roundly criticized them, claiming their actions were contributing to a slippery slope towards widespread access to abortion. It was also the year that Youth Defence launched a nationwide campaign of giant-sized, graphic billboards under the title 'Abortion tears her life apart' to coincide with a parliamentary private member's bill calling for legislation on the X Case. The bill was introduced by Clare Daly who was then a Socialist Party TD, with the support of the Irish Family Planning Association (IFPA), a reproductive healthcare provider that has always campaigned for abortion access. Youth Defence's actions angered a new layer of younger activists including those within the anarchist-feminist group RAG (short for Revolutionary Anarcha-Feminist Group) who called a public meeting that spawned the short-lived Irish Choice Network. Angela Coraccio, a member of RAG, remembers how people were frustrated that liberal feminist groups, especially the NWCI, were doing nothing about the abortion ban. Nor was the Labour Party, which also claimed to be pro-choice and did vocally object to government policy, but they put no real effort into mobilizing for change outside of cordial negotiations, a pattern that highlighted a repeated reluctance to jeopardize cooperative relationships with potential coalition partners no matter what the issue was.

Both the Labour Party and the NWCI did participate in the first March for Choice which took place in September 2012 with an attendance of around 2,500. Within weeks of this march, an Indian woman living in Galway named Savita Halappanavar died of septicaemia soon after being refused an abortion. She was miscarrying but was denied the treatment that would have saved her because doctors could detect a foetal heartbeat. This aroused the already growing pro-repeal movement. The Abortion Rights Campaign (ARC) emerged from the Irish Choice Network with RAG effectively dissolving into this new entity. Meanwhile ROSA (Reproductive Rights against Oppression, Sexism and Austerity) was formed from within the Socialist Party. By 2013, a Coalition to Repeal the Eighth had been convened by Ailbhe Smyth and Sinéad Kennedy, providing a united front for these groups as well as other grassroots campaigners, trade unions, artists, journalists, political parties and healthcare providers in calling for a referendum on abortion. Over the next five years, this 'repeal movement' created a constant flow of protest, consciousness-raising public meetings and highly visible street art that continually reminded the public that everyday women's lives were being put at risk and that people were travelling overseas or were breaking the law by buying abortion pills. Eventually, a Fine-Gael-led government gave in to domestic and international pressure by first outsourcing the decision to a citizens' assembly which recommended a referendum, then referring their decision to a parliamentary cross-party committee which sat from April to December 2017.

The Campaign Against Church Ownership of Women's Healthcare

In the middle of this hive of activity, activists were forced to expand their campaign when the government unexpectedly announced that Ireland's €1 billion future flagship National Maternity Hospital (NMH) would be gifted to a private company called St Vincent's Healthcare Group (SVHG). Maybe we shouldn't have been surprised. The proposal perfectly matched the neoliberal extension of private over public healthcare which, to that point, had mostly focused on pushing people into private insurance plans but was now moving towards a fully operational privatized model of care. The announcement might have passed quietly and even with public support had it not transpired that the majority shareholders of SVHG were the Sisters of Charity; one of four religious orders who ran Magdalene Laundries throughout the 1900s and who have never contributed to the financial redress scheme. Some NMH board members reacted negatively to the announcement, including Dr Peter Boylan who resigned his seat in 2017. Dr Chris Fitzpatrick, former clinical lead at the Rotunda Maternity Hospital also resigned from the Health Service Executive (HSE) board managing the project in support of Boylan's views. The public nature of these resignations was significant. One campaigner, Sarah Murphy recalls, 'it was Dr Boylan who set the cat amongst the pigeons' and spurred some feminists within already established pro-repeal groups to seek to stop the deal. The Campaign Against Church Ownership of Women's Healthcare was quickly formed, mainly from members of a group in Dublin Bay North that had formed to campaign for the removal of the Eighth Amendment. It quickly spread beyond this cluster including to another local cluster Wicklow for Choice within which Sarah Murphy was active. Wicklow for Choice's involvement was strategically important as this was the constituency of Simon Harris, then Minister for Health and the government's front face of the deal. Wicklow for Choice carried out two leaflet drops and organized a well-attended public meeting at which Ailbhe Smyth, Siobhan Donoghue from TFMR, a speaker from Doctors for Choice and Róisín Shortall, the then leader of the Social Democrats addressed the crowd. 'I was pregnant at the time,' Sarah recalls, 'and there was a lot of talk about having to go in front of the bulldozers and stuff like that. The public meeting raised so many issues.'

In the midst of a media frenzy that shone a light on the need for Vatican permission, the government realized they had mis-judged the situation and the Sisters of Charity announced that they would be severing all ties with SVHG. All that remained was permission from the pope that they could pass the land on to the state.

Together for Yes

In January 2018, with the issue of the maternity hospital seemingly settled, the Irish government eventually announced that a referendum on abortion would be held that June. Immediately, a 'Yes' vote coalition campaign group called 'Together for Yes' (TfY) was formed led by ARC, the Coalition to Repeal the Eighth, the NWCI (whose established policy now mirrored the Fine Gael government's pro-choice perspective) and the IFPA. Together for Yes became the umbrella under which up to 20,000 people began actively canvassing the length and breadth of Ireland. One contributor to this research captures the mood across hundreds of canvasser groups: 'Repeal the 8th, what can I say, I campaigned with Kerry for Choice and meeting likeminded activists was a joy. It was a tough campaign, and many difficult conversations were had. I felt for the first time that women's voices were being heard.'

There is no doubt that the explosion of grassroots activism within Irish feminism will be remembered for many years. But the TfY phase was the movement's most conservative. Many activists struggled with what they believed was a toned-down medicalized message that over-relied on stories of tragedy that ignored feminist concerns about patriarchal and paternalistic attitudes within obstetrics. There were legitimate concerns about the obliteration of working-class, disabled, LGBTQIA+ and migrant voices, and criticisms of what appeared from the outside to be a strategic decision to forge new alliances with liberal feminist organizations and conservative politicians that did not represent, or indeed understand, the grassroots nature of the movement.[30] It was also challenging for those on the inside who had to deal with a very different reality. Sinéad Kennedy, a member of the TfY executive, remembers the dynamics like this:

> When all the mainstream political parties come on board, the centre of gravity shifts so you become a minority and the voice of the left, the far left who in many ways do all the groundwork to take you there and then the centre come in and take all the credit … And I

suppose in some ways as the campaign becomes more mainstream, and more liberal, it is disciplined, and domesticated and some of the more radical aspects of it are lost.

There were advantages to this united front including that the national conversation undoubtedly shifted from the realm of morality and towards reproductive healthcare. A united front also ensured the disunity evident in 1983 didn't play into the hands of the anti-abortion movement. In the end, 66.4 per cent of the electorate voted to remove the constitutional ban, an overwhelming endorsement of the national desire for affordable, safe and legal abortion.

Issues associated with the individualist, legalistic, pro-choice tone of the campaign would linger especially for Migrants and Ethnic Minorities for Reproductive Justice (MERJ) who had held firm on a radical analysis that stressed the practicalities of abortion access especially for marginalized population groups. MERJ, formed in 2018 and mostly from within ARC, were unhappy about the absence of migrant voices in the TfY campaign and about their own positioning in some feminist spaces. This perspective is captured by one of MERJ's supporters, Amel Yacef who shares her experience of Irish-based feminism telling me, '[D]espite the effort of a few individual white women, I never felt welcome in the movement, the individual efforts did not compensate for the absence of a collective, intentional effort to welcome me'. At the same time, '[T]here was so much labour for us to catch up with the white Irish feminists and there weren't any efforts made to slow down to make sure that the process was participative'. Amel continues:

> I could see that it was complicated for the individual allies to negotiate space for us, and that their allyship could cost them their own credibility. I feel that our issues, the issues of the migrant women, or women of colour in Ireland, were perceived as always going to be issues about asylum seeking, immigration, family reunification, employment, language, whatever. These are issues that white Irish feminists can feel sympathy for, but they would not see what the relevance of those issues is in the Irish feminist struggle. So, it's an afterthought, or a kind of 'oh, yeah, we will come to you, but these are social issues, they're not specifically feminist issues' ... I had to prove so many times that I knew what I was talking about, just to make sure I wasn't dismissed or patronised, I had to prove I knew my stuff

in terms of repeal, in terms of an Irish context, understanding the history, knowing the Constitution, understanding when and what happens, knowing the main players, you know, like and having to throw in all these references so that they could see that I understood and therefore might value what I had to say, might value how the struggles are fundamentally interconnected.

This sounds like an exhausting role to occupy. Others too spoke out against aspects of the campaign including some disabled activists who talked about an environment where they were sometimes pushed forward to speak for the cause without any concern for their well-being and with very little emphasis on the violations of disabled people's reproductive rights. These violations continue to this day including denying people basic information, providing services that are inaccessible for many people and embedding ongoing ableist attitudes by healthcare professionals that hugely influence the choices people are offered.[31]

Although the referendum campaign was imperfect, it was not to blame for the conservativism of Ireland's *The Health (Regulation of Termination of Pregnancy) Act* (2018). This law ensures abortion remains a criminal offence outside of strictly defined rules each of which contravenes WHO guidelines. Abortion is only allowed on demand before twelve weeks and only with a three-day pause period. After that, it is only allowed for foetal fatality (not foetal anomaly) and where the life or health of the pregnant person is at risk. This continues a chill effect for healthcare professionals who must still make complex medical decisions, often in emergency situations, when dealing with miscarriages, ectopic pregnancies and other obstetric complications with the risk of prosecution hanging in the air if they are determined to have made the wrong call. There is also an opt out conscientious objection clause for healthcare workers which falsely personifies a foetus then honours the values of the conscientious objector over the rights of the pregnant person. There are other problems too including how only *c.* 15 per cent of GPs have registered with the public platform MyOptions.ie mostly because they are already overwhelmed with heavy patient loads within a system that falls well below OECD averages on GPs per head of population.[32] And not all maternity hospitals provide abortion care despite being fully funded by the public purse. Because of these barriers, people still travel either to other countries or across Ireland, and the same people who were most impacted by the Eighth Amendment continue to suffer the most. This includes people with very little money including low-income migrants, disabled people, those living with violence and coercion, those with heavy care loads, people who can't take time off work and those with irregular periods which can sometimes be a symptom of addiction or other health concerns.

Birthing rights and the Irish maternity care system

Most pregnancies do not end in abortions, rather they result in the birth of healthy children. Although many women experience birth as liberating and joyous, it can also be traumatic and can negatively impact a person's capacity to bond with their baby, adjust to parenthood and plan their future family.[33] Typically, the root of the problem is the medicalization of pregnancy and childbirth, a framing that places little or no emphasis on a person's experience outside of this lens. Anyone who has given birth in a medical setting will confirm the extent to which our bodies are routinely subjected to a range of unpleasant, unnecessary, often humiliating procedures such as vaginal examinations and sweeps, rupturing of the amniotic sac and being asked to birth in unnatural positions that are normalized in hospitals. Domestic and international studies have found that only basic consent is typically sought with most women receiving minimal information on the procedures carried out on them.[34] Meanwhile the rates of caesarean sections are skyrocketing, sometimes because they are needed and sometimes because of maternal choice but mostly as an inevitable consequence of the accumulated impact of the interventions described above. Little wonder that many women leave hospital carrying shame, stigma and feelings of failure when they don't give birth 'naturally'. Increasingly active management practices in maternity care settings are being classified as a form of obstetric violence including within a United Nations special report on reproductive health.[35] One 2024 UK parliamentary enquiry into birth trauma went so far as to conclude that good maternity care was the exception and not the rule.[36]

This is the same maternity system within which minoritized and migrant bodies are further subjugated; something that can begin before they even enter the healthcare system if they are unaware of their entitlements or fear that coming forward will result in deportation. They may not know how to access care within a system where it is hard to get a GP and where there is an over-reliance on familiarity with the English language. In 2021, the voluntary organization, Amal

Women's Association, carried out extensive research on the experiences of Muslim women in Irish maternity hospitals which uncovered overt racism, negative attitudes and a failure to support often the most basic cultural needs.[37] The researchers (of which I was one) proposed immediate and inexpensive improvements including stable funding for a cultural advocacy and mediation programme, support for Amal to collaborate with maternity services beyond their current voluntary commitment, and offers to provide culturally responsive education to staff in seeking to combat the institutional racism that stems from white supremacy. These inexpensive recommendations were presented to a cross-party government committee, but nothing has been done to action them. Where is the feminist outrage for these women? Indeed, as Rafia Zakaria notes, many Western feminists are much more focused on condemning obstetric and gender-based violence in other countries than acknowledging the obstetric violence that has become so normalized in the West.[38]

#MakeOurMaternityOurs

The absence of feminist outrage for these women is important to highlight especially when the repeal movement has re-formed on more than one occasion since the 2018 referendum including in 2022 when the issue of the NMH resurfaced with a bang. This was when broken promises surrounding the Sisters of Charity's supposed extraction from Ireland's future national maternity hospital became public. The nuns hadn't gifted ownership of their church-owned land to the state as had been widely reported. Instead, the permission they received (or perhaps sought) from the Vatican was to transfer ownership to another private company called St Vincent's Holdings whose company documents clearly state adherence to Catholic values that typically prohibit tubal ligations, abortion on demand and vasectomies. Immediately, the campaign against the transfer of the NMH was reactivated, this time under the hashtag #MakeOurMaternityHospitalOurs. Thousands took to the streets including Dr Peter Boylan, the NWCI and some sitting politicians and much work was done to decipher sometimes-complex legal jargon and technical company law that was being drip fed to the public. Concerns immediately began to surface about the deal. Ivana Bacik, leader of the Labour Party and a legal expert in reproductive healthcare, described the arrangements as 'byzantine' whilst independent TD and barrister Catherine Connolly said she was 'deeply troubled' by the governance arrangements being proposed. Other legal experts also expressed concerns, most of which centred on the risk of future religious interference.[39] These objections were sometimes expressed with reference to patterns in the United States where some hospitals with no overtly religious ethos have been sold to private companies that also outwardly seem to have no religious ethos but whose contract for services sometimes dangerously limits reproductive healthcare. Often, people arrive at these hospitals unaware of restrictions and without knowing that the options being laid out before them do not represent the full range of possible medical options.[40]

The coalition government of Fianna Fáil, Fine Gael and the Green Party insisted that all the necessary legal safeguards were put in place, faced down dissenters in their own parties and dismissed what were clearly credible concerns including objections to the transfer of a €1 billion hospital project to a private company. When the cabinet eventually signed off on the deal, then leader of the Social Democrats Róisín Shortall captured the public mood when she remarked, 'I think today is a bad day for Ireland. I think it's a bad day for the taxpayer. It's a bad day for women's health. It's a bad day for the Public Health Service.'[41] JoAnne Neary of Leitrim for Choice, who also volunteers with #MakeOurMaternityOurs captures what she believes is a shift in Irish feminism in its aftermath:

> Mná na hÉireann [women of Ireland], there is a different energy, we are not going back, and we are not going to be messed with. They have made a massive mistake with the national maternity hospital ... I think they have been bullish and said, we need to get on with this, but it is women who will suffer.

The right to parent

It is no harm repeating that the reproductive justice lens I am applying focuses on three basic rights: the right to have children, the right to not have children and the right to parent in healthy and safe environments without undue interference from others. This broader understanding connects reproductive rights with factors that can otherwise be ignored such as race, gender, citizenship status and dis/ability. It also brings housing to the fore, something that requires urgent attention given that thousands of people currently live in unsuitable emergency hostel or hotel accommodation, often for years on end. This has a particular impact on women who are parenting alone. The housing activist Clare O'Connor grimly describes her own experiences of working with 'women who are in one room with all of their children, and maybe there is a child who is crawling, another one with developmental delays or health issues and they are going into the toilet to cry so their kids don't see them, and they see no future for themselves'.

The right to parent also encompasses cultural attitudes that can define certain people as unfit parents including poorer women who parent alone who already endure high levels of surveillance from welfare officers.[42] Judgements about the capacity to parent are based on a range of arbitrary and subjective benchmarks, such as being the wrong social class, being disabled, too young or too old, religious or not religious enough, being in a same-sex relationship, being trans, or being the wrong race. One population group that is particularly targeted are Ireland's Roma community, one in five of whom will experience extreme poverty during their lifetime – meaning they will live without food, electricity and water.[43] Across Europe, Roma have endured historical assimilation policies that removed children from families, including in Ireland, sometimes solely because of social and economic conditions that could have been rectified through investment in public housing, education and welfare. Irish-based research acknowledges that this has created understandable fear amongst Roma populations which is compounded by discriminatory child protection actors who assume families are not able or willing to raise and educate their children.[44] The right to parent is also denied to other population groups including prisoners, with the number of women being imprisoned growing mostly amongst those who have backgrounds of financial poverty, homelessness, addiction, or family breakdown. These include Traveller women who are 18–22 times more likely to be imprisoned than their settled counterparts.[45] Travellers are also seven times more likely to have their children taken into care, as are children of African descent and disabled children.[46]

Retreats to conservativism despite pro-choice advances

There are many other ways that the right to parent is denied, which I do not have the space to explore in just one chapter. These include growing numbers of disabled children being denied school places, legal recognition for same-sex parents, access to fertility treatments and the conditions under which the women in Direct Provision who opened this chapter must continue to parent often with the threat of deportation looming large. What I hope I have done is highlight just how enormous the struggle for reproductive justice is and illuminate the failures of pro-establishment governments to truly partner with feminist campaigns.

Certainly, there have been significant improvements. Contraception is now freely available and often on demand, assuming you can get a GP. Great strides have also been made in making hormone replacement therapy available for menopause and a regulatory system has been introduced for fertility treatment which, before 2024 was completely out of the reach of many people. But there have been significant betrayals and broken promises on abortion rights, amidst a global attack on abortion laws worldwide that were mostly initiated by the 2022 SCOTUS reversal of abortion rights in the United States. Since then, several opportunities to improve Irish law have been ignored including inaction on legal reforms recommended within the state's own independent review which was published in 2023. This review would not have happened at all if it weren't for sustained pressure by pro-abortion activists who were forced into launching a #repealreview campaign two years earlier when it became obvious that a promised independent and external review was to be replaced with the 'in-house job' then Minister for Health Simon Harris had assured us would not happen.[47] The most straightforward way to improve Ireland's law would be to back a 2023 private member's bill brought by TD Bríd Smith which mirrored the same recommendations of the government's own review. But they chose not to do so. Compare these actions to the response to the SCOTUS ruling in the Netherlands, which ditched the five-day-wait period and extended prescriptive authority beyond dedicated abortion clinics. Or in France, which immediately passed a cross-party bill that paved the way for making abortion a constitutional right, with one National Assembly member Marie-Pierre Rixain exclaiming, '[W]hat happened elsewhere must not happen in France'.[48] Irish politicians might reject this analysis and point to the introduction of a law that now bans protesters from harassing and intimidating people outside abortion services as evidence of progress. But this *Health (Termination of Pregnancy Services) (Safe Access Zones) Act 2024* mostly came about because of a sustained campaign by the Limerick-based group Together for Safety.

The absence of holistic, natural birthing environments that this chapter highlighted is also unlikely to change any time soon and there is no doubt that its absence has contributed to a growing free-birthing movement which involves labouring and giving birth at home without a doctor or midwife. In 2024, free-birthing took the life of Naomi James, who died in hospital soon after giving birth at home. The concern for her passing from medical providers was welcome but little has been done at a structural level to expand and improve public home-birthing services which are increasingly restrictive and usually underfunded.

Many feminists see little wrong with obstetric norms and fail to consider structural problems in reproductive healthcare, especially from the viewpoint of minoritized population groups and disabled people. Failures within feminism including left-wing feminism are important to reflect on and our evaluation of winning abortion rights must include concerns raised by marginalized voices and our mission for reproductive justice should encourage alliances of solidarity that hold firm on a political analysis. Building these will form part of the discussion in the next and final chapter.

I find it frustrating that many feminists don't call out the key issue as capitalism. You're not a bad feminist or selling out the sisterhood or benefitting from patriarchy because you believe patriarchy wouldn't exist without capitalism and want to work on dismantling capitalism instead of just striving for equality on a male scale of measurement.

– People before Profit member and convener of their feminist caucus

Chapter 7

DOING FEMINISM

In 1984, the philosopher and social activist bell hooks described feminism as 'a struggle to end sexist oppression and male domination' and therefore, 'necessarily a struggle to eradicate the ideology of domination that permeates Western culture on various levels as well as a commitment to reorganizing society so that the self-development of people can take precedence over imperialism, economic expansion, and material desires'.[1] In reaching this conclusion, hooks, who was black, drew from her childhood in the rural, segregated town of Hopkinsville, Kentucky, in the United States locating her experience as 'in the margin' and therefore 'part of the whole but outside the main body' – thus a unique vantage point that her oppressors lacked.[2] Although centring sexism and male domination, hooks positions feminism within its capitalist context and repeatedly exposes the falsehood of universalizing patriarchy – a standpoint that betrays millions of women, girls, other marginalized genders and many men by upholding what hooks determines the *white-supremacist-capitalist-patriarchy*.

The idea that there are two souls to feminism runs through this book – the intersectional and anti-capitalist version that hooks speaks to, and a pro-neoliberal, pro-establishment version that doesn't just passively permit income inequality, environmental catastrophe and imperialist expansion, it co-opts feminism and weaponizes it in advancing this white-supremacist-capitalist-patriarchy. Liberal feminism might preach equality, often eloquently, but its actions betray a deeper commitment to preserving the status quo. By way of example, one current instance of performativity that some feminists support is the Athena SWAN initiative, which seeks gender-equality in universities, especially in sciences, tech and engineering. Athena SWAN was established in the UK in 2005 but has since spread to other countries including Ireland. The reality of Athena SWAN is that it is mostly a tick-box, administratively burdensome task that helps universities win awards (bronze, silver or gold) so they can improve their international rankings. Because increased prestige typically leads to higher college fees, this makes these institutions less accessible to poorer students. Nothing about Athena SWAN substantively addresses the issues faced by the lecturers, tutors, researchers, housekeeping and other staff I talked about in Chapter 3 who are employed on low-paid, precarious contracts across European universities.

Dismissing innovations like Athena SWAN and other liberal initiatives is not an agreed standpoint for all feminists and some people (including some of you reading this book) might prefer to steer clear of the either/or political polarization I offer, viewing it as an oversimplification of more complex realities. Instead, you might choose a seemingly neutral stance. By way of example, the Irish-based Women for Election (est. 2012, which I talked about in Chapter 2) describes itself as 'a non-partisan, independent, not-for-profit organisation' that seeks to 'inspire, equip, and support the full diversity of women to succeed in politics'.[3] Feminists who take this liberal stance often use *diversity* in this way, wiping it clean of the relations of power that create difference in the first place. Being neutral isn't apolitical; it upholds the logic of capitalism. This abortion rights activist sums up the core contradiction: 'There's no equality in capitalism so to be a feminist and a capitalist is a contradiction.'

Others that resist an either/or argument are those whose ontologies view reality as less stable, including some feminists who uphold identity politics. This contested concept mostly describes a political perspective that rejects single axis theories of oppression – mostly class, in favour of incorporating a range of equal identities including, but not limited to, race, sexuality, disability and, of course, gender. The expression *identity politics* was first used by the radical US-based black feminist collective the Combahee River Collective (est. 1974) whose members included Audre Lorde, Beverly Smith and Angela Davis. But it was appropriated and watered-down by white-liberal university-based feminists who claimed that the ideas expressed by the Combahee River Collective were already part of their work.[4] Today, identity politics is mostly an all-purpose expression that replaces the concept of structural inequality with the concept of opportunity; an individualist perspective that overemphasizes personal responsibility and individual effort. This depoliticization has provided fertile ground for far-right political actors who hijack its meaning and extend their once central anti-immigration and nationalist rhetoric to include other 'identities' specifically LGBTQIA+ people, ethnic minorities and, of course, women.[5]

7. Doing Feminism

Why we still need feminism

Sometimes, it can be tempting to abandon the word *feminism* altogether. To borrow the words of Françoise Vergès, 'why defend feminism when these terms are so corrupted that even the far right can appropriate them?' Some of the people I met with agreed and often with good reason. Amel Yacef explains how 'a lot of women of colour would think of feminism as white feminism so they don't want to have anything to do with it'. Clare O'Connor, puts it like this:

> [T]here are issues in Irish feminism, middle-class and white feminism, with liberal feminism, because it can become a talking shop about progressive national things that need to change in a way that forgets women living in poverty. Poverty needs to be the central ... class is so central to our experiences ... that is if you truly want to address the issues affecting women.

And another contributor, who prefers to stay anonymous resists the word altogether because of 'the persistent issue of middle-class feminism in a lot of activist groups', making it 'hard to know what the solution is'.

I share these concerns. But I also think we need feminism as much as we ever did, not just because it is still mostly women who carry domestic and care labour, fall victim to gender-based violence, are discriminated against in work, and are more impacted by imperialist war and climate change, but because our feminist history reveals that important reforms can and have been won through feminist struggle. Victories include the right to vote, to sit on juries, to better working conditions, to have fewer children, if at all, to express an opinion, to not be raped by our husbands, to open a bank account, and to run for government all of which have been fought for and won because of bottom-up grassroots activism. But the capacity to exercise these rights is asymmetric in part because the struggles to secure them have focused on individualized, single-issue campaigning that isolates each oppression from the other.

Rethinking feminism

Rethinking feminism means placing those who are the most discriminated against at the centre of our struggle. It means moving away from the idea that there is only one version of feminism, accepting that certain feminist hierarchies are harmful and embracing the objectives of justice, dignity and care as we seek to unite people towards a common cause – to end sexist oppression and drastically reorganize society. Victories that have been won are not unimportant; in fact they can help people a great deal. For instance, it is essential to establish abortion clinics that are fully funded by the state. But these clinics will never address the fact that economic hardship accompanying large recessions can be the catalyst that leads people to terminate unplanned pregnancies.[6] And they don't address the barriers to care that disability, poverty, or citizenship status create or pay attention to the working conditions in clinics, especially for low-paid workers. Instead, individualist solutions fall on the side of sustaining and nourishing injustice by dehumanizing those most impacted by structural inequality and expecting them to express gratitude and indebtedness to their own oppressors.

Many feminist victories started out with bolder ambitions than what is eventually won as was the case with Ireland's pro-abortion movement, the backbone of which has always been anarchist and socialist feminists. Long-time abortion rights activist and socialist Sinéad Kennedy describes the movement as 'not just about abortion but about all sorts of things – housing, gender, sexuality, healthcare, about education, about welfare and about communities'. But these ambitions were watered down, especially by the political elite but also by feminists including radical feminists. As Fiona de Londras writes when reflecting on the white-led campaign's willingness to shelve its own intersectional lens, 'there was an uncomfortable tension between what we believed in and what we thought we needed to do or say to win the referendum. The apprehension of a loss was weighty and sometimes overbearing; in truth many of us did, wrote and said what we thought would work to secure a 50.1 per cent vote for "yes".'[7] This willingness to leave our own political analysis outside the door, de Londras argues, was undoubtedly influenced by previous feminist defeats and the fear that this might happen again.

Feminist theory is essential to rethinking feminism and to reclaiming identity politics as it was originally outlined by the Combahee River Collective, who described their oppression amidst three overlapping realms – society at large, the civil rights movement and white liberal feminism. Their statement, and indeed their wider Marxist-influenced activism, sought liberation for themselves only as part of the struggle for equality for everyone. They determined that their own unique form of oppression 'embodied in the concept of identity politics' was 'the

7. Doing Feminism 159

most profound and potentially most radical politics to come directly out of our own identity, as opposed to working to end somebody else's oppression.'[8] As Sara Salem notes, the Combahee River Collective and the wider radical black feminist movement they were part of pinpointed the central role of race and racism in capitalist development and explained *why* intersections happen by analysing the root causes of historical and materialist exploitation.[9] These feminists did not see being black as secondary to class but as intersecting with it where neither is inevitable and where neither should be talked about in isolation. Olúfẹ́mi Táíwò agrees with Salem in emphasizing that readings of the Combahee River Collective statement are best understood in the context of the parallel neoliberal hegemonic expansion outlined in Chapter 1 making it the obvious target for its 'elite capture'.[10]

One manifestation of elite capture that Táíwò focuses on is the practice of centring stories of oppression where the very people who are most impacted by a particular oppression, are encouraged to repeatedly share their personal narratives, often very publicly and mostly without being paid for their time. This is because they are seen as the only voices that carry authenticity. This member of the People before Profit feminist caucus, who preferred to stay anonymous, sums up the problem perfectly:

> You aren't allowed have an opinion, or even to organise things unless you 'out yourself' as being directly affected by the issue and this is often used to shut down political debate. For example, if someone says, as an abuse survivor 'I think x-y-z' on a topic, you can't challenge this unless you are also starting the conversation as a survivor of abuse because you will get piled on for attacking an abuse survivor otherwise.

Listening to, learning from and indeed centring the knowledge and experiences of those at the receiving end of oppression has always been a guiding principle of feminism and can be an effective tool in bringing about positive change. Bringing our own experiences to the fore is a crucial aspect of consciousness raising education which seeks to unpack and validate our personal struggles as symptomatic of broader societal issues. This is the basis from which we build solidarity and collectively challenge the status quo. However, the practice today is often the exact opposite and one which Táíwò describes as 'passing the mic' where sharing personal struggles has become an end in itself without any attempt to mix this with an anti-capitalist analysis. Passing the mic also feeds into what Emma Dabiri identifies as a pattern where some white activists are preoccupied with creating platforms for people of colour to share their experience of racism in a way that mostly serves to centre white supremacy all over again.[11] Instead of being an act of liberation, Táíwò explains the result as a discourse of 'attentional injustice' that effectively takes the focus off the real controllers of the narrative, namely the corporations and algorithms that ensure international conversations deflect our attention from 'the root political issues that explain why everything is so fucked up'.[12]

Doing anti-capitalist feminism

The alternative, Táíwò argues, is 'constructive politics' which doesn't exclude or silence people, but ensures our focus is on creating alternative systems and structures and not just including marginalized voices in an otherwise-largely unchanged world. There is no straightforward set of practices that I can prescribe for achieving this, and it can be hard to keep going when we might not see the benefits of our actions. Many recent global feminist movements have fallen short in their ambitions. These include the Ni Una Menos (Not One Woman Less) movement against femicide and machismo in Latin America, the anti-corporatist 'women's strike' movement which sought international alliance in emphasizing paid and unpaid work and for women's rights more broadly,[13] Iranian protests against hijab rules from 2017 onwards and protests in Poland against abortion restrictions. In Afghanistan, bans on education, employment and even being seen in public continue to escalate despite the best efforts of the Revolutionary Association of the Women of Afghanistan (RAWA, est. 1977) and other underground feminist groups. Similarly, the ecofeminist centring of environmental justice proposed by Françoise d'Eaubonne in *Le Féminisme ou la Mort* (which translates as Feminism or Death) has only brought limited reforms as is true for the wider environmental movement. As these and other social movements fail to grow as rapidly as we think they should, the far right is managing to fill the void as people struggle in the face of the consequences of capitalism.

It is easy to feel hopelessness given these setbacks, especially in the face of deep and perpetual injustices. But the lives of many women are profoundly different from just one generation ago because of the actions of feminists. In some respects, our biggest challenge is to cultivate hope. As the Brazilian educationalist and philosopher Paulo Freire writes,

'[H]opelessness paralyzes us, immobilizes us. We succumb to fatalism, and then it becomes impossible to muster the strength we absolutely need for a fierce struggle that will re-create the world.'[14] But hope alone cannot change the world indeed, to believe so, Freire argues, is a sign of the very naivety that embeds hopelessness even further. The task he sets us is to create the conditions of hope and to do this through struggle. bell hooks, whose writings were influenced by Freire, also determined that 'hope emerges from those places of struggle where I witness individuals positively transforming their lives and the world around them'.[15]

Sometimes it can be difficult to know where to start, especially if there is no obvious political organization to join. But if you are reading this book, you probably agree that something must be done to at least try to make the world a better place for everyone. One start may be to take the lead from the feminist writer and independent scholar Sara Ahmed whose concept of the *feminist killjoy* describes how even seemingly small acts of disruption can become a political tool that cuts through the social norms that perpetuate inequality. Some acts of defiance can go unnoticed, as captured by this abortion rights campaigner who believes 'individuals can engage in feminist activism outside organisations, groups and networks, like teaching our children to question and critique patriarchal power structures, pushing back against sexism in the workplace and calling out friends on misogynistic jokes and behaviour'. Other times, individual acts can touch many lives and have a lasting impact. When the global Me Too movement resulted in the exposure of some high-profile perpetrators of misconduct, this included Michael Colgan, the former director of the Gate Theatre. His systemic sexual harassment and bullying were open secrets in some circles of the art world but weren't negatively impacting his career. When Grace Dyas wrote a blog about her own experiences with Colgan, it went viral across the internet. Dyas had first attempted to effect change through more formal channels. 'I went to people who were in positions of potential power,' she told me, 'And they told me not to do anything about it and that if I did, that he would ruin my life and I just felt, hang on a minute, that is mad.' So, she took it upon herself to share her unpleasant encounters with Colgan with as wide an audience as possible. Her blog, which was read by thousands of people, included the expression 'I believe you before you open your mouth', which she borrowed from the campaigner and survivor of Ireland's industrial school complex Christine Buckley (1947–2014). With this mantra as a guide, Dyas invited readers to send her direct messages sharing their own stories. Six-hundred people took up this invitation in an outpouring of expression that, Dyas tells me, has helped shape the direction of her artistry. Colgan had already retired at the time of the blog posts. However, in its aftermath the Gate Theatre commissioned an independent review by workplace relations expert Gaye Cunningham, regarding allegations of inappropriate behaviour and abuse of power. The review concluded that 'credible and consistent testimonies' about Colgan's behaviour indicated he had 'a case to answer' about his behaviour, and an apology to victims was issued by the theatre.[16] Most impactfully the review led to the establishment of government-funded 'safe to create' dignity at work programme for the arts.

Individual actions can also have a global impact. In July 2024, Benjamin Netanyahu, the Prime Minister of Israel, addressed a joint session of the US Congress amidst a military incursion into Palestine that the International Court of Justice ruled as a violation of international law by an apartheid state and that there was a plausible case to be made that Israel was committing genocide. In response to Netanyahu's presence, Rashida Tlaib, the Michigan representative for the US Democratic Party took her seat in Congress wearing a keffiyeh and holding up a sign that read 'war criminal' on one side and 'guilty of genocide' on the other. Her actions didn't prevent the US government from continuing to arm Israel; within weeks, the United States approved a further $20bn in weapons transfers, despite international condemnation of Israel's routine violations of international law in Gaza and the occupied West Bank. But what if Tlaib's audience isn't her colleagues in government? What if her audience is us, the wider public who are increasingly backing the BDS movement, a non-violent Palestinian-led initiative that promotes boycotts, divestments and economic sanctions against Israel. Recent milestones by the BDS movement include forcing the world's largest private security company Allied Universal to sell its business interests in Israel and pressuring the insurance giant AXA to divest from Israeli banks. As Chapter 3 detailed, lessons can be taken from how a simple action by Irish trade unionists kickstarted Ireland's engagement with similar boycott appeals against the historical apartheid regime in South Africa.

Other feminist killjoy actions that Sara Ahmed encourages include a willingness to constantly question the way things are, even when you are repeatedly dismissed, asserting people's right to occupy spaces they are typically excluded from, calling out carceral policies that manage the complainant and not the complaint, and, for feminists who are white, not asserting a dominant presence in feminist spaces that positions their ethnicity as most powerful.[17] But, as Ahmed concludes, 'we are louder when we are heard together' and collectivizing our actions is essential. There are ways we can do this. If we are trade unionists, we can push for consciousness-raising by initiating discussions that highlight connections between workplace struggles and social justice issues more broadly thereby forcing our unions to adopt a more politicized approach, if we are not trade unionists, we can become one. We should also be inspired by the work of ROSA (est. 2013), a political collective that has consistently featured throughout this book, which always challenges mainstream feminist discourse and calls out those who claim to be on the left but whose actions reveal something different. I heard from Eva (a pseudonym) who joined ROSA in 2018 when she was canvassing during the abortion referendum and 'was looking for a group to join that sought to understand the world but also to change it'. She explains how they work as follows:

> In ROSA we have discussions centred around topical issues through a socialist feminist lens. These might include gender-based violence, trans rights, abortion rights, racism, the housing crisis, art, COVID, etc. We use these discussions to try to analyse and understand the world we are living in, but also to come up with the best strategy to enact change and get more people actively involved in left wing feminist politics.

ROSA was central to building Ireland's repeal movement, has always supported and sometimes led trans-affirming activism and was a key organizer in the resistance to 'the horrendous handover of the National Maternity Hospital to the Sisters of Charity' (Eva's words, see Chapter 5). They have organized community-based demonstrations in support of migrants and against gender-based violence. Their actions recognize how local and personal issues intersect with global systems of patriarchal power. For example, ROSA have organized protests in solidarity with the French woman Giséle Pelicot, who, in 2024, bravely waived her own anonymity so that the more than fifty men who abused her over decades whilst she was unconscious would be publicly named. Her rejection of legal protections supposedly in place to protect survivors has rightly shifted the locus of shame away from herself and onto the shoulders of her rapists. As was Pelicot's intention, ROSA have linked her case to all survivors of gender-based violence highlighting systemic failures in criminal justice solutions in preventing shame. But ROSA doesn't view any issue in isolation, but as part of a wider movement for change.

'Even when there is not an obvious struggle or movement happening in society, ROSA always aims to agitate and continue the fight for all oppressed and exploited,' Eva explains.

Other examples of collective actions that move beyond single-issue activism and towards a collective effort against the structures and symptoms of capitalism include pushbacks against the far right as happened when, in 2023, the Carlow Women's Refuge Campaign (est. 2017) responded to anti-migrant protests outside a local building earmarked to accommodate International Protection applicants by launching a flier that condemned the protests and rejected the trope of the 'unvetted male' as having anything to do with women's safety. Or when Dublin-based Google workers moved beyond borders and joined thousands worldwide in staging a walkout against sexual harassment in the workplace.

A recurrent theme that emerged when writing this book was the extent to which anti-capitalist feminism should engage with non-profit state-funded feminist groups, if at all. Many radical writers are sceptical about collaboration with any state structures. Sara Jaffe, Angela Davis and, perhaps most famously, Audre Lorde have argued against any reliance on existing structures in our quest for liberation. Lorde sees radical feminism as 'learning how to stand alone, unpopular and sometimes reviled, and how to make common cause with those other identified as outside the structures in order to define and seek a world in which we can still flourish'. She continues, '*For the master's tools will never dismantle the masters house.* They may allow us temporarily to beat him at his own game, but they will never enable us to bring about genuine change. And this fact is only threatening to those women who still define the masters house as their only source of support.'[18] Some of the activists I spoke to believe that grassroots anti-capitalist feminists should resist the allure of state funding as this inevitably leads to the sort of co-option experienced by the anti-violence movement as discussed in Chapter 5. Others called on state-funded organizations to be more vocal. One community worker argues:

> I understand the dilemma of 'if we speak out, we won't get our funding; we won't be able to do these other things over here.' But organisations need to be calling out government, and they need to be calling out female politicians who are allowing people to feel like their funding is being threatened.

Mostly, the people that I spoke to backed continued engagement with state-funded feminist organizations, many of which provide vital services, and where employees often hold more radical perspectives than their employers.[19] These are the people who work tirelessly, sometimes precariously and on average salaries, as they mop up the symptoms of structural inequality. Many of these organizations are members of the NWCI which, more recently have provided access to resources and public platforms that have helped amplify causes that historically, they were less likely to pay any attention to; indeed they have repeatedly shown solidarity with anti-capitalist feminist activism in recent years. We cannot ignore how difficult it can be to hold an anti-capitalist political analysis in these spaces when doing so antagonizes the neoliberal politicians who hold the purse-strings. Engaging with state-funded organizations like the NWCI doesn't mean abandoning the belief that change comes from below, it means being open to a united front and ensuring our anti-capitalist spaces do not become insular and exclusionary where would-be radicals share solidarity and support in their own echo chamber.

What we must do is maintain theoretical clarity when entering spaces that we know will never realize fundamental change as modelled by revolutionary-left politicians from People before Profit Solidarity and other independent anti-capitalist politicians when participating in cross-party parliamentary committees including those on health, climate change, employment affairs and social protection, transport and justice and equality. They give these and other similar spaces their time only when being there might minimize harm and call out their undemocratic nature. They never allow this engagement to distract them from the need to build a mass collaborative movement amidst civil society campaigns for change when there is a sufficient ideological match.

Building a united front

Successfully building this united front means uniting our struggle with non-governmental organizations, environmentalists, trade unionists, disability activists, trans activists, the revolutionary-left and all social actors who have had enough of the stark inequalities that capitalism breeds and are united in the belief that another world is possible. Our fight is for a society where resources are shared, where the market is based on need and not greed, and where there is a universal basic income along with universal basic services. Spaces for strategizing can and should include actors from within not-for-profit state-funded groups, but the requirement is that they act in solidarity, something

Lola Olufemi describes as about 'working across difference, standing together in the face of shared oppression, and standing alongside those with whom you do not share a common experience of the world'.[20]

A strong educational component is essential. According to bell hooks, our feminism must incorporate theory not as 'an oppressive hierarchy' but in a way that is accessible, democratic and resistant to the 'false assumption that theory is not a social practice'.[21] She writes:

> Within revolutionary feminist movements, within revolutionary black liberation struggles, we must continuously claim theory as necessary practice within a holistic framework of liberatory activism. We must do more than call attention to ways theory is misused. We must do more than critique the conservative and at times reactionary use some academic women make of feminist theory. We must actively work to call attention to the importance of creating theory that can advance renewed feminist movements, particularly highlighting that theory which seeks to further feminist opposition to sexism and sexist oppression.[22]

Our political education should nurture leadership, model dynamic consciousness-raising, learn from the past and draw tactics from others. Praxis is its core, a cyclical process of reflection and action that is directed at the structures we seek to transform. Political education must be truly dialogic and democratic. There are examples of radical feminist education in Ireland. In the last quarter of 2024 alone these include a day-school on Gender Oppression and Liberation hosted by Rebel News and the Socialist Workers Network, a Solidarity and Struggle event by community-based feminists with university activists and a Feminist Climate Justice event organized as part of the NWCI backed Feminist Communities for Justice Campaign. Across these and similar events, we must recognize and address problematic power-dynamics in our own feminist circles which are dominated by white-Western ways of being and which rarely encourage seasoned practitioners to confront their own knowledge limitations or let go of their own sense of authority. This, bell hooks reminds us, can be alienating for newer, younger activists who can feel embarrassed to contribute for fear of getting things wrong.[23] This might seem like a minor point, but it is essential if we are to sustain movements of resistance and avoid high levels of attrition especially when we know just how crippling activist burnout can be.

The real feminists are not the ones in the centre-left who have failed to construct a counter-hegemony to neoliberal capitalism and have provided a vacuum for far-right ideas to ferment. And they are not the ones who are joining single-issue campaigns that claim to be neutral, but actually function as instruments that further uphold the logic of the status quo. They are the ones who critically engage with reality and seek transformational change as part of a global movement. It might feel like a different fight from what was the case in the twentieth century, but for many thousands of people in Ireland, many features remain the same including the very real dangers of gender-based violence, the absence of childcare, limits to reproductive healthcare and workplace inequality. Newer struggles include the extension of racism beyond Traveller experiences to include Ireland's growing ethnic minority population, the rise in right-wing populism and transphobia and the more acutely obvious struggle for climate justice.

Building a united front is easier said than done. But as the negative effects of capitalism like climate change, housing insecurity, precarious work and wealth concentration affect more and more people, being anti-capitalist isn't as radical an opinion as it once was. In some respects, it has become more common to encounter anti-capitalist activism outside of feminism where liberal frameworks continue to focus on reforming rather than dismantling capitalist structures. Rethinking feminism means bucking this trend by ensuring that our feminist struggles always focus on systemic inequalities and root causes. After all, what else can we do?

NOTES

Chapter 1

1 World Economic Forum, 2024.
2 Oxfam International, 2021.
3 Stapleton, Polakowski, & Quinn, 2022.
4 For detailed statistics on abortion worldwide see https://www.who.int/news-room/fact-sheets/detail/abortion. Accessed 5 June 2023.
5 Enright & Russell, 2020, p. 8.
6 Lawlor, 2005, p. 430.
7 There are divisions on the feminist left. Some Marxist feminists remain committed to a form of economic reductionism that sees other 'identities' as secondary to class and can be reluctant to incorporate radical intersectionality and the complexity of social relations in analysing and addressing social and economic oppression. Meanwhile anarchist feminism, which has a rich history in an Irish context both through the Workers Solidarity Movement (1984–2021) and Revolutionary Anarcha-Feminist Group (RAG, 2005–13), holds a different view to Marxism, especially on authority and hierarchy in political organizing.
8 Fitzsimons, 2021.
9 Olufemi, 2020, p. 13.
10 hooks, 1984, p. 41.
11 in Broder, 2022.
12 Farris, 2017, p. 4.
13 Butler, 1990, p. 33.
14 Rogers, 2016.
15 Allen, 2017, p. 21.
16 Marx & Engels, 1848/2018, pp. 13–4.
17 Sangari, 2020, p. 269.
18 Engels, 2001 [1884], p. 69.
19 Ibid, p. 89.
20 Engels, 2001 [1884], p. 65.
21 Ibid, p. 67.
22 Vogel, 2013, p. 94.
23 Holborow, 2024, p. 43.
24 Davis, 1981, p. 203.
25 Russell, Raffaele, McGinnity, & Privalko, 2019, p. xi.
26 Davis, 1981, p. 206.
27 Ferguson, 2020, p. 18.
28 Mitchell & Fazi, 2017.

29 Harvey, 2005, p. 22.
30 Taken from the Margaret Thatcher Foundation website: https://www.margaretthatcher.org/document/106689 dated 23 September 1987. Interview for Woman's Own ('No Such Thing as Society'). Retrieved 16 April 2023.
31 Harvey, 2005, p. 21.
32 Chancel, Piketty, Saez and Zucman, 2022.
33 Bale, 2023.
34 O'Brien, 2023.
35 https://www.unitetheunion.org/news-events/news/2023/april/tesco-accused-of-rampant-profiteering-as-obscene-profits-published/. Accessed 11 September 2023.
36 See corporate.primark.com/en-us/newsroom/corporate-news/a-summary-of-primarks-rana-plaza-response/n/4c985c3e-17af-4b87-abe8-9c64faf42eb5 for a full detail on their response.
37 Rottenberg, 2018, pp. 36–9.
38 hooks, 2000, p. ix.
39 Bryson, 2021, p. 50.
40 Sangari, 2020, p. 270.
41 Collins, 2005, p. 83.
42 Manne, 2017, p. 63.
43 Das, 2022.
44 Peterson, 2018.
45 Bohrer discusses the many tensions between both schools of thought and encourages us to draw from often under-discussed anti-capitalist women of colour histories that have always straddled the divide between two theories most notably the Combahee River Collective which included Angela Davis (Bohrer, 2018).
46 Sweeney & Lajoie, 2022, p. 2.
47 Ferguson, 2019, p. 61.
48 Hartnett, 2011, pp. 26–7.
49 Zakaria, 2021, p. 175.
50 Pavee Point, 2015.

Chapter 2

1 Casserly, 2018, p. 10.
2 Dooley, 2009.
3 McCabe, 2021, p. 7.
4 Dooley, 2009.
5 National Library of Ireland, 2022.
6 Connelly, 2015, p. 5.
7 Ryan, 2020, p. 18.

8 It was this version of suffrage that allowed the nationalist Constance Markievicz to run for office. When she was elected to Westminster in 1919 (before being elected to the Irish Parliament in 1923), she became the first female minister in Europe.
9 Maguire, 2018.
10 She used this expression during a television interview on the Late Late Show on 20 of January 2023 when appearing alongside Holly Cairns to talk about their experiences as politicians.
11 Moore, 2021.
12 For instance, when Bertie Ahern was leader of Fianna Fáil during the 1990s and 2000s, he hired a chief party fundraiser to organize the party's now infamous Galway Races event so that property developers could gain direct access to government ministers.
13 Marx & Engels, 1848/2018, p. 13.
14 Allen, 2016, pp. 112–13.
15 Kathleen Clarke, Linda Kearns, Constance Markievicz, Dorothy McArdle, Margaret Pearse and Hannah Sheehy-Skeffington (Naughton, 2016, p. 285).
16 Murray, 2024.
17 They are not mentioned in an extensive account of events in Cullen-Owen (2005, chapter 10).
18 Hill, 2003, p. 100.
19 Padbury, 2018.
20 If you supported the 1921 Anglo-Irish Treaty which partitioned Ireland into north and south you voted Fine Gael, if you didn't you voted Fianna Fáil.
21 Ferriter, 2004, p. 369.
22 Luddy, 2005, p. 192.
23 Lentin, 1998.
24 Cullen-Owens, 2005, p. 281.
25 Connolly, 2002, pp 8–10.
26 Internationalist connections included with Irish Friends of the Spanish Republican Committee, Irish Friends of Soviet Russia, The Women's International League and The League Against Imperialism. This extensive doctoral thesis uses a biographical analysis to track the feminist activism of Constance Markievicz, Eva Gore-Booth, Hanna Sheehy Skeffington, Rosamond Jacob, Patricia Lynch, Sighle Humphreys, Kathleen Lynn, Nora Connolly O'Brien, Charlotte Despard and Helena Molony (Kyte, 2018). This quote is from page 219.
27 Farrell, 2011, p. 49.
28 Ibid, p. 53.
29 Cullen-Owens, 2005, pp. 292–3.
30 De Haan, 2015.
31 Connolly, 2002, p. 94.
32 Sweetman, 2020, p. 146.
33 Stopper, 2006, p. 151.

Notes

34 The H-Block campaign was a protest movement against the ill-treatment of republican prisoners in the Maze Prison in Northern Ireland whose political prisoner status was revoked in 1976.
35 This comes from an article called 'Irish Women Uniting?' written by M. McAdams and published in the August edition of the Socialist Worker which is archived at this link: https://archive.org/details/The_Worker_Volume_1_No_30_July_August_1975/page/n1/mode/2up?view=theater. Accessed 14 August 2024.
36 Thank you to Irish Left Archive who provide a scanned copy of the 7th edition of *Banshee* at this link: https://www.leftarchive.ie/document/1894/. Accessed 22 July 2024.
37 Bastiat, 2011, p. 185.
38 Mac Donagh, 1975.
39 O'Keefe, 2017, p. 167.
40 Ibid, p. 176.
41 Debating with her party colleague Alice Glynn https://www.youtube.com/watch?v=t507IF7XrCY. Accessed 22 October 2023.
42 Dillon, 1993, pp. 73–4.
43 Harvey, 2016, pp. 7–8.
44 This interview was part of an earlier project on community work and is reproduced with the contributor's permission.
45 Fitzsimons, 2017, pp. 195–224.
46 Larraghy, 2014, p. 190.
47 Arlow, 2020, p. 121.
48 Smyth and Conroy shared this information during an interview by Ruth Wallsgrove which was published in *Off Our Backs, a Women's Newsjournal* (Smyth, Conroy, & Wallsgrove, 1989, p. 12).
49 No other country in the EU legally required and that all centrist mainstream political parties backed In 2008, the electorate rejected the Lisbon Treaty but instead of respecting this result, the government repeated the referendum with the express intention of getting the answer that was more compatible with the EU's neoliberal agenda.
50 They were Ruth Coppinger in Dublin West, Paul Murphy in Dublin South-West, Mick Barry in Cork North Central, Richard Boyd Barrett in Dún Laoghaire, Gino Kenny in Dublin Mid-West and Bríd Smith in Dublin South-Central.
51 Cronin, 2012, p. 31.
52 Siggins, 2016.
53 I witnessed this pattern first hand when I visited the count centre of the local and European elections of 2024 and observed how common it was for voters to place a left-wing candidate at the top of their ballot then choose a right-wing candidate as their second choice and vice versa.
54 Allen, 2024.
55 Jazayeri, 2015, p. 322.

Chapter 3

1. The event was recorded and is available to view at: https://www.youtube.com/watch?v=OXvG5ED6mmM&t=3557s. Accessed 14 August 2024.
2. These themes are discussed throughout *Dark Academia, How Universities die* (Fleming, 2021).
3. O'Keefe & Courtois, 2019.
4. Nugent, Pembrook, & Taft 2019, p. 3.
5. Ruggi, 2023, pp. 69–70.
6. James, 1973.
7. TASC, 2016, p. 1.
8. O'Connor, 2022.
9. https://emn.ie/migrants-in-the-labour-force-in-2022/. Sourced January 2024.
10. Lawrence, Kelly, McGinnity, & Curristan, 2023.
11. Joseph, 2019.
12. Curran, 2021.
13. The Irish Human Rights and Equality Commission, 2023.
14. Hiltzik, 2014.
15. https://www.irishexaminer.com/news/arid-30677292.html. Sourced January 2024.
16. Ahmed, 2021.
17. McAlevey defines a strike as 'a worker led action in which all the workers walk off the job, united, with purpose, and shutter the production and seriously hamper the employer's ability to get much of anything done, including to make money' (2020, pp. 18–19).
18. Tristan, 1843/1983, p. 83.
19. D'Arcy, 1994.
20. Their levels of involvement can be traced through Jones, 1988.
21. In 2014, Dublin's latest bridge across the River Liffey was named the Rosie Hackett Bridge. This is only the second of twenty-three bridges across the Liffey named after a woman and only came about because of a trade-union-led campaign. It is both a testament to her and a sad reflection of the esteem women are held in Irish history.
22. Jones, 1988, p. 11–13.
23. See chapter 2 Allen (1997).
24. Ferriter, 2004, p. 421; Hill, 2003, p. 79.
25. Hill, 2003, pp. 99–100.
26. Irish Countrywomen's Association. I have listed the reference in the bibliography without a date as this is not included in the publication.
27. Taken from oral histories gathered by Mary Muldowney and archived with Digital Repository Ireland.
28. Galligan, 1998, p. 70.
29. Jones, 1988, pp. 174–6.
30. Allen, 1997, pp. 88–94.

31 Russell, McGinnity, & O' Connell, 2017, p. 398.
32 Galligan, 1998, pp. 76–9.
33 Ayres, 2011, p. 89.
34 Daly, 1997, p. 227.
35 McCafferty, 2004, p. 295.
36 Levine, 1982, p. 230.
37 Allen, 1997, p. 147.
38 Galligan, 1998, p. 69.
39 Beale, 1986, p. 158.
40 Allen, 2000, pp. 59–60.
41 Larraghy (2014) dedicates chapter nine of his book *Asymmetric Engagement* to the experiences of the NWCI in social partnership negotiations, pp. 183–208.
42 Kane, 2023, pp. 32–3.
43 Geary & Belizon, 2021, p. 5.
44 Monaghan, 2020.
45 Holland, 2021.
46 The case had begun in 2016 when, after months working to unionize riders, the Independent Workers Union of Great Britain made a formal request to Deliveroo to recognize them for collective bargaining purposes in respect of riders in certain geographical areas of London.
47 European Federation for Agriculture and Tourism Trade Unions, 2020, p. 10.
48 Rogan, 2023.
49 Alberti, Holgate, & Turner, 2014, p. 117.
50 https://www.forsa.ie/snas-back-new-pay-scale-point-in-forsa-ballot/. Sourced 27 January 2024.
51 Geary & Belizon, 2021, p. 8.
52 Luxemborg, 2010, pp. 110–11.
53 McAlevey, 2020, p. 244.

Chapter 4

1 Gleeson & O'Rourke, 2021, p. 14.
2 Serano, 2016, p. 24.
3 Ibid, p. 15.
4 Fausto-Sterling, 2000, p. 31.
5 Malatino, 2019, p. 18.
6 O'Keefe, 2021.
7 In 1917–18, US-based Alan Hart became one of the first men to transition with medical support (Gill-Peterson, 2018, p. 60).
8 Chou, Kilmer, Campbell, DeGeorge, & Stranyx, 2023.
9 Neff, 2022.

10 Barbee, Hassan, & Liang, 2024, p. 125.
11 Allen, Watson, Egan, & Moser, 2019; and Kaltiala, Heino, Työläjärvi, & Suomalainen, 2020 are just two examples. A quick academic search will reveal many more.
12 Zazanis, 2021, p. 43.
13 Keogh, Carr, Doyle, Higgins, Morrissey, Sheaf, & Jowett, 2023.
14 Turban, Beckwith, Reisner, & Keuroghlian, 2020, p. E2.
15 Vernon, 2000, p. 38.
16 Serano, 2016, p. 120.
17 Smyth, 2010.
18 Egan, 2019.
19 Gender Recognition Advisory Group, 2011. The report is available at https://www.marriageequality.ie/download/pdf/gender_recognition_advisory_group_report.pdf. Sourced 20 March 2024.
20 One was by the TD Aengus O'Snodaigh of Sinn Féin and one by the independent Senator Katherine Zappone which was written with the support of trans activists in TENI.
21 McBride, Neary, & Gray, 2020, p. 4.
22 McNeil, Bailey, Ellis, & Regan, 2009, p. 8.
23 One example that did get some coverage was when, in March 2023, a woman in her forties was attacked by at least two men one of whom was wielding a crutch who pulled up beside her in a car whilst she was out walking, jumped out, then beat her around the head and body leaving her with several head lacerations and a fractured hand before fleeing the scene (English, 2023).
24 https://www.garda.ie/en/about-us/our-departments/office-of-corporate-communications/press-releases/2023/march/an-garda-siochana-2022-hate-crime-data-and-related-discriminatory-motives.html. Sourced 4 March 2024.
25 https://www.gov.uk/government/statistics/hate-crime-england-and-wales-2022-to-2023/hate-crime-england-and-wales-2022-to-2023. Sourced 4 March 2024.
26 ILGA Europe, 2023, p. 5.
27 Stryker, p. 153.
28 https://translegislation.com/
29 Carlisle, 2022.
30 Tebbutt, 2015, p. 724; Pieper, 2016, p. 1.
31 Pieper, 2016, p. 3.
32 Roy-Steier, 2021, p. 1.
33 Corrêa, 2017.
34 Taken from Judith Butler's excellent account of the role of the Vatican in their 2024 publication *Who's Afraid of Gender* (2024, p. 38).
35 Roy-Steier, 2021, p. 1.
36 Congregation for Catholic Education, 2019, p. 13.
37 Taken from the senior cycle available at this link: https://ncca.ie/media/6269/draft-sc-sphe-for-consultation.pdf. Accessed 17 June 2024.

38 Osborne & Nolan, 2023.
39 McCormack & Gleeson, 2014, pp. 398–402.
40 Raymond, 1994, p. 28.
41 Stryker, 2017, pp. 151–2.
42 Available at: https://meetinggroundonline.org/wp-content/uploads/2013/10/GENDER-Statement-InterActive-930.pdf. Accessed 24 March 2024.
43 Silva, Araújo, Santana, Moura, Ramalho, & Abreu, 2022.
44 De Beauvoir, 1949, p. 249.
45 De Beauvoir, 1949, p. xvi.
46 Butler, 2024, pp. 139–41.
47 Butler, 1990, p. 7.
48 Namaste, 2000, pp. 10–13.
49 Frazer, 1998, pp. 144–5; Arruzza, 2015, pp. 34–6.
50 Bettcher, 2014, pp. 387–8; Lee, 2021.
51 Butler, 2024, p. 165.
52 Shaw, 2023.
53 Donohue, 2018.
54 Full article available at this link: https://www.irishtimes.com/opinion/bill-to-ban-conversion-therapy-poses-problems-for-therapists-1.4642164.
55 This was at the Education and Training Board Ireland Annual conference, 2022.
56 Her address is available here: https://www.youtube.com/watch?v=M48-mL_OYc.
57 The NWCI have endured demonstrations outside events and online backlash when they signed a statement along with human rights and LGBTQIA+ groups that condemned the transphobia.
58 Dáil records for 18 April 2023. https://www.oireachtas.ie/en/debates/debate/dail/2023-04-18/5/#s6.
59 Gleeson and O'Rourke, 2021, p. 22.
60 Butler, 2024, pp. 263–4.

Chapter 5

1 Safe Ireland, 2019, p. 13.
2 Moore, 2024.
3 Full transcript from the Oireachtas committee meeting is available at https://www.oireachtas.ie/en/debates/debate/joint_committee_on_justice/2021-11-03/3/#spk_29. Sourced 5 June 2023.
4 https://commission.europa.eu/strategy-and-policy/policies/justice-and-fundamental-rights/gender-equality/gender-based-violence/what-gender-based-violence_en. Accessed 24 June 2024.
5 https://www.alwayshere.ie/. Accessed 4 June 2024.
6 See https://www.womensaid.ie/get-informed/facts/.

7   Bleakley, 2023.
8   Hearne, 2022, pp. 213–14.
9   https://www.iom.int/news/iom-chief-nearly-100-disappeared-or-dead-mediterranean-2024-underscoring-need-regular-pathways.
10 Eran, Boerma, Akseer, Langer, Malembaka, & Okiro, 2021.
11 UN Women, 2024.
12 Amnesty International, 2024, p. 20.
13 McCann, 2018, p. 50.
14 Pickering, 2002, p. 195.
15 Vergès, 2022, p. 4.
16 Diver, 2019, p. 179.
17 My decision to not capitalize 'black' is inspired by Emma Dabiri who, in *What White People Can do Next* (2021) makes the case for a small 'b' arguing that the opposite is a form of labelling that retains our actions within the constraints of racial hierarchies.
18 Dabiri, 2021, p. 35.
19 Jones, 1988, p. 176.
20 The Irish Women's Liberation Movement, 1970, p. 21.
21 Quote taken from Feminist Archives: https://feministarchives.isiswomen.org/publications/isis-international-bulletin/51-isis-international-bulletin/isis-international-bulletin-5-october-1977/675-international-solidarity
22 McKay, 2005, p. 16.
23 Ibid, p. 7.
24 Saidléar, 2015.
25 INCITE! Women of Colour Against Violence, 2018.
26 Loughran, 1986, p. 60.
27 Ibid, p. 65.
28 Walker, 2021.
29 This is from an archived interview in 2019 that is stored by the Irish Qualitative Data Archive open to academic researchers.
30 Galligan, 1998, p. 116.
31 Diver, 2019, p. 233.
32 United Nations Office of the High Commissioner, 2022.
33 Office of the Tánaiste, 1997.
34 Wilson, 2022, p. 50.
35 McKay, 2005, p. 221.
36 Davis, Dent, Meiners, & Richie, 2022, p. 103.
37 *First National Strategy on Domestic, Sexual and Gender-Based Violence* was from 2010 to 2014, the second from 2016 to 2021 and the third ongoing strategy from 2022 to 2026.
38 Group of Experts on Action against Violence against Women and Domestic Violence, 2023.
39 O'Brien, 2023, pp. 38–9.
40 Safe Ireland, 2014, p. 11.
41 Leahy, 2023, p. 5.

42 The full recording of her speech is available at https://www.ilovelimerick.ie/natasha-obrien-protest/. Sourced 24 June 2024.
43 Many of these images had been filmed without consent. Others were weaponized following consent for filming for private use. There was public outcry when people realized that this wasn't a criminal offence. Image-based sexual abuse was criminalized when the *Harassment, Harmful Communications and Related Offences Act* (2020), or 'Coco's Law', was passed. This name is to honour a young woman called Nicole 'Coco' Fox Fenlon who died by suicide after enduring years of severe online abuse. Her mother, Jackie Fox, campaigned tirelessly for legal reform to prevent a similar situation arising again.
44 Huber, 2023.
45 Olufemi, 2020, p. 111.
46 Blackstock, 2023.
47 In 2021, an internal investigation into the cancellation of thousands of 999 calls found that 3,000 of these related to domestic violence (Lally, 2021).
48 Ward, 2021.
49 Safe Ireland, 2014, pp. 38, 68, 90.
50 This topic is discussed in detail in *Police Wife: The Secret Epidemic of Police Domestic Violence* by Alex Roslin (2017).
51 Lally, 2021.
52 Garda Ombudsman, 2012.
53 Diversity Matters, 2024, pp. 20–6.
54 Joyce, O'Reilly, O'Brien, Joyce, Jennifer, & Haynes, 2017.
55 Ó Scannáil, 2019.
56 Press statement available at https://www.finegael.ie/west-can-still-take-action-to-help-refugees-and-defend-womens-rights-in-afghanistan-madigan/. Sourced 25 February 2023.
57 Zakaria, 2021, pp. 69–70.
58 Carroll-MacNeill, 2024.
59 Frazier, 2017, pp. 9–11.
60 Gruber, 2020, p. 198.
61 Rape Crisis Network Ireland, 2014.
62 Davis, Dent, Meiners, & Richie, 2022, p. 128.

Chapter 6

1 Government of Ireland, 2020, p. 7.
2 https://www.who.int/news/item/09-09-2020-every-woman-s-right-to-a-companion-of-choice-during-childbirth. Accessed 25 May 2024.
3 Tobin & Murphy Lawless, 2014.
4 Lyons, Clarke, Staines, & O'Keefe, 2008, pp. 264–9.

5   This extensive study uncovered the experiences of over 100 self-selecting Muslim women of minoritized ethnicities (Fitzsimons, Hassan, Nwanze, & Obasi, 2021).
6   CDE Ireland, 2019, p. 3.
7   O'Hare, Manning, Corcoran, and Greene, 2023, p. 17.
8   McGinnity, Privalko, Russell, Curristan, Stapleton, & Laurence, 2022.
9   Kennedy, 2022, p. 4.
10 Centre for Reproductive Rights, 2021.
11 Arguing against abortion ignores the fact that for centuries, ending a pregnancy before 'the quickening' (i.e. when foetal movement is felt) wasn't controversial and how there is unproblematic references to abortion in most religious texts (Kissling, 2018, pp. 1–2). The Catholic Church, the largest anti-abortion movement in the world today, didn't take a firm stance until 1869 when they declared all abortion murder (Hovey, 1985, p. 18), a standard position that remains to this day. The only historic concerns ever raised related to the particular dangers of late-abortions (Riddle, 1992, pp. 4–7) or the poisonous nature of certain remedies (Potts & Campbell, 2009). The first laws were mostly to protect women from unscrupulous vendors who peddled unsafe medicines and not because of moral concerns (Kissling, 2018, p. 2).
12 Ní Aodha, 2016.
13 McCord, 2013.
14 Delay, 2019.
15 Kelly, 2023, pp. 225–6.
16 Ibid, p. 227.
17 Levine, 1982, p. 139.
18 Kelly, 2023, p. 244.
19 Kennedy, 2022, p. 7.
20 Horgan held this role until six months before the vote then handed the reins to another left-wing activist Eddie Conlon.
21 Levine, 1982, p. 74.
22 There was also a referendum in 2002 which sought to remove the threat of suicide and introduce penalties for illegal abortion, it was defeated by 50.4 per cent, with a turnout of just 43 per cent.
23 In McIntosh (2023) from research carried out by the group Pregnant and Screwed.
24 The commission was chaired by a Justice Mella Carroll (a Judge) and included Francis Fitzgerald and Carmel Foley from the Women's Council, Catherine Byrne from the Irish Congress of Trade Unions as well as other trade unionists, women from business and others (Houses of the Oireachtas, 1990).
25 Horgan, 2001, p. 106.
26 Coakley & Healy, 2007, p. 6.
27 Coalition Against the Deportation of Irish Children, 2008, p. 3.
28 The full transcript of the interview is available at https://repository.dri.ie/catalog/zs269j39x#dri_download_modal_id. Accessed 15 August 2024.

29 Breen, Haynes, & Devereux, 2006, pp. 5–6.
30 Fitzsimons, 2021, p. 157.
31 Flynn, Dagg, Ní Fhlatharta, & Burns, 2023, p. 5.
32 https://www.imo.ie/news-media/news-press-releases/2021/imo-hugely-concerning-rec/index.xml. Accessed 25 May 2024.
33 Alcorn, O'Donovan, Patrick, Creedy, & Devilly, 2010, p. 1849.
34 Chadwick, 2017, pp. 497–501; AIMS, 2014.
35 UN, 2019, pp. 5–6.
36 The All-Party Parliamentary Group on Birth Trauma, 2024.
37 Fitzsimons, Hassan, Nwanze, & Obasi, 2021, pp.77–8.
38 Zakaria, 2022, pp. 138–40.
39 Both Professor of law at UCC Deirdre Madden and a board member of the HSE (along with Dr Sarah McLoughlin, patient advocate) dissented to the board's approval stating they 'continued to have concerns regarding legal ownership of the site and building, and the governance and control' (https://www.irishtimes.com/news/politics/proposals-to-ensure-independence-of-national-maternity-hospital-approved-1.4860785). Solicitor Simon McGarr (2022) raises a number of issues about missing documents, and a rent agreement where the €10 a month deal repeatedly touted as 'as good as state ownership' is not what is defined in the lease rather is conditional on the new NHM adhering to certain conditions set out by St Vincent's Holdings including a condition surrounding 'clinical appropriateness'.
40 Mincer, 2016.
41 Moore, 2022.
42 The investigative journalist Aoife Moore has published several examples of this including repeated spot-checks from sometimes intimidatory social welfare officers whose principal concern is to weed out romantic partners. In one of the stories Moore exposes, one officer produced a social media post that had been deleted some time ago as proof that her relationship status wasn't single. See, for example, Moore, 2021.
43 Pavee Point Traveller and Roma Centre & Department of Justice and Equality, 2018, pp. 63–4.
44 Pavee Point Travellers Centre, 2012, pp. 17–8.
45 www.iprt.ie/site/assets/files/6332/iprt_position_paper_on_women_in_the_criminal_justice_system.pdf/ Accessed 24 March 2021.
46 Gilligan, 2019, p. 229.
47 Fitzsimons, 2022, p. 153.
48 Cited in Mahdawi, 2022.

Chapter 7

1 hooks, 1984, p. 24.
2 hooks, 1984, p. viii.

3 Buckley & Keenan, 2021, p. 6.
4 Salem, 2018, p. 406.
5 Weeks & Allen, 2023, p. 935.
6 Lima, Reeves, Billari, McKee, & Stuckler, 2016, pp. 518–19.
7 de Londras, 2020, p. 136.
8 The Combahee River Collective, 2017, p. 19.
9 Salem, 2018, p. 410.
10 Táíwò, 2022, p. 23.
11 Dabiri, 2021, p. 108.
12 Táíwò, 2022, p. 72.
13 Arruzza, 2017, p. 194.
14 Freire, 1992, p. 2.
15 hooks, 2003, p. xiv.
16 https://www.gatetheatre.ie/the-board-of-the-gate-theatre-issues-apology/. Accessed 21 September 2024.
17 Ahmed explores these ideas feminist killjoy activism across several books and publications including *Living a Feminist Life* (2017) and summarizes this theory in the 2023 publication *The Feminist Killjoy*.
18 Lorde, 1983, p. 99.
19 Fitzsimons, 2017, p. 61.
20 Olufemi, 2020, p. 100.
21 hooks 1994, pp. 65–6.
22 hooks, 1994, pp. 69–70.
23 hooks, 2003, p. 200.

BIBLIOGRAPHY

Ahmed, S. (2021). *Complaint!* London: Duke University Press.
Ahmed, S. (2023). *The Feminist Killjoy Handbook*. UK: Allen Lane an imprint of Penguin Books.
Alberti, G., Holgate, J., & Turner, L. (2014). Opportunities and Choice for Unions Organising Migrant Workers: A Comparison across Unions and Countries. In L. Adler, M. Tapia, & L. Turner (eds.), *Mobilising against Inequality: Unions, Immigrant Workers and the Crisis of Capitalism* (pp. 109–30). New York: Cornell University Press.
Alcorn, K. L., O'Donovan, A., Patrick, J. C., Creedy, D., & Devilly, G. J. (2010). A prospective longitudinal study of the prevalence of post-traumatic stress disorder resulting from childbirth events. *Psychological Medicine*, 40(11), 1849–59.
Allen, K. (1997). *Fianna Fáil and Irish Labour 1926 to the Present*. London: Pluto Press.
Allen, K. (2000). *The Celtic Tiger: The Myth of Social Partnership*. Manchester and New York: Manchester University Press.
Allen, K. (2016). *1916 Ireland's Revolutionary Tradition*. London: Pluto Press.
Allen, K. (2017). *Marx and the Alternative to Capitalism*. London: Pluto Press.
Allen, K. (2024). Local and EU elections: We can wipe the smile from their faces. *Rebel*. Retrieved 15 August 2024, from https://www.rebelnews.ie/2024/06/10/local-and-eu-elections-we-can-wipe-the-smile-from-their-faces/.
Allen, L. R., Watson, L. B., Egan, A. M., & Moser, C. N. (2019). Well-being and suicidality among transgender youth after gender-affirming hormones. *Clinical Practice in Pediatric Psychology*, 7(3), 302–11.
Amnesty International (2024). '*You feel like you are subhuman*' *Israel's Genocide again Palestinians in Gaza*. London: Amnesty International.
Arlow, J. (2020). Antifa without fascism: The reasons behind the anti-fascist movement in Ireland. *Irish Political Studies*, 35(1), 115–37.
Arruzza, C. (2015). Gender as social temporality: Butler (and Marx). *Historical Materialism*, 23(1), 28–52.
Arruzza, C. (2017). From Social Reproduction Labour to the Women's Strike. In T. Bhattacharya (ed.), *Social Reproduction Theory* (pp. 192–6). London: Pluto Press.
Arruzza, C., Bhattacharya, T., & Fraser, N. (2019). *Feminism for the 99%*. New York: Verso Books.
Atuhairwe, S., Gemzell-Danielsson, K., Byamugisha, J., Kaharuza, F., Mbona Tumwesigye, N., & Hanson, C. (2021). Abortion related near-miss morbidity and mortality in 43 health facilities with differences in readiness to provide abortion care in Uganda. *BMJ Global Health*, 6(2), 1–12. doi:10.1136/bmjgh-2020-003274.

Ayres, M. (2011). Equal pay for women: Words not deeds? *Saothar*, *36* (Women: Special Issue), 89–96.

Bale, C. (2023). *Ireland's Two Richest People Have More Wealth – €15 Billion – than Half of the Irish Population Who Have €10.3 Billion*. Retrieved 25 January 2023, from Oxfam Ireland: https://www.oxfamireland.org/blog/press-releases.

Barbee, H., Hassan, B., & Liang, F. (2024). Postoperative regret among transgender and gender-diverse recipients of gender-affirming surgery. *JAMA Surgery*, *159*(2), 125–6. doi:10.1001/jamasurg.2023.6052.

Bastiat, B. (2011). Banshee, an Irish feminist newspaper: (March 1976–October 1978): Style and themes*. *ABEI Journal: The Brazilian Journal of Irish Studies*, *7*, 185–92. Retrieved from https://www.revistas.usp.br/abei/article/download/184273/170616.

Beale, J. (1986). *Women in Ireland*. London: MacMillan Education.

Bettcher, T. M. (2014). Trapped in the wrong theory: Rethinking trans oppression and resistance. *Signs*, *39*(2), 383–406.

Blackstock, B. C. (2023). *An Independent Review into the Standards of Behaviour and Internal Culture of the Metropolitan Police Service*. London: Metropolitan Police. Retrieved 4 May 2024, from https://www.met.police.uk/SysSiteAssets/media/downloads/met/about-us/baroness-casey-review/update-march-2023/baroness-casey-review-march-2023a.pdf.

Bleakley, P. (2023). 'Would your level of disgust change?' Accounting for variant reactions to fatal violence against women on social media. *Criminology & Criminal Justice*, *23*(5), 845–60.

Bohrer, A. (2018). Intersectionality and Marxism: A critical historiography. *Historical Materialism*, *26*(2), 46–74.

Breen, M., Haynes, A., & Devereux, E. (2006). Citizens, Loopholes and Maternity Tourists: Irish Print Media Coverage of the 2004 Citizenship Referendum. In M. Peillion, & M. Corcoran (eds.), (5th ed.), *Irish Sociological Chronicles* (pp. 59–70). Dublin: Institute of Public Administration.

Broder, D. (2022). Hillary Clinton is wrong: Electing a far-right woman is not a step forward for women. *Jabobin*. Retrieved 16 July 2023, from https://jacobin.com/2022/09/hillary-clinton-women-far-right-italy-giorgia-meloni-feminism.

Bryson, V. (2021). *The Futures of Feminism*. Manchester: Manchester University Press.

Buckley, F., & Keenan, L. (2021). *More Women – Changing the Face of Politics: Women's Experience of Running for Election in Ireland*. Dublin: Department of Housing, Local Government and Heritage.

Butler, J. (1990). *Gender Trouble*. New York: Routledge.

Butler, J. (2024). *Who's Afraid of Gender*. Great Britain: Allen Lane.

Cahill, A. (2014). UN: Irish abortion law treats women as 'vessels'. *The Irish Examiner*. Retrieved 28 June 2021, from https://www.irishexaminer.com/news/arid-20275578.html.

Cahill, H. (2001). Male appropriation and medicalization of childbirth: An historical analysis. *Journal of Advanced Nursing, 33*(3), 334–42.

Carlisle, M. (2022). Pediatricians who serve trans youth face increasing harassment. Lifesaving care could be on the line. *Time*. Retrieved 10 March 2024, from https://time.com/6146269/doctors-trans-youth-gender-affirming-care-harassment/.

Carr, J. (2016). *Experiences of Islamophobia: Living with Racism in the Neoliberal Era*. London: Routledge.

Carroll-MacNeill, J. (2024). We need to double defence spending to €3bn a year so we can defend ourselves. *The Irish Independent*. Retrieved 20 July 2024, from https://www.independent.ie/opinion/comment/jennifer-carroll-macneill-we-need-to-double-defence-spending-to-3bn-a-year-so-we-can-defend-ourselves/a654840820.html?registration=success®=true.

Casserly, M. (2018). Suffragette's City: a Walking Tour of the Suffrage Movement in Dublin City. In M. Casserly, & B. Kelly (eds.), *History on Your Doorstep: Six Stories of Dublin History* (pp. 9–19). Dublin: Dublin City Council.

CDE Ireland (2019). *Confidential Maternal Death Enquiry Ireland: Data Brief No. 4*. Cork: MDE Ireland. Retrieved 26 November 2020, from https://www.ucc.ie/en/media/research/nationalperinatalepidemiologycentre/MDEDataBriefNo4December2019.pdf.

Chadwick, R. (2017). Ambiguous subjects: Obstetric violence, assemblage and South African birth narratives. *Feminism and Psychology, 27*(4), 489–509.

Chancel, L., Piketty, T., Saez, E., Zucman, G. (2022). *World Inequality Report 2022*. World Inequality Lab. Retrieved from wir2022.wid.world.

Chapple, T. (2020). Transphobic hate crime reports have quadrupled over the past five years in the UK. *BBC*. Retrieved 15 April 2022, from https://www.bbc.com/news/av/uk-54486122.

Chou, J., Kilmer, H. L., Campbell, C., DeGeorge, B. R., & Stranyx, Y. J. (2023). Gender-affirming surgery improves mental health outcomes and decreases anti-depressant use in patients with gender dysphoria. *PRS Global Open: International Open Access Journal of American Society of Plastic Surgeons, 11(6 Suppl)*, p. 1. doi:10.1097/01.GOX.0000944280.62632.8c.

Coakley, L., & Healy, C. (2007). *Looking Forward, Looking Back: Experiences of Irish Citizen Child Families*. Dublin: Integrating Ireland, Commissioned by the CADIC Coalition.

Coalition Against the Deportation of Irish Children (2008). *Evaluation of CADIC Achievements 2006–2007. Final Report*. Dublin: CADIC.

Collins, R. W. (2005). *Masculinities*. Cambridge: Polity Press.

Congregation for Catholic Education (2019). *'Male And Female, He Created Them' towards a Path of Dialogue on the Question of Gender Theory in Education*. Vatican City: Vatican City. Retrieved 16 April 2022, from http://www.educatio.va/content/dam/cec/Documenti/19_0997_INGLESE.pdf.

Connelly, K. (2015). Sylvia Pankhurst, the First World War and the struggle for democracy. *Revue Française de Civilisation Britannique, XX-1*, 1–13. doi:10.4000/rfcb.275.

Connolly, L. (2002). *The Irish Women's Movement: From Revolution to Devolution*. London: Palgrave MacMillan.

Connolly, L. (2020). *The Story of Ireland's First Commission on the Status of Women*. Retrieved 2 November 2022, from RTE.ie Brainstorm: https://www.rte.ie/brainstorm/2020/1201/1181579-first-commission-on-the-status-of-women-ireland-1970/.

Connolly, L. (2020). Towards a Further Understanding of the Sexual and Gender-Based Violence Women Experienced in the Irish Revolution. In L. Connolly (ed.), *Women and the Irish Revolution* (pp. 103–28). Kildare: Irish Academic Press.

Connolly, L., & O'Toole, T. (2005). *Documenting Irish Feminisms: The Second Wave*. Dublin: The Woodfield Press.

Corrêa, S. (2017). Gender ideology: Tracking its origins and meanings in current gender politics. Retrieved 9 April 2022, from https://blogs.lse.ac.uk/gender/2017/12/11/gender-ideology-tracking-its-origins-and-meanings-in-current-gender-politics/.

Cronin, D. (2012). Women and austerity. *Irish Marxist Review, 1*(1), 30–3.

CSO (2021). *Gender Balance in Business Survey*. Retrieved 2 December 2022, from Central Statistics Office: https://www.cso.ie/en/releasesandpublications/er/gbb/genderbalanceinbusinesssurvey2021/.

Cullen-Owens, R. (2005). *A Social History of Women in Ireland 1870–1970*. Dublin: Gill and Macmillan.

Curran, D. (2021). *Inside-out Hospitality: A Study of Working Conditions in the Hospitality Sector in Ireland*. NUI Galway. Retrieved 5 January 2023, from https://doi.org/10.13025/EVCK-0X89.

Dabiri, E. (2021). *What White People Can Do Next*. Dublin: Penguin.

Daly, M. (1997). *Women and Work in Ireland*. Dublin: Economic and Social History Society of Ireland.

D'Arcy, F. (1994). Irish trade unions before congress. 18th–19th century social perspectives, 1. *History Ireland, 2*(2), Summer 1994, 25–30. Retrieved 25 January 2025, from https://historyireland.com/irish-trade-unions-before-congress-by-fergus-darcy/.

Das, S. (2022). Inside the violent, misogynistic world of TikTok's new star, Andrew Tate. *The Guardian*. Retrieved 12 November 2022, from https://amp.theguardian.com/technology/2022/aug/06/andrew-tate-violent-misogynistic-world-of-tiktok-new-star.

Davidson, M. (2022). *Transgender Legal Battles: A Timeline*. Retrieved 9 March 2024, from Politics and History, Jstor Daily: https://daily.jstor.org/transgender-legal-battles-a-timeline/.

Davis, A. (1981). *Women, Race & Class*. New York: Vintage Books.

Davis, A. Y., Dent, G., Meiners, E. R., & Richie, B. E. (2022). *Abolition. Feminism. Now.* UK: Hamish Hamilton, an imprint of Penguin Books.

De Beauvoir, S. (1949). *The Second Sex*. New York: Bantom books.

De Haan, J. (2015). McQuaid's 'old granny'. *Twentieth Century Social Perspectives, 23*(1). Retrieved 12 August 2023, from https://www.historyireland.com/mcquaids-old-granny/.

Delay, C. (2019). Pills, potions, and purgatives: Women and abortion methods in Ireland, 1900–1950. *Women's History Review, 28*(3), 479–99.

de Londras, F. (2020). Intersectionality, Repeal, and Reproductive Rights in Ireland. In S. Atrey, & P. Dunne (eds.), *Intersectionality and Human Rights Law* (pp. 125–45). Oxford: Harte Publishing, an imprint of Bloomsbury Publishing.

Department of Social Protection (2023). *Minister Humphreys and Minister Coveney Announce Lowest Levels of Unemployment in over 20 Years*. Retrieved February 2024, from Gov.ie: https://www.gov.ie/en/press-release/49ae5-minister-humphreys-and-minister-coveney-announce-lowest-levels-of-unemployment-in-over-20-years.

Devlin Trew, J., Bloomer, F., Pierson, C., MacNamara, N., & Mackle, D. (2017). *Abortion as a Workplace Issue: A Trade Union Survey North & South of Ireland*. Dublin: Unite the Union.

Dillon, M. (1993). *Debating Divorce: Moral Conflict in Ireland*. Kentucky, KY: University Press of Kentucky.

Diver, C. (2019). *Marital Violence in Post-Independence Ireland, 1922–96: A Living Tomb for Women*. Manchester: Manchester University Press.

Diversity Matters (2024). *Policing and Racial Discrimination in Ireland: A Community and Rights Perspective*. Dublin: Irish Council for Civil Liberties and Irish Network Against Racism.

Dole, N., Savitz, D. A., Siega-Riz, A. M., Hertz-Picciotto, I., McMahon, M. J., & Buekens, P. (2004). Psychosocial factors and preterm birth among African American and white women in Central North Carolina. *American Journal of Public Health, 94*(8), 1358–65.

Donohue, K. (2018). Ireland says no to TERFs. *Gay Community News*. Retrieved 23 March 2024, from https://gcn.ie/ireland-says-no-to-terfs/

Dooley, D. (2009). *Wheeler, Anna Doyle*. https://doi.org/10.3318/dib.008987.v1.

Egan, O. (2019). *Queer Republic of Cork: Cork LGBT History*. Retrieved 23 March 2024, from Cork LGBT Archive: https://corklgbtarchive.com/blog/.

Engels, F. (2001 [1884]). *The Origins of the Family, Private Property and the State*. London: The Electric Book.

English, E. (2023). Gardaí probe armed attack on transgender woman in Cork. *The Irish Examiner*. Retrieved 21 April 2023, from https://www.irishexaminer.com/news/munster/arid-41084185.html#:~:text=The%20victim%20was%20walking%20along,removed%20to%20hospital%20for%20treatment.

Enright, S., & Russell, H. (2020). *Gender Balance at Work, a Study of an Irish Civil Service Department*. Dublin: Economic and Social Research Institute. https://doi.org/10.26504/rs115.

Eran, B., Boerma, T., Akseer, N., Langer, A., Malembaka, E. B., & Okiro, E. A. (2021). The effects of armed conflict on the health of women and children. *The Lancet, 397*(10273), 522–32. doi:10.1016/S0140-6736(21)00131-8.

European Federation for Agriculture and Tourism Trade Unions. (2020). *Covid-19 Outbreaks in Slaughterhouses and Meat Processing Plants: State of Affairs and Demands for Action at EU Level*. EFFAT. Retrieved 21 January 2024, from https://effat.org/wp-content/uploads/2020/09/Covid-19-outbreaks-in-slaughterhouses-and-meat-processing-plants-State-of-affairs-and-demands-for-action-at-EU-level-7.09.2020.pdf.

European Union (2020). *Precarious Work from a Gender and Intersectionality Perspective, and Ways to Combat It*. Brussels: Policy Department for Citizens' Rights and Constitutional Affairs Directorate-General for Internal Policies: European Union. Retrieved 28 November 2022, from https://www.europarl.europa.eu/RegData/etudes/STUD/2020/662491/IPOL_STU(2020)662491_EN.pdf.

Farrell, A. (2011). 'Harassed housewives fight the consumer's battle': The formation of the Irish Housewives Association and the campaign for price control, clean food, and equitable distribution in the Ireland of 'the emergency'. *Saothar* (Women: Special Issue), *36*, 49–58.

Farris, S. (2017). *In the Name of Women's Rights: The Rise of Femonationalism*. Durham, NC: Duke University Press.

Fausto-Sterling, A. (2000). *Sex/Gender: Biology in a Social World*. New York: Routledge.

Fennell, N. (1974). *Irish Marriage: How Are You!* Cork: The Mercier Press.

Fennell, N. (2009). *Nuala Fennell: Political Woman. A Memoir*. Dublin: Curragh Press.

Ferguson, S. (2020). *Women and Work: Feminism, Labour, and Social Reproduction*. London: Pluto Press.

Ferriter, D. (2004). *The Transformation of Ireland 1900–2000*. London: Profile Books.

Fitzsimons, C. (2017). *Community Education and Neoliberalism: Philosophies, Practices and Policies in Ireland*. Zurich: Palgrave-Macmillan.

Fitzsimons, C. (2021). *Repealed, Ireland's Unfinished Fight for Reproductive Rights*. London: Pluto Press.

Fitzsimons, C. (2022). *Irish Healthcare Workers Experiences of Anti-Abortion Protesters and the Case for Safe Access Zones*. Maynooth University. Retrieved 2 January 2023, from https://mural.maynoothuniversity.ie/16215/.

Fitzsimons, C., & Kennedy, S. (2021). Ireland's Dark History of Injustices against Women. In C. Fitzsimons (ed.), *Repealed, Ireland's Ongoing Fight for Reproductive Rights* (pp. 45–64). London: Pluto Press.

Fitzsimons, C., & Nwanze, L. (2023). Can critical education help address racial discrimination in Irish maternity settings? *Journal of Critical Education Policy Studies, 20*(3), 215–42.

Fitzsimons, C., Hassan, B., Nwanze, L., & Obasi, P. (2021). *Researching the Experiences of Muslim Women in Irish Maternity Settings*. Dublin: Amal Women's Association and the Irish Human Rights and Equality Commission.

Fleming, P. (2021). *Dark Academia: How Universities Die*. London: Pluto Press.

Flynn, E., Dagg, J., Ní Fhlatharta, M., & Burns, E. Q. (2023). *Re(al) Productive Justice: Final Report*. Galway: University of Galway. https://doi.org/10.13025/70jg1s95.

Fraser, N. (2009). Feminism, capitalism and the cunning of history. *The New Left Review*, 56, Mar/Apr, 97–117.

Frazer, N. (1998). Heterosexism, misrecognition and capitalism: A response to Judith Butler. *New Left Review I/228*, 140–9.

Frazier, J. (2017). *Women's Antiwar Diplomacy during the Vietnam War Era*. Chapel Hill, NC: University of North Carolina Press.

Freire, P. (1992). *Pedagogy of Hope*. New York: Continuum

Gallagher, C., & Mackin, L. (2017). Seven women allege abuse and harassment by Michael Colgan. *The Irish Times*. Retrieved 29 December 2022, from https://www.irishtimes.com/news/ireland/irish-news/seven-women-allege-abuse-and-harassment-by-michael-colgan-1.3279488.

Gallagher, N. (2021). We need to recognise Irish participation in the British colonial story. *The Irish Times*. Retrieved 21 May 2023, from https://www.irishtimes.com/opinion/we-need-to-recognise-irish-participation-in-the-british-colonial-story-1.4498224.

Galligan, Y. (1998). *Women and Politics in Contemporary Ireland: From the Margins to the Mainstream*. London and Washington, DC: Pinter.

Garda Ombudsman (2012). *Report Pursuant to Section 103 of the Garda Síochána Act 2005 into Alleged Comments Made by Gardaí on 31 March 2011, Relating to Two Female Protesters Arrested at a 'Shell to Sea' Demonstration at or near Aughoos, Erris, co. Mayo*. Garda Ombudsman. Retrieved 25 January 2025, from https://www.gardaombudsman.ie/publications/investigation-reports/?download=file&file=631.

Geary, J., & Belizon, M. (2021). *Union Voice in Ireland: First Findings from the UCD Working in Ireland Survey*. Dublin: University College Dublin. Retrieved 13 May 2023, from https://www.smurfitschool.ie/t4media/7791%20NERI%20UCD%20Union%20Voice.pdf.

Gender Recognition Advisory Group (2011). *Report to Joan Burton, T.D., Minister for Social Protection*. Gender Recognition Advisory Group. Retrieved 10 March 2024, from https://www.marriagequality.ie/download/pdf/gender_recognition_advisory_group_report.pdf.

Gill-Peterson, J. (2018). *Histories of the Transgender Child*. Minneapolis, MN: University of Minnesota Press.

Gilligan, R. (2019). The family foster care system in Ireland – Advances and challenges. *Children and Youth Services Review*, 100(3): 221–8.

Gleeson, J. J., & O'Rourke, E. (2021). *Transgender Marxism*. London: Pluto Press.

Government of Ireland (1924). *Regulations by Minister of Finance under Section 9 of the Civil Service Regulation Act, 1924*. Retrieved 19 December 2022, from Electronic Irish Statute Book: https://www.irishstatutebook.ie/eli/1924/sro/950/made/en/print.

Government of Ireland (2020). *Mother and Baby Homes Commission Final Report*. Dublin: Government of Ireland. Retrieved 7 August 2023, from https://assets.gov.ie/118565/107bab7e-45aa-4124-95fd-1460893dbb43.pdf.

Government of Ireland (2020). *Report of the Advisory Group on the Provision of Support including Accommodation to Persons in the International Protection Process*. Dublin: Government of Ireland. Retrieved 24 May 2022, from https://www.gov.ie/en/publication/ee7d5-report-of-the-advisory-group-on-the-provision-of-support-including-accommodation-to-persons-in-the-international-protection-process/.

Group of Experts on Action against Violence against Women and Domestic Violence (2023). *GREVIO Baseline Evaluation Report Ireland*. Strasbourg Cedex: Council of Europe.

Gruber, A. (2020). *The Feminist War on Crime: The Unexpected Role of Women's Liberation in Mass Incarceration*. Oakland, CA: University of California Press.

Hamad, R. (2020). *White Tears/Brown Scars: How White Feminism Betrays Women of Colour*. London: Trapeze.

Hartnett, J. (2011). *Historical Representation and the Postcolonial Imaginary: Constructing Travellers and Aborigines*. Edited by Michael O hAodha. Cambridge: Cambridge Scholars Publishing.

Harvey, B. (2016). Local and Community Development in Ireland: An Overview. In C. Forde, D. O'Byrne, R. O'Connor, F. Ó Hadhmaill, & C. Power (eds.), *The Changing Landscape of Local and Community Development in Ireland: Policy and Practice* (pp. 7–14). Cork: University College Cork.

Harvey, D. (2005). *A Brief History of Neoliberalism*. New York: Oxford University Press.

Hassan, S. M., Leavy, C., & Rooney, J. S. (2019). *Exploring English Speaking Muslim Women's First-Time Maternity Experiences: A Qualitative Longitudinal Interview Study*. BMC Pregnancy and Childbirth. 19:156 1-10. doi.org/10.1186/s12884-019-2302-y.

Hearne, R. (2022). *Gaffs: Why No One Can Get a House and What We Can Do about It*. Dublin: Harper Collins.

Hill, M. (2003). *Women in Ireland: A Century of Change*. Belfast: The Blackstaff Press.

Hiltzik, M. (2014). Did Sheryl 'lean in' Sandberg turn her back on Boston hotel workers? *The Los Angeles Times*. Retrieved 3 January 2024, from https://www.latimes.com/business/hiltzik/la-fi-mh-sheryl-lean-in-sandberg-20140528-column.html.

Holborow, M. (2024). *Homes in Crisis Capitalism: Gender, Work and Revolution*. London: Bloomsbury Academic.

Holland, K. (2021). Ex-Debenhams workers end 406-day dispute and. *The Irish Times*. Retrieved 4 January 2024, from https://www.irishtimes.com/news/social-affairs/ex-debenhams-workers-end-406-day-dispute-and-accept-3m-training-fund-1.4570579.

hooks, b. (1982). *Ain't I a Woman: Black Women and Feminism*. London: Pluto Press.

hooks, b. (1983). *Teaching to Transgress: Education as the Practice of Freedom*. New York: Routledge.

hooks, b. (1984). *Feminist Theory from Margins to Center*. Boston, MA: South End Press.

hooks, b. (1994). *Teaching to Transgress: Education as the Practice of Freedom*. New York: Routledge.

hooks, b. (2000). *Feminism Is for Everybody: Passionate Politics*. London: Pluto Press.

hooks, b. (2003). *Teaching Community: A Pedagogy of Hope*. London: Routledge.

Horgan, A. (2021). *Lost in Work: Escaping Capitalism*. London: Pluto Press.

Horgan, D. (2001). Childcare provision in Ireland: Themes and issues. *Irish Journal of Applied Social Studies*, 2(3), 104–17. doi:10.21427/D72H9D

Houses of the Oireachtas (1990). Commission on the status of women. Retrieved 30 June 2024, from https://opac.oireachtas.ie/AWData/Library3/Library2/DL038378.pdf.

Hovey, G. (1985). Abortion: A history. *Plan Parent Review*, 5(2), 18–21. PMID: 12340403.

Huber, A. R. (2023). Image-based sexual abuse: Legislative and policing responses. *Criminology & Criminal Justice*, 0(0): https://doi.org/10.1177/17488958221146141.

ILGA Europe (2023). *Annual Review of the Human Rights Situation of Lesbian, Gay, Bisexual, Trans and Intersex People in Europe and Central Asia*. Brussels: ILGA Europe. Retrieved 21 April 2023, from https://www.ilga-europe.org/report/annual-review-2023/.

INCITE! Women of Colour Against Violence (2018). *Colour of Violence, the INCITE! Anthology*. Durham, NC, and London: Duke University Press.

Irish Countrywomen's Association (n.d.). *Brief History*. Retrieved 17 December 2022, from ICA: https://www.ica.ie/about-us/brief-history/.

Jaffe, S. (2021). *Work Won't Love You Back*. London: Hurst.

James, S. (1973). Women, the unions and work: Or what is not to be done. *Radical America*, 7(4–5), 51–71.

Jardine, J., Walker, K., Gurol-Urganci, I., Webster, K., Muller, P., Hawdon, J., & Van Der Muelen, J. (2021). Adverse pregnancy outcomes attributable to socioeconomic and ethnic inequalities in England: A national cohort study. *The Lancet*, (*10314*) 1905–12. doi:10.1016/S0140-6736(21)01595-6.

Jazayeri, M. (2015). Revolution. In S. Mojab (ed.), *Marxism and Feminism* (pp. 305–30). London: Zed Books.

Jones, M. (1988). *These Obsterperous Lassies*. Dublin: Gill and Macmillan.

Joseph, E. (2019). The centrality of race and whiteness in the Irish labour market. *Beyond Hate Crime: Perspectives on Racism in Ireland*. Retrieved 29 December 2023, from http://enarireland.org/the-centrality-of-race-and-whiteness-in-the-irish-labour-market/.

Joseph, E. (2020). *Critical Race Theory and Inequality in the Labour Market*. Manchester: Manchester University Press.

Joyce, S., O'Reilly, O., O'Brien, M., Joyce, D., Jennifer, S., & Haynes, A. (2017). *Irish Travellers' Access to Justice*. Limerick: Limerick University. Retrieved 12 May 2024, from https://researchrepository.ul.ie/articles/report/Irish_Travellers_Access_to_Justice/20179889.

June, L. (1982). *Sisters*. Dublin: Attic Press.

Kaltiala, R., Heino, E., Työläjärvi, M., & Suomalainen, L. (2020). Adolescent development and psychosocial functioning after starting cross-sex hormones for gender dysphoria. *Nordic Journal of Psychiatry, 74*(3), 213–19.

Kane, A. (2023). *Trade Unions*. Cork: Cork University Press.

Kelly, L. (2023). *Contraception and Modern Ireland*. Cambridge: Cambridge University Press.

Kennedy, S. (2022). A tale of two referendums: A comparative study of the anti-amendment campaign and together for yes. *Feminist Encounters: A Journal of Critical Studies in Culture and Politics, 6*(1), 1–15. doi:10.20897/femenc/11748.

Keogh, B., Carr, C., Doyle, L., Higgins, A., Morrissey, J., Sheaf, G., & Jowett, A. (2023). *An Exploration of Conversion Practices in Ireland*. Dublin: School of Nursing and Midwifery, Trinity College Dublin.

Kissling, E. A. (2017). *From a Whisper to a Shout*. New York: Random House Inc.

Klien, N. (2023). *Doppelganger: A Trip into the Mirror World*. London: Allen Lane, an imprint of Penguin.

Kyte, E. (2018). Feminist fusions: Irish socialist feminists, 1900s–1940s. Doctoral thesis. Cork: University College Cork. Retrieved from https://hdl.handle.net/10468/6277.

Lally, C. (2021). More Gardaí expected to come forward to reveal barring orders. *The Irish Times*. Retrieved 9 May 2024, from https://www.irishtimes.com/news/crime-and-law/at-least-21-barring-orders-issued-against-gardai-since-start-of-2019-figures-show-1.4702680.

Lally, C. (2021). More than 3,000 domestic violence 999 calls marked 'cancelled' by Garda. *The Irish Times*. Retrieved 9 May 2024, from https://www.irishtimes.com/news/crime-and-law/more-than-3-000-domestic-violence-999-calls-marked-cancelled-by-garda-1.4601760.

Larraghy, J. (2014). *Asymmetric Engagement: The Community and Voluntary Pillar in Irish Social Partnership*. Manchester and New York: Manchester University Press.

Lawlor, S. (2005). Disgusted subjects: The making of middle-class identities. *The Sociological Review, 53*(3), 429–46.

Lawrence, J., Kelly, E., McGinnity, F., & Curristan, S. (2023). *Wages and Working Conditions of Non-Irish Nationals in Ireland*. Dublin: ESRI. Retrieved 5 August 2023, from https://www.esri.ie/publications/wages-and-working-conditions-of-non-irish-nationals-in-ireland.

Leahy, S. (2023). Still a private matter? Evaluating the Irish State's response to domestic abuse. *International Journal of Law, Policy and the Family*, 23(ebad008), 1–20. doi:10.1093/lawfam/ebad008.

Lee, R. (2021). Judith Butler's Scientific Revolution: Foundations for a Transsexual Marxism. In J. J. Gleeson, E. O'Rourke, & J. Rosenberg (eds.), *Transgender Marxism* (pp. 62–9). London: Pluto Press.

Lentin, R. (1998). 'Irishness', the 1937 constitution, and citizenship: A gender and ethnicity view. *Irish Journal of Sociology*, 8(1), 5–24.

Levine, J. (1982). *Sisters*. Dublin: Ward River Press.

Lima, J. M., Reeves, A., Billari, F., McKee, M., & Stuckler, D. (2016). Austerity and abortion in the European union. *European Journal of Public Health*, 26(3), 518–19. doi:10.1093/eurpub/ckw026.

Livingstone, E. (2021). *Make Bosses Pay – Why We Need Unions*. London: Pluto Press.

London Edinburgh Weekend Group (2020). *In and against the State: Discussion Notes for Socialists*, edited by S. Wheeler (2nd ed.). London: Pluto Press.

Lorde, A. (1983). The Masters Tools Will Never Dismantle the Masters House, Comments at the 'Personal and the Political' Panel. (Second Sex Conference 29 October 1979). In C. Moraga, & G. Anzaldúa (eds.), (2nd ed.), *This Bridge Called My Back: Writings by Radical Women of Colour* (pp. 98–101). New York: Women of Colour Press.

Loughran, C. (1986). Armagh and feminist strategy: Campaigns around republican women prisoners in Armagh jail. *Feminist Review*, 23(1), 59–79.

Luddy, M. (2005). A 'sinister and retrogressive' proposal: Irish women's opposition to the 1937 draft constitution. *Transactions of the Royal Historical Society*, 15, 175–95.

Luxemborg, R. (2010). *Rosa Luxemborg: Selected Writings Socialism or Barbarism*. London: Pluto Press.

Lyons, S., Clarke, A., Staines, A., & O'Keefe, F. (2008). Cultural diversity in Dublin maternity services: The experiences of maternity service providers when caring for ethnic minority women. *Ethnicity & Health*, 13(3), June, 261–76.

Mac Donagh, P. (1975). *Socialist Republic: Paper of the Revolutionary Marxist Group*, p. 10. Retrieved from https://www.leftarchive.ie/document/view/487/.

Maguire, S. (2018). *Barriers to Women Entering Parliament and Local Government*. University of Bath, Institute for Policy Research. Retrieved 16 July 2023, from https://www.bath.ac.uk/publications/barriers-to-women-entering-parliament-and-local-government/attachments/barriers-to-women.pdf.

Mahdawi, A. (2022). French lawmakers propose bill to inscribe abortion rights in constitution. *The Guardian*. Retrieved 15 October 2022, from https://www.theguardian.com/world/2022/jun/25/french-lawmakers-propose-bill-abortion-rights-constitution.

Malatino, H. (2019). *Queer Embodiment: Monstrosity, Medical Violence, and Intersex Experience*. Lincoln, NE: University of Nebraska Press.

Manne, K. (2017). *Down Girl: The Logic of Misogyny*. New York: Oxford University Press.

Manning, E. (2014). *Establishing a Maternal Death Enquiry in a Low Maternal Mortality Context*. World Health Organisation. Retrieved from https://www.who.int/maternal_child_adolescent/epidemiology/maternal-death-surveillance/case-studies/ireland/en/

Marx, K., & Engels, F. (1848/2018). *The Communist Manifesto*. Minneapolis, MN: Lerner Publishing Group.

McAlevey (2020). *A Collective Bargain: Unions, Organizing, and the Fight for Democracy*. New York: Ecco.

McBride, R.-S., Neary, A., & Gray, B. (2020). *The Post-Primary School Experiences of Trans Gender and Gender Diverse Youth in Ireland*. Limerick and Dublin: University of Limerick and the Transgender Equality Network of Ireland. Retrieved 15 April 2022, from https://www.teni.ie/wp-content/uploads/2020/08/0309-UL-Report-Body_online.pdf.

McCabe, H. (2021). 'Political … civil and domestic slavery': Harriet Taylor Mill and Anna Doyle Wheeler on marriage, servitude, and socialism. *British Journal for the History of Philosophy*, 29(2), 226–43.

McCafferty, N. (2004). *Nell*. Dublin: Penguin Ireland.

McCann, E. (2018). *War and an Irish Town* (3rd ed.). Chicago, IL: Haymarket Books.

McCord, R. (2013). The mother and child scheme – The role of Church and State. *The Irish Story*. Retrieved 29 June 2024, from https://www.theirishstory.com/2013/06/19/the-controversy-of-womens-health-the-mother-and-child-scheme-the-role-of-church-and-state/.

McCormack, O., & Gleeson, J. (2014). Curriculum, culture, ideology and ownership: The case of the exploring masculinities programme. *Irish Educational Studies*, 31(4), 397–414.

McGarr, S. (2022). *The Maternity Hospital's Difficult Birth*. Retrieved 12 July 2024, from The Gist: https://www.thegist.ie/the-gist-maternity-hospital-difficult-birth/.

McGinnity, F., Privalko, I., Russell, H., Curristan, S., Stapleton, A., & Laurence, J. (2022). *Origin and Integration: Housing and Family amongst Migrants in the 2016 Irish Census*. Dublin: Economic and Social Research Institute. Retrieved 23 May 2022, from https://www.esri.ie/system/files/publications/BKMNEXT422_0.pdf.

McIntosh, K. (2023). Patching up childcare. *Community Practitioner: The Journal of the Community Practitioners' & Health Visitors' Association*, 96(2), 8–10.

Bibliography

McKay, S. (2005). *Without Fear: 25 Years of the Dublin Rape Crisis Centre*. Dublin: New Island.

McNeil, J., Bailey, L., Ellis, S., & Regan, M. (2009). *Speaking from the Margins: Trans Mental Health and Wellbeing in Ireland*. Dublin: TENI.

MERJ (2018). *We've Come a Long Way: Reproductive Rights of Migrants and Ethnic Minorities in Ireland* (2nd ed.). Dublin: Editora Urutau.

Mincer, J. (2016). *Watchdog Finds Much Larger Catholic Influence on U.S. Hospitals*. Retrieved 29 May 2024, from Reuters: https://www.reuters.com/article/idUSKCN0XW1HC/.

Mitchell, W., & Fazi, T. (2017). *Reclaiming the State: A Progressive Vision for Sovereignty for a Post-Neoliberal World*. London: Pluto Press.

Monaghan, K. (2020). *Investigation into Sexual Harassment and the Management of Sexual Harassment Complaints within the GMB*. GMB. Retrieved 25 January 2025 from https://www.gmb.org.uk/assets/media/documents/independent-investigation/monaghan-report.pdf.

Moore, A. (2021). Catherine Martin 'disappointed' Greens won't sanction Brian Leddin over WhatsApp remarks. *The Irish Examiner*. Retrieved 9 June 2024, from https://www.irishexaminer.com/news/politics/arid-40575623.html.

Moore, A. (2022). Cabinet signs off on maternity hospital as Hourigan to be 'denied opportunity' to vote against government. *The Irish Examiner*. Retrieved 28 July 2024, from https://www.irishexaminer.com/news/politics/arid-40874426.html.

Moore, J. (2024). Over half of domestic violence shelters across the country are full. *The Journal.ie*. Retrieved 6 April 2024, from https://www.thejournal.ie/domestic-violence-refuges-6298145-Feb2024/#:~:text=Safe%20Ireland%20offers%20a%20list,Domestic%20Abuse%3A%201800%20816%20588.

Murray, A. (2024). Opinion: What does article 42B mean for disabled people? *Irish Legal News*. Retrieved 9 June 2024, from https://www.irishlegal.com/articles/opinion-what-does-article-42b-mean-for-disabled-people.

Namaste, V. (2000). *Invisible Lives: The Erasure of Transsexual and Transgender People*. London: The University of Chicago Press.

National Library of Ireland (2022). *Revealing History: Hanna Sheehy-Skeffington. Feminist, Nationalist, Activist*. Dublin: National Library of Ireland. Retrieved 14 August 2023, from https://www.nli.ie/sites/default/files/2022-12/nli-revealing-history-hanna-sheehy-skeffington.pdf.

National Rapporteur on Human Trafficking (2023). *Trafficking in Human Beings in Ireland: Second Evaluation of the Implementation of the EU Anti-Trafficking Directive: A Digest*. Dublin: Irish Human Rights and Equality Commission. Retrieved 6 June 2024, from https://www.ihrec.ie/app/uploads/2023/09/Trafficking-in-Human-Beings-in-Ireland-Digest_FA_web-Fin.

Naughton, L. (2016). *Markievicz: A Most Outrageous Rebel*. Dublin: Merrion Press.

Neff, K. (2022). The function, demand, limits and future of the national gender service. *The Irish Times*. Retrieved 4 March 2024, from https://www.irishtimes.com/life-and-style/health-family/the-function-demand-limits-and-future-of-the-national-gender-service-1.4755189.

Ní Aodha, G. (2016). State apology: 399 women given up to €150,000 each for symphysiotomy procedures. *The Journal.ie*. Retrieved 29 May 2024, from https://www.thejournal.ie/symphysiotomy-scheme-2-3095739-Nov2016/.

Nugent, C. S., Pembrook, S., & Taft, M. (2019). *Precarious Work in the Republic of Ireland*. Dublin: Research for New Economic Policies. Retrieved 13 May 2023, from https://www.nerinstitute.net/sites/default/files/research/2019/precarious_work_in_the_republic_of_ireland_july_19_final.pdf.

O'Brien, C. (2023). Tesco Ireland sales rose 3% in 2022 despite inflation challenge. *The Irish Times*. Retrieved 8 July 2023, from https://www.irishtimes.com/business/2023/04/13/tesco-expects-flat-annual-profit-after-inflation-hit/.

O'Brien, M. E. (2023). *Family Abolition, Capitalism and the Communizing of Care*. London: Pluto Press.

O'Connor, P. (2022). Why do we consider some work as less valuable than others? *The Irish Examiner*. Retrieved 1 December 2022, from https://www.irishexaminer.com/opinion/commentanalysis/arid-41017571.html.

O'Connor, P., & Irvine, G. (2020). Multi-level state interventions and gender equality in higher education institutions: The Irish case. *Administrative Sciences*, *10*(98), 1–21.

Office of the Tánaiste (1997). *Report of the Task Force on Violence against Women*. Dublin: Stationary Office.

O'Hare, M. F., Manning, E., Corcoran, P., Greene R. A. on behalf of MDE Ireland (2023). *Confidential Maternal Death Enquiry in Ireland, Report for 2019 2021*. Cork: MDE Ireland.

O'Keefe, C. (2021). Gardaí get 120 domestic abuse calls every day. *The Irish Examiner*. Retrieved 11 April 2023, from https://www.irishexaminer.com/news/arid-40724256.html.

O'Keeffe, E. (2021). *Queering Irish History: What Damage Done to Irish Genderqueer Identities by Colonialism?* Retrieved 23 March 2024, from Medium: https://medium.com/p/d4f4d2a356c1.

O'Keefe, T. (2017). Mother Ireland, Get Off Our Backs. In L. Bosi, & G. De Fazio (eds.), *The Troubles in Northern Ireland and Theories of Social Movements* (pp. 165–84). Amsterdam: Amsterdam University Press.

O'Keefe, T., & Courtois, A. (2019). 'Not one of the family': Gender and precarious work in the neoliberal university. *Gender Work Organisation*, *26*(4), 463–79. doi:/10.1111/gwao.12346.

Olufemi, L. (2020). *Feminism Interrupted*. London: Pluto Press.

One Family. (2022). *Pre Budget Submission*. Dublin: One Family. Retrieved 11 March 2023, from file:///C:/Users/cfitzsimons/OneDrive%20-%20Maynooth%20University/Desktop/OneFamilyPBS_2022-1.pdf.

Bibliography

Osborne, M., & Nolan, D. (2023). Hundreds attend event opposing inclusion of transgender information in primary school course. *The Irish Independent*. Retrieved 18 June 2024, from https://www.independent.ie/irish-news/hundreds-attend-event-opposing-inclusion-of-transgender-information-in-primary-school-course/a282191517.html.

Ó Scannáil, M. (2019). 'More feminist women needed for leadership roles as we haven't achieved full equality' – Madigan. *The Irish Independent*. Retrieved 24 April 2024, from https://www.independent.ie/irish-news/more-feminist-women-needed-for-leadership-roles-as-we-havent-achieved-full-equality-madigan/37728100.html.

Oxfam International (2021). *Not All Gaps Are Created Equal: The True Value of Care Work*. Retrieved 18 April 2022, from https://www.oxfam.org/en/not-all-gaps-are-created-equal-true-value-care-work.

Padbury, J. (2018). A mixture of flattery and insult. *History Ireland; 20th Century Social Perspectives*(3 [May/June]). Retrieved 17 December 2022, from https://www.historyireland.com/a-mixture-of-flattery-and-insult/.

Pavee Point (2015). *Traveller Women Fact Sheet*. Retrieved 23 July 2023, from Pavee Point Traveller and Roma Centre: https://www.paveepoint.ie/wp-content/uploads/2015/04/Factsheets-Pavee-Point-WOMEN.pdf.

Pavee Point Traveller and Roma Centre & Department of Justice and Equality (2018). *Roma in Ireland: A National Needs Assessment*. Dublin: Pavee Point.

Pavee Point Travellers Centre (2012). *Roma Communities in Ireland and Child Protection Considerations*. Dublin: The Irish Health Repository.

Peterson, J. (2018). Jordan Peterson debate on the gender pay gap, campus protests and postmodernism. (C. 4. News, Interviewer) Retrieved 28 November 2022, from https://www.youtube.com/watch?v=aMcjxSThD54.

Pickering, S. (2002). *Women, Policing and Resistance*. Belfast: Beyond the Pale Publications.

Pieper, L. P. (2016). *Sex Testing: Gender Policing in Women's Sports*. Urbana, IL: University of Illinois Press.

Potts, M., Campbell, M., Global library of women's medicine, (ISSN: 1756-2228). doi: 0.3843/GLOWM.1037.

PwC (2022). *Women in Work Index*. Retrieved 24 January 2023, from https://www.pwc.ie/reports/women-in-work-index-2022.html.

Rape Crisis Network (2014). *Asylum Seekers and Refugees Surviving on Hold*. Dublin: Rape Crisis Network. Retrieved 15 August 2024, from https://www.rcni.ie/wp-content/uploads/RCNI-Asylum-Seekers-and-Refugees-Surviving-on-Hold.pd.

Raymond, J. G. (1994). *The Transsexual Empire: The Making of a She-Male*. New York: Teachers College Press.

Reagan, L. (1997). *When Abortion Was a Crime: Women, Medicine, and Law in the United States, 1867–1973*. Berkeley, CA: University of California Press.

Riddle, J. (1992). *Contraception and Abortion from the Ancient World to the Renaissance*. New York: Harvard University Press.

Rogan, A. (2023). 'Large group' of Irish Google workers turn to union as tech crunch bites. *The Business Post*. Retrieved 4 January 2024, from https://www.businesspost.ie/news/large-group-of-irish-google-workers-turn-to-union-as-tech-crunch-bites/.

Rogers, N. (2016). Ireland, slavery, antislavery, post-slavery and empire:an historiographical survey. *Slavery & Abolition*, 37(3), 489–504. http://dx.doi.org/10.1080/0144039X.2016.1208915.

Roslin, A. (2017). *Police Wife: The Secret Epidemic of Police Domestic Violence*. Canada: Sugar Hill Books.

Ross, L. J., & Solinger, R. (2017). *Reproductive Justice: An Introduction*. Oakland, CA: University of California Press.

Ross, L. J., Roberts, L., Derkas, E., Peoples, W., & Bridgewater Toure, P. (2017). *Radical Reproductive Justice*. New York: Feminist Press.

Rottenberg, C. (2018). *The Rise of Neoliberal Feminism*. New York: Oxford University Press.

Roy-Steier, S. (2021). Coming up short: The Catholic Church's pastoral response to the transgender crisis in America. *Religions*, 12(337), 1–20. doi:10.3390/rel12050337.

Ruggi, L. (2023). Three conditions for equality: Feminist organising at the university of Galway. *Journal of Gender, Globalisation and Rights*, 4, 61–80. doi:10.13025/fzwq-bn80.

Russell, H., McGinnity, F., & O' Connell, P. J. (2017). Gender equality in the Irish labour market 1966–2016: Unfinished business? *The Economic and Social Review*, 48(4), 393–418.

Russell, H., Raffaele, G., McGinnity, F., & Privalko, I. (2019). *Caring and Unpaid Work in Ireland*. Dublin: Irish Human Rights and Equality Commission and The Economic and Social Research Institute. doi:10.26504/bkmnext382.

Ryan, L. (2020). Nationalism and Feminism: The Complex Relationship between the Suffragist and Independence Movements in Ireland. In L. Connolly (ed.), *Women and the Irish Revolution* (pp. 17–32). Kildare: Irish Academic Press.

Safe Ireland (2014). *The Lawlessness of the Home*. Safe Ireland. Retrieved 7 August 2023, from https://www.safeireland.ie/wp-content/uploads/SAFE-IRELAND-The-Lawlessness-of-the-Home.pdf.

Safe Ireland (2019). Gender matters 2019: Summary findings of research on public attitudes to gender equality and roles, domestic abuse, and coercive control in Ireland. Safe Ireland. Newbridge: Irish Academic Press. Retrieved 15 August 2024, from https://www.safeireland.ie/policy-publications/#dflip-df_7296/1/17-32).

Saidléar, C. (2015). *Making Choice to Seek Help Is a Big Decision – 80% of Sexual Violence Cases Go Unreported*. Retrieved 11 April 2023, from Rape Crisis Network Ireland: https://www.rcni.ie/making-choice-seek-help-big-decision-80-sexual-violence-cases-go-unreported/.

Salem, S. (2018) Intersectionality and its discontents: Intersectionality as traveling theory. *European Journal of Women's Studies*, 25(4), 403–18.
Sandberg, S. (2013). *Lean In*. New York: Wh Allen.
Sangari, K. (2020). Patriarchy/Patriarchies. In S. Mojab (ed.), *Marxism and Feminism* (pp. 259–86). London: Bloomsbury Academic & Professional.
Schoen, J. (2005). *Choice and Coercion: Birth Control, Sterilization, and Abortion in Public Health and Welfare*. Chapel Hill, NC: University of North Carolina Press.
Serano, J. (2016). *Whipping Girl* (2nd ed.). Emeryville, CA: Seal Press.
Shaw, D. (2023). A tale of two feminisms: Gender critical feminism, trans inclusive feminism and the case of Kathleen Stock. *Women's History Review*, 32(5), 768–80.
Siggins, L. (2016). Galway West's Catherine Connolly says Labour has 'lost its soul'. *The Irish Times*. Retrieved 17 August 2023, from https://www.irishtimes.com/news/politics/galway-west-s-catherine-connolly-says-labour-has-lost-its-soul-1.2549837.
Silva, I., Araújo, E., Santana, A., Moura, J., Ramalho, M., & Abreu, P. (2022). Gender violence perpetrated against trans women. *Revista brasileira de enfermagem*, 75(2), 1–8.
Smyth, A. (1988). The contemporary women's movement in the republic of Ireland. *Women's Studies International Forum*, 11(4), 331–41.
Smyth, A., Conroy, R., & Wallsgrove, R. (1989). Two sides of Ireland: Feminist press. *Off Our Backs*, 19(10), 12–13.
Smyth, J. (2010). Lydia Foy began legal fight for recognition in 1997. *The Irish Times*. Retrieved 5 August 2023, from https://www.irishtimes.com/news/lydia-foy-began-legal-fight-for-recognition-in-1997-1.681281.
Stapleton, A., Polakowski, M., & Quinn, E. (2022). The integration of non-EU migrant women in Ireland. *ESRI Research Series 148*. Dublin: Irish National Contact Point of the European Migration Network.
Stopper, A. (2006). *Monday at Gaj's: The Story of the Irish Women's Liberation Movement*. Dublin: The Liffey Press.
Stryker, S. (2017). *Transgender History: The Roots of Today's Revolution*. New York: Seal Press.
Sweeney, R., & Lajoie, A. (2022). *Budget 2022 Gender Analysis*. Dublin: TASC. Retrieved 11 September 2023, from https://www.nwci.ie/images/uploads/Budget_2022_Gender_analysis_final.pdf.
Sweetman, R. (2020). *Feminism Backwards*. Cork: Mercier Press.
Táíwò, O. O. (2022). *Elite Capture How the Powerful Took over Identity Politics and Everything Else*. London: Pluto Press.
TASC (2016). *Low Pay Commission: Submission on the Underlying Reasons for the Preponderance of Women on Minimum Wage*. Dublin: Think Tank for Action on Social Change. Retrieved 29 December 2022, from https://www.tasc.ie/assets/files/pdf/tasc_low_pay_commission_women_final.pdf.

Tebbutt, C. (2015). The spectre of the 'man-woman athlete': Mark Weston, Zdenek Koubek, the 1936 Olympics and the uncertainty of sex. *Women's History Review*, *24*(5), 721–38.

The All-Party Parliamentary Group on Birth Trauma (2024). *Listen to Mums: Ending the Postcode Lottery on Perinatal Care*. Appg, Birth Trauma. Retrieved 30 June 2024, from https://www.theo-clarke.org.uk/sites/www.theo-clarke.org.uk/files/2024-05/Birth%20Trauma%20Inquiry%20Report%20for%20Publication_May13_2024.pdf.

The Combahee River Collective (2017). The Combahee River Collective Statement. In K.-Y. Taylor (ed.), *How We Get Free: Black Feminism and the Combahee River Collective* (pp. 15–27). Chicago, IL: Haymarket Books.

The Irish Human Rights and Equality Commission (2023). *Trafficking in Human Beings in Ireland: Second Evaluation of the Implementation of the EU Anti-Trafficking Directive: A Digest*. Dublin: Irish Human Rights and Equality Commission. Retrieved from https://www.ihrec.ie/app/uploads/2023/09/Trafficking-in-Human-Beings-in-Ireland-Digest_FA_web-Final.pdf.

The Irish Women's Liberation Movement (1970). *Irishwomen – Chains or Change*. Dublin: IWLM.

The National Office for the Prevention of Domestic, Sexual and Gender-Based Violence (2010). *National Strategy on Domestic, Sexual and Gender Based Violence 2010–2014*. Dublin: Department of Justice, Equality and Law Reform. Retrieved 15 April 2023, from https://www.tusla.ie/uploads/content/Domestic_nationalstrategy.pdf.

Tordoff, D. M., Wanta, J. W., Collin, A., Cesalie, S., Inwards-Breland, D. J., & Ahrens, K. (2022). Mental Health Outcomes in Transgender and Nonbinary Youths. *JAMA Network Open*, *5*(2), 1–13. doi:10.1001/jamanetworkopen.2022.0978.

Tobin, C.,. & Murphy-Lawless, J. (2014). Irish midwives' experiences of providing maternity care to non-Irish women seeking asylum. *International Journal of Women's Health*, *6*, 159–69.

Tristan, F. (1983). The Workers' Union. In B. Livingston (ed.), *Flora Tristan: The Workers' Union. Translated with an Introduction by Beverly Livingston* (pp. 30–138). Urbana, Chicago, IL, London: University of Illinois Press.

Turban, J. L., Beckwith, N., Reisner, S. L., & Keuroghlian, A. S. (2020). Association between recalled exposure to gender identity conversion efforts and psychological distress and suicide attempts among transgender adults. *JAMA Psychiatry*, *77*(1), 68–76.

UN (1979). *Convention on the Elimination of All Forms of Discrimination against Women*. New York: United Nations General Assembly. Retrieved 23 May 2022, from https://www.ohchr.org/sites/default/files/cedaw.pdf.

UN (2019). *A Human Rights-Based Approach to Mistreatment and Violence against Women in Reproductive Health Services with a Focus on Childbirth and Obstetric Violence*. New York: United Nation General Assembly. Retrieved 17 December 2020, from https://undocs.org/A/74/137.

United Nations (2020). *World Social Report 2020, Inequality in a Rapidly Changing World*. New York: United Nations Department of Economic and Social Affairs. Retrieved 7 December 2022, from https://www.un.org/development/desa/dspd/wp-content/uploads/sites/22/2020/02/World-Social-Report2020-FullReport.pdf.

United Nations (2023). *UK: Discrimination against People of African Descent Is Structural, Institutional and Systemic, Say UN Experts*. Retrieved 21 July 2023, from United Nations: https://www.ohchr.org/en/press-releases/2023/01/uk-discrimination-against-people-african-descent-structural-institutional.

United Nations Human Rights (2022). *Transgender*. Retrieved from United Nations Free and Equal: https://www.unfe.org/wp-content/uploads/2017/05/UNFE-Transgender.pdf.

United Nations Office of the High Commissioner (2022). *Declaration on the Elimination of Violence against Women*. Retrieved 17 November 2022, from United Nations Office of the High Commissioner: https://www.ohchr.org/en/instruments-mechanisms/instruments/declaration-elimination-violence-against-women.

United Nations Office on Drugs and Crime (2021). *Killings of Women and Girls by Their Intimate Partner or Other Family Members: Global Estimates, 2020*. Vienna: United Nations Office on Drug Crime. Retrieved 24 January 2023, from https://www.unodc.org/documents/data-and-analysis/statistics/crime/UN_BriefFem_251121.pdf.

UN Women (2017). *Women Migrant Workers and Remittance: Policy Briefing No. 3*. New York: United Nations. Retrieved 11 March 2024, from https://www.unwomen.org/sites/default/files/Headquarters/Attachments/Sections/Library/Publications/2017/Policy-brief-Women-migrant-workers-and-financial-remittances-en.pdf.

UN Women (2024). *Gender Alert: The Gendered Impact of the Crisis in Gaza*. New York: UN Women Regional Office for the Arab States.

Vergès, F. (2022). *A Feminist Theory of Violence*. London: Pluto Press.

Vernon, J. (2000). 'For some queer reason': The trials and tribulations of Colonel Barker's masquerade in interwar Britain. *Signs*, 26(1), 37–62.

Vogel, L. (2013). *Marxism and the Oppression of Women: Toward a Unitary Theory*. Leiden and Boston, MA: Brill.

Walker, L. (2021). Lynda Walker, Communist Party of Ireland, NICRA, women's rights movement, Northern Ireland women's coalition, and international brigades. (I. l. Archive, Interviewer)

Ward, J. (2021). *Gardaí Explanations for Cancelled 999 Calls 'Perplexing in the Extreme'*. Retrieved 5 May 2024, from Breaking News.ie: https://www.breakingnews.ie/ireland/gardai-explanations-for-cancelled-999-calls-perplexing-in-the-extreme-1206145.html.

Weeks, A. C., & Allen, P. (2023). Backlash against 'identity politics': Far right success and mainstream party attention to identity groups. *Politics, Groups and Identities*, 11(5), 935–53.

WHO (2014). *Framework for Ensuring Human Rights in the Provision of Contraceptive Information and Services*. Geneva: WHO. Retrieved 2 January 2023, from https://apps.who.int/iris/bitstream/handle/10665/133327/9789241507745_eng.pdf.

WHO (2021). *Abortion: Key Facts*. Retrieved 15 October 2022, from World Health Organization: https://www.who.int/news-room/fact-sheets/detail/abortion.

WHO (2022). *Abortion Care Guidelines*. Geneva: World Health Organization. Retrieved 29 May 2022, from https://www.who.int/publications/i/item/9789240039483.

Wilson, N. (2022). Thinking together: A feminist collaborative inquiry into pedagogical approaches for domestic violence work in Ireland. Doctoral Thesis. Kildare: Maynooth University. Retrieved 25 January 2025, from https://mural.maynoothuniversity.ie/id/eprint/15844/.

Workers Solidarity Movement (2013). *On the RAG – Interview with Revolutionary Anarcha-Feminist Group*. Retrieved 15 January 2023, from Workers Solidarity Movement: http://www.wsm.ie/c/rag-interview-revolutionary-anarcha-feminist-group-mar2013.

World Economic Forum (2024). *Global Gender Gap Report 2024. Insight Report*. Geneva: World Economic Forum. Retrieved 15 September 2024, from https://www.weforum.org/publications/global-gender-gap-report-2024/.

World Federation of Trade Unions (2011). *Constitution of the World Federation of Trade Unions*. Athens: WFTU. Retrieved 30 December 2023, from https://www.wftucentral.org/?wpfb_dl=241.

Zakaria, R. (2021). *Against White Feminism*. UK: Penguin.

Zazanis, N. (2021). Social Reproduction and Social Cognition: Theorizing (Trans)gender Identity Development in Community Context. In J. J. Gleeson and E. O'Rourke (ed.), *Transgender Marxism* (pp. 33–46). London: Pluto Press.

ACKNOWLEDGEMENTS

This book only exists because of the many people who generously gave their time, expertise and energy. An enormous thank you to those I interviewed and those who got in touch with me online. Thank you to the feminist and other researchers who came before me including those who archived their previous work across such platforms as Digital Repository Ireland, Irish Left Archive and the Irish Election Literature archive. Thank you to Maynooth University Social Sciences Institute (MUSSI) who gave me a small grant that allowed me to transcribe interviews; this was a big help. To people who give guidance and advice along the way by reading aspects of the work, specifically Marnie Holborow, Miriam Hamilton, Dilara Demir Bloom, Clare Tebbutt, Anna MacNeill and Gary Branigan. An enormous thanks to Olivia Dellow and everyone in Bloomsbury Publishing and also to Pritha Suriyamoorthy; it was an absolute pleasure working with you. Thanks to my family, Isobel, Dylan, Anna and Brian for all of the time, space and love that you gave me. And to my comrades across a range of social activist spaces who offered encouragement and guidance along the way.

INDEX

A, B and C v Ireland 44, 141
Abolish Direct Provision 127, 129, 138
abolitionist feminism 112, 117, 120, 123
abortion 5–6, 8, 38–9, 41–6, 48, 67, 84, 96, 130–7, 141–8, 151–2, 156, 158
Abortion Rights Campaign (ARC) 44, 96, 142, 144–5
abuse 102–3, 108, 117–21, 159
    online 4, 27, 94, 177 n.43
    sexual 18, 119, 121
Action, Information, Motivation (AIM) 108, 110
Ahern, Bertie 170 n.12
Ahmed, Sara 58, 161–3, 180 n.17
AIMS Ireland (Association for the Improvement in Maternity Services) 2
AkiDwA 139
All Nations Church 89
'Always Here' campaign 104
Amal Women's Association 147–8
Amini, Mahsa (death of) 1–2
Amnesty International 106
Anti-Amendment Campaign (AAC) 135–6
Anti-Austerity Alliance-People Before Profit (AAA-PbP) 45
anti-capitalist feminism 8, 12, 19, 21–2, 48–9, 58, 67, 160–5
anti-establishment feminism 18, 36–7
Anti-Fascist Action Ireland (AFA) 42
anti-violence movement 110–12, 115, 124, 164
Apple company 29
Ardern, Jacinda 49

Association of Business and Professional Women 34
Athena SWAN 155–6

Banshee, media analysis 36
Barnes, Monica 35, 38
BDS movement 162
Belacy, Neira 103
Belfast Women's Collective 37
Bell, Ollie 95–7
Benedict, Nex (death of) 86
Berry, Megan 20–1, 121
biological sex 88, 93
birthing rights 147–8
Blanckensee, Sam 85, 94, 97
Boylan, Peter 143, 148
Browne, Noel 131–3
Buckley, Christine 161
bullying 57, 86–7, 119, 161
Burton, Joan 46, 57
Butler, Judith 10, 91–2, 96

caesarean section 132, 141, 147
Caherty, Therese 43, 60, 67, 113
Cairns, Holly 3
Campaign Against Church Ownership of Women's Healthcare 143–4
Campaign Against Rape (CAR) 110
capitalism 10–19, 21, 29, 49, 55, 57, 72, 78, 92, 95–7, 105–7, 112, 156, 160, 164–5, 167
carceral feminism 122–4
Carlow Women's Refuge Campaign 164
Carroll-MacNeill, Jennifer 122
Catholic Church 30, 34, 36, 38–9, 88–90, 132–3, 137, 178 n.11
Catholic Primary Schools Management Association 89

Chains and Change (publication) 109–10, 133
childcare 66, 137–9, 167
The Child Care Act (1991) 138
cis feminists 78
cisgender 79, 97
cis-heteronormativity 80, 83
Clinton, Bill 130
Clinton, Hillary 9
Coalition Against the Deportation of Irish Children (CADIC) 139–40
coercion/coercive control 4, 6, 84, 107, 117–18, 120–1, 147
Colgan, Michael 161–2
Collins, Joan 44
Combahee River Collective 156, 158–9, 169 n.45
Commission on the Status of Women (1990) 138
Communist Party of Ireland (CPI) 33, 37, 113
community development 39–41
community employment (CE) 138
Concannon, Helen 31
Congress of Catholic Schools Parent Association (CSAP) 89
Connolly, Catherine 46
Conroy, Roisin 43
conservative politics 36, 38
conservativism 63–5, 146, 150–2
Constitution of Ireland 30–1, 135, 140, 146
constructive politics 160
contraception 41, 43, 61, 131–5, 137, 151
Contraceptive Action Programme (CAP) 134–5
Conway, Vicky 120, 171 n.48
Coppinger, Ruth 45–6
Coraccio, Angela 142
Coroners (*Amendment*) *Act 2019* 128
Cosc (National Office for the Prevention of Domestic, Sexual and Gender-based Violence) 116
Council for the Status of Women (CSW) 34–5, 38, 40–1, 62, 108, 114, 138–9
Covid-19 pandemic 105, 128, 163
Criminal Justice (*Victims of Crime*) *Act* (2017) 116–17
Criminal Justice Bill 114
Criminal Law (*Sexual Offences*) *Act* (2017) 116
Criminal Law Amendment Act 83
Crotty, Cathal 118
Cumann na mBan 27
Cumann na nGaedheal political party 30

Dáil Éireann and Seanad Éireann 28–32, 35, 37–8, 43–8, 95
Daly, Clare 44, 142
Daly, Mary 62
Davidson, Madge 37
Dawson, Juno, *This Book Is Gay* 94
de Beauvoir, Simone, *The Second Sex* 91
Deif, Mohammed 107
Deliveroo workers 68–9
De Valera, Eamonn 34
Devlin-McAliskey, Bernadette 36
DeVun, Leah, *The Shape of Sex* 81
Direct Provision (DP) 124, 127–9, 150
disability 31, 132
discrimination 81–5, 104, 128, 130
  double 60
  face 79, 103
  gender-based 6, 56, 70
  pay 62
  work-based 58
diversity 20, 32, 67, 79, 81, 85, 156
Divorce Action Group (DAG) 38–9
Doctors for choice 143
domestic violence 19, 54, 101–3, 105, 108, 111, 115–18, 120–1, 123

Domestic Violence Act (2018) 117
Doyle, Anna Wheeler 25
Dublin Abortion Rights Group (DARG) 137
Dublin Rape Crisis Centre (DRCC) 104, 111, 114–16
Dunnes Stores strike 64–5, 68
Dyas, Grace 4, 161–2

eco-feminism 160
economic nationalism 30
Eighth Amendment 135–7, 141, 143, 146
elite capture 159
Engels, Friedrich 11–12, 72
  Communist Manifesto 11, 59
  The Origins of the Family, Private Property and the State 12
English Language Students' Union 69
EU Lisbon Treaty 43
European Commission (EC) 29, 103–5
European Convention on Human Rights (ECHR) 69, 84
European Court of Human Rights 141
exclusion, history of 59–61
'Exploring Masculinities' (school subject) 89–90

Fagan, Rita 40–1, 101–4, 108, 111, 123
FairPlé, work of 70
far-right politics 5, 18, 28, 42, 47–8, 77, 94–5, 97, 156–7, 160, 164, 167
Farris, Sara, *Femonationalism* 10
fast fashion 16
female trade unionists 60–3
feminism 155–60. *See also* politics and feminism
  performance 18–21
  in 1960s 34–7
  souls of 6–10

Feminist Communities for Justice Campaign 166
Feminist Forum 113
feminist killjoy activism 161–3, 180 n.17
Feminist Open Forum 43
feminist theory 27, 158–9, 166
Fennell, Nuala 35, 108
Fianna Fáil political party 19, 30–3, 38, 42, 134, 149
Fine Gael political party 29, 31, 35–6, 38–9, 44–6, 122, 142, 144, 149
Fitzgerald, Gareth 35
Fitzpatrick, Chris 143
Flynn, Tara 4
Fórsa, trade union 71
Fox, Megan 119
Foy, Lydia 84–5
Fraser, Nancy 91
Freire, Paulo 160–1

Garda Síochána/Gardaí (Police Force in Ireland) 44, 65, 68, 86, 95, 120–1
gender-based discrimination 6, 56, 70
gender-based violence 5, 7, 21, 43, 57, 94, 103–5, 107, 111–12, 114, 123, 148, 157, 163, 167
gender-critical feminists 90–2
gender equality 27, 57, 155
gender identity 8, 84, 86–7, 89, 93
gender quotas (in politics) 28
Gender Recognition Act 79, 84–5, 90
Gender Recognition Advisory Group 85
gender variance 78–81, 83
gender verification testing 87
Ghey, Brianna (murder of) 86, 92
gig economy 56
Gomperts, Rebecca 137
Gordon, Mary 39
Green Party 3, 27, 31, 44, 149

Grimes, Lorraine 105, 116
Griswold v. Connecticut 135
Group of Experts on Action against Violence against Women and Domestic Violence (GREVIO) 117

Halappanavar, Savita (death of) 1, 45, 142
Hamilton, Miriam 72
Harney, Mary 138
Harris, Simon 53–5, 143, 151
Haughey, Charles 39
H-Block campaign 113, 171 n.34
Health (Family Planning) Act 134
The Health (Regulation of Termination of Pregnancy) Act (2018) 146
health and safety bills 87
Health Service Executive (HSE) 82, 143
Holland, Kitty 141
Home Rule bill 26–7
hooks, bell 9, 17, 155, 161, 166
Horgan, Goretti 135, 141, 178 n.20
Hourigan, Niamh 27
housing 2, 7, 15, 19, 29, 35–6, 46–8, 73, 102, 105–6, 127, 129, 149–50
human trafficking 57
Hussey, Gemma 35–6, 38

identity politics 19, 156, 158
Imbugna, Samone 139–40
imperialist violence 112–13
Inchicore Domestic Violence Centre 111
INCITE! Women of Colour Against Violence 112
Independent Workers Union 69, 173 n.46
Industrial Relations Act 61, 65
institutionalized sexism 17

International Organization for Migration 106
International Women's Day 53, 93
interpersonal violence 37, 86, 107–10, 114–16, 124
intersectionality 18–20, 168 n.7
intersex variation 80, 89, 95–6
Irish Anti-Apartheid Movement 65
Irish Congress of Trade Unions (ICTU) 62, 65, 69
Irish Council for Civil Liberties 139
Irish Countrywomen's Association (ICA) 61
Irish Distributive and Administrative Union (IDATU) 64
Irish Family Planning Association (IFPA) 44, 142
Irish Federation of University Teachers (IFUT) 72
Irish Housewives Association (IHA) 33–4, 61
Irish Museum of Modern Art (IMMA) 3
Irish Rugby Football Union (IRFU) 87
Irish Transport and General Workers Union (ITGWU) 59–60, 62
Irish Women's Franchise League (IWFL) 26
Irish Women's Liberation Movement (IWLM) 35, 108–9, 133–5
Irish Women United (IWU) 36–7, 43, 62, 134–5
Irish Women Workers' Union (IWWU) 32–3, 43, 59–62
Istanbul Convention 116–17
Istanbul Convention Action Against Violence Against Women 19

James, Naomi (death of) 152
Johnson, Marsha P. 95
Joyce, Nan 36
Justice for Cleaners campaign 70–1

Kellie-Jay Keen (Posie Parker) 77–8, 93
Kelly, Linda 43, 71
Kennedy, Sinéad 141–2, 158
Kenny, Enda 45
Kenny, Mary 35
Keynesian economics 13
Khelif, Imane 87
Klein, Naomi, *Doppelganger* 47–8
Knight, Eden (death of) 86

labour movement 60, 67, 72
Labour Party, The 33, 36, 38–9, 42–6, 49, 57, 92, 142, 148
The Late Late Show 35
left-wing revolutionary parties 41–8, 56, 65, 91, 113, 152
Levine, June 133–5
LGBTQIA+ community 4, 18, 28, 43, 77, 79, 85–7, 93, 95–6, 144, 156
liberal feminism 7–9, 16–17, 20–2, 28, 37–8, 40, 46, 49, 57, 62, 110, 122, 135, 137–8, 142, 144, 155, 157–8
Litster, Alice 109
Lloyds pharmacy workers 69
Lorde, Audre 18–19, 164
Lower Price Council (LPC) 33
Luxemburg, Rosa 72

Madigan, Josepha 122
Magdalene Laundries 109, 143
#MakeOurMaternityHospitalOurs 148–9
male-female binary 80
marriage bars 30, 34, 60
Martin, Aoife 81–2, 94, 97
Marx, Karl, *Communist Manifesto* 11, 29, 59, 72
masculinity 10, 12, 17, 79, 92, 94
maternity care system 147–8
maternity hospital 109, 140, 144, 146, 148–9

Mathis, Coy 87
McArdle, Dorothy 33, 38
McCarthy, Justine 141
McCormack, Micheline 111
McDermott, Mary 102–3, 108, 123
McDonald, Mary Lou 48
McDowell, Michael 140
McEntee, Helen 53, 57
McGee, Mary 134–5
McQuaid, Charles, C. 34, 132–3
Meloni, Georgio 9, 87–8, 95
Men's Aid Ireland 104
Me Too movement 6, 103, 161
middle-class women 7–8, 13, 18, 21, 28–9, 35–6, 41, 58, 81, 109, 157
Midwives in the Community 2
Migrant Rights Centre of Ireland (MRCI) 70
migrants 56–7, 138, 139, 147, 163
children rights 137–9
Migrants and Ethnic Minorities for Reproductive Justice (MERJ) 145
militarization 122–4
Moore, Aoife 179 n.42
Mother and Baby Homes 2–3, 46, 108–10
Movement of Asylum Seekers in Ireland (MASI) 48, 70
Muldowney, Mary 42, 136–7
Murphy, Ashling (death of) 105
Murphy, Paul 95, 171 n.50
Murphy, Sarah 143
Murray, Alannah 31
Murray, Andrea 77–8

National Gender Service (NGS) 82
National Health Service (NHS) 132
National Maternity Hospital (NMH) 143, 148
National Minimum Wage Act 70
National Wage Agreement 62
National Women's Council of Ireland (NWCI) 31, 41, 43,

66, 93–4, 96, 104, 139–40, 142, 144, 148, 165–6
neoliberalism 13–16, 35, 41, 54
Netanyahu, Benjamin 107, 162
Ni Una Menos (Not One Woman Less) movement 160
Noonan, Liz 36
Northern Ireland 2, 27, 28, 37, 60–1, 77, 107, 113
Northern Irish Women's Rights Movement (NIWRM) 37

O'Brien, Natasha 118–19
obstetric violence 147–8
O'Carroll, Maureen 33
O'Connor, Clare 47, 150, 157
O'Connor, Orla 43, 66, 94
O'Gorman, Rodrick, *Mother and Baby Institution Payment Bill* 3
O'Leary, Dale, *The Gender Agenda* 88
O'Malley, Stella 92–3
O'Neill, Michelle 48
online abuse 4, 27, 94, 177 n.43
Open Door Counselling 136

Palestinian people 106
parental alienation syndrome 117
Parker, Posie. *See* Kellie-Jay Keen (Posie Parker)
patriarchy/patriarchies 12, 17–19, 21, 25, 32, 40, 48–9, 60, 90–1, 97, 108, 111–12, 115–16, 123, 144, 155, 161, 163
pay discrimination 62
Pearse, Margaret 31
Pelicot, Giséle 163
People before Profit (PbP) 42–5, 48, 63, 95, 159
People's Democracy 36
Peterson, Jordan 18
Phillips, Sara 93
pinkwashing 95–6

politics and feminism 25–8
   Catholic Church 30, 34
   far-right political parties 47–8
   left-wing revolutionary parties 41–7
   party loyalty 37–9
   problems 28–9
   in 1960s 34–7
   state role 29–30
   women in 30–4
poverty 47, 49, 109, 131, 150, 157
praxis 22, 124, 166
pregnancy 12, 109, 127, 132–5, 139–41, 146–7
pro-abortion movement 45, 111, 135, 137, 151, 158
Pro-Life Amendment Campaign (PLAC) 135

queer activism 95–7
Quigley, Dara 121
Quinn, Emma 7

race/racism 21, 109, 121, 127–9, 148, 150, 159, 160, 167
rape 46, 107, 110–11, 114, 118, 121
Raymond, Janice, *The Transsexual Empire ...* 90
'Reclaim the Night' march 110
Redmond, Bridget 31
Redmond, William 31
Refugee Act 1996 70
Relationships and Sexuality Education (RSE) 89
repeal movement 141–3, 148, 163
Reproductive Rights against Oppression, Sexism and Austerity (ROSA) 1, 7, 77, 96, 119, 142, 163–4
#RespectForSNAs campaign 71
Revolutionary Anarcha-Feminist Group (RAG) 42–3, 142, 168 n.7

Revolutionary Association of the Women of Afghanistan (RAWA) 160
right to parent 129, 149–50
Right to Work Campaign 70
Rivera, Sylvia 95
Rixain, Marie-Pierre 151
Roe v. Wade ruling 135
Roma community 150
Rowling, J. K. 87, 92
Ruane, Lynn 46–7, 123
Ryder, Mary 39–40, 113

Sandberg, Susan, *Lean In* 7, 57
Serano, Julia, *Whipping Girl* 78–9, 83
Services Industrial Professional and Technical Union (SIPTU) 69–70, 140
sexism 5, 7–8, 17, 27–8, 37, 42, 63–5, 68, 155, 161, 166
sexual abuse 18, 119, 121
sexual harassment 63–4, 70, 88, 103, 119, 161, 164
sexual violence 103, 120, 124, 127
Sheehy-Skeffington, Hanna 26, 33, 56, 60
Shortall, Róisín 149
Sinn Féin political party 37, 44, 48
Sisterhood 9–10, 93
Smith, Bríd 42, 63–4, 151
Smyth, Ailbhe 1, 43, 113, 141–3, 171 n.48
socialism 25, 33
Socialist Worker newspaper 36
Socialist Workers Movement (SWM) 39, 42
Socialist Workers Party 137
social partnership 65–6
social reproductive labour 11–13, 18, 32
Society for the Protection of the Unborn Child (SPUC) 136
'Speak Up for Women's Rights' conference 93

Special Needs Assistants (SNAs) 71
Speed, Ann 62–3
Spillane, Alison 44–6
Starmer, Keir 92, 95
state violence 119–22
Stock, Kathleen 92–3
St Vincent's Healthcare Group (SVHG) 143–4
St Vincent's Holdings 148
suffragette movement 8, 25–8, 30, 33
Sunak, Rishi 92, 95
Sunday World newspaper 63, 111
Survivors Informing Services and Institutions (SISI) 117
Sustainable Development Goal (SDG) 4
Sustaining Progress 66

Task Force Report 115–16
Tate, Andrew 18
Teachta Dálas (TDs) 27, 31, 33, 38, 42, 45–6, 141, 148
Termination for Medical Reasons (TFMR) 141
Thatcher, Margaret 14–15, 138
Thompson, William 25
Tlaib, Rashida 162
Together for Safety 151
Together for Yes (TfY) 144–7
trade union movement 43, 56, 58–63, 65–73
trans 78–9
  crimes against 86
  rights 78–80, 85–6, 96–7
  visibility 81–5
Trans and intersex Pride 95–7
trans-exclusionary radical feminists (TERFs) 90–2, 94–5
Transgender Equality Network of Ireland (TENI) 85
trans liberation 21, 77–81
  queer activism 95–7
transmisogynistic violence 86
transmisogyny 79

transphobia 79, 86, 167
Travellers 20–1, 32, 36, 103, 121, 150, 167
Tristan, Flora 59
Trump, Donald 18
Tserendorj, Urantsetseg (death of) 105
'turn on the tap' campaign 61
Tweedy, Hilda 33–4
Twenty-seventh Amendment 139–41

United Left Alliance (ULA) 43–4
United Nations Committee on Human Rights 132
University College Dublin (UCD) 113
US Supreme Court (SCOTUS) ruling 135, 151

Vatican 89, 144, 148

Walker, Linda 37
Wallace, Mick 44
waves, feminist 8–9
Weinstein, Harvey 6
Well Woman Centre 136
What We Stand For (IWU manifesto) 36
white-supremacist-capitalist-patriarchy 155
white supremacy 58, 148, 160
Wicklow for Choice 143
Wilde, Oscar 83
Wilson, Niamh 114–16
Winchester, Noreen 110
Wollstonecraft, Mary, *Vindication of the rights of women* 25

Women Against Imperialism (WAI) 37, 113
'Women Demand Better' rally 2
Women of African Descent for Reproductive Justice 130
women of colour 5, 7, 28, 112, 145, 157
Women of Honour 119
Women's Advisory Committee (WAC) 62
Women's Aid 104, 114–15
Women's Political Association 35–6
Women's Right to Choose Group (WRCG) 113, 130, 135
Women's Social and Progressive League (WSPL) 33
women4women (South Dublin network) 42
Workers Solidarity Movement 168 n.7
Workers Solidarity Party 137
working-class women 7–8, 12–13, 26, 28, 32–3, 41, 47, 58–9, 109–10, 123, 134
Working Women's Charter 62
workplace inequality 57–8
Workplace Relations Commission 70
'work to rule' 59
World Health Organization (WHO) 5, 84, 104, 128, 130, 146
  guidelines on abortion care 5, 146

Yacef, Amel 145, 157
Youth Defence 42, 141–2

zero-tolerance approach 112, 118